PUBLIC RELATIONS AS DRAMATISTIC ORGANIZING

A Case Study Bridging Theory and Practice

THE HAMPTON PRESS COMMUNICATION SERIES
Communications and Social Organization
Gary L. Kreps, series editor

Conflict and Diversity
  Claire Damken Brown, Charlotte Snedeker, and *Beate Sykes (eds.)*

Power and Public Relations
  Jeffrey L. Courtright and *Peter M. Smudde (eds.)*

Community at Work: Creating and Celebrating Community
  in Organizational Life
  Patricia K. Felkins

Qualitative Research: Applications in Organizational Life (2nd ed.)
  Sandra L. Herndon and *Gary L. Kreps (eds.)*

Building Diverse Communities: Applications of Communication Research
  Trevy A. McDonald, Mark P. Orbe, and *Trevellya Ford-Ahmed (eds.)*

Terrorism: Communication and Rhetorical Perspectives
  Dan O'Hair, Robert Heath, Gerald Ledlow, and *Kevin Ayotte (eds.)*

Communication and Social Action Research
  Joseph J. Pilotta

Organizational Communication and Change
  Philip Salem (ed.)

Ethics and Organizational Communication
  Matthew W. Seeger

Engaging Communication, Transforming Organizations:
  Scholarship of Engagement in Action
  Jennifer Lyn Simpson and *Pamela Shockley-Zalabak (eds.)*

Inspiring Cooperation and Celebrating Organizations: Genres, Message
  Design and Strategies in Public Relations
  Peter M. Smudde and Jeffrey L. Courtright

Public Relations as Dramatistic Organizing: A Case Study
  Bridging Theory and Practice
  Peter M. Smudde

Communicating with Customers: Service Approaches, Ethics and Impact
  Wendy S. Zabava-Ford

# PUBLIC RELATIONS AS DRAMATISTIC ORGANIZING

A Case Study Bridging Theory and Practice

Peter M. Smudde

Illinois State University

HAMPTON PRESS, INC.
CRESSKILL, NEW JERSEY

Copyright © 2011 by Hampton Press, Inc.

All rights reserved. No part of this publication may be reproduced, stored in a retrieval system, or transmitted in any form or by any means, electronic, mechanical, photocopying, microfilming, recording, or otherwise, without permission of the publisher.

Printed in the United States of America

Library of Congress Cataloging-in-Publication Data

Smudde, Peter M.
  Public relations as dramatistic organizing : a case study bridging theory and practice / Peter M. Smudde.
     p. cm. -- (The Hampton Press communication series. Communication and social organization)
  Includes bibliographical references and index.
  ISBN 978-1-57273-954-3 (hbk.) -- ISBN 978-1-57273-955-0 (pbk.)
  1. Public relations--Case studies. 2. Organizational sociology--Case studies. 3. Industrial organization--Case studies. I. Title.
  HD59.S537 2010
  659.2--dc22
                                    2010052861

Hampton Press, Inc.
23 Broadway
Cresskill, NJ 07626

For my family, Patty, Matthew, and Jeffrey,
and for my parents, Tony and Alyce.

CONTENTS

Acknowledgements   xi

1 Introduction: Public Relations Contexts   3
    Thesis and Research Questions   4
    Project Justification   5
    Literature Review   8
    Content Preview   28

2 Dramatistic Organizing as Method   31
    Theoretical Framework   31
    Framework for Textual Analysis   44
    Methodological Program Summarized   54

3 Logological Description of the Case   57
    Order   58
    Pollution   60
    Guilt   62
    Purification   67
    Redemption   70
    Quantitative Corroboration of the Logological Analysis   73
    Epilogue: An "Ill-defined" Issue   79

4 Microscopic Textual Analysis of the Case   81
    Organizing the Issue   82
    Key Messages   84
    A Representative Text   86
    The Cornerstone to Redemption   89

5 Macroscopic Textual Analysis of the Case	91
PR Discourse Before *Dateline NBC*	92
The Turning Point: *Dateline NBC*'s Report	95
PR Discourse After *Dateline NBC*	97
Thoughts on Texts and Process	121
6 Lessons From the Method and Case	123
Evaluating the Success of the Case	123
What the Case Teaches Us	126
How Well the Method Works	136
Implications	138
7 Conclusion: Strategic Planning For and Value of Public Relations	141
The Impacts of History, Tactical Bias and Semantic Baggage	142
Using Rhetorical Theory in Practice	149
Prospective, Strategic and Rhetorical Public Relations	156
A Strategy for the Dramatistic Organizing of Public Relations	164
Public Relations' Value Contribution	172
Appendix A Sample Public Relations Discourse About the C/K Pickup Issue	177
Prepared Statement	178
Press Release	179
Backgrounder	180
Written Correspondence	182
Pitch Letter	183
Written Correspondence	184
Appendix B Public Awareness and Opinion About the Case	187
Awareness of C/K Truck Fuel Tank Issue (February 1993–November 1994).	188
GM Right Direction vs. Wrong Track: CK Truck Events (August 1992–November 1994).	189
Appendix C General Motors Public Relations Texts Used	191
Notes	199
References	205
Author's Biography	225
Author Index	227
Subject Index	233

Figures and Tables

Table 2.1.	Complementary Terms and Unifying Concepts Between Kenneth Burke and Karl Weick.	44
Table 2.2.	Representative Genre Set for Public Relations Discourse	47
Figure 3.1.	Cycle of Terms for Order Present in the C/K Pickup Issue.	59
Figure 3.2.	Comparison between full-size C/K pickup truck designs, 1973-1987 models and thereafter (Weiser, 1993).	61
Figure 3.3.	The logological evolution of the case.	72
Figure 6.1.	Model for the dramatistic organizing of public relations.	127
Figure 7.1.	Strategic planning process model.	148
Figure 7.2.	Four-phase logological progression of public relations matters.	158
Table 7.1.	The Pentad and Public Relations Discourse Examples	162

ACKNOWLEDGEMENTS

I express my heartfelt gratitude to a number of people who have been instrumental in helping me along the way toward publishing this volume. My wife, Patty, and sons, Matt and Jeffrey, have given me their love and support, especially during lengthy periods of seclusion to do my work. My parents, Tony and Alyce, kept a high level of interest and pride in my work, and their love and support has been immeasurable.

This book is largely the product of my doctoral dissertation research, completed in 2000 at Wayne State University, and my subsequent research, teaching, and practice. It has been amazing to see how the fields I address in this work have blossomed in new ways, while much has remained strong and fruit-bearing. I am grateful for the sage counsel on my dissertation from Ellen Barton; the late Bernie Brock, who was my advisor; Jack Kay; and Matt Seeger.

I am also indebted to a number of people who have been there for me in various ways at various times. First is Gary Kreps, who, as Hampton Press' series editor, believed in this book and gave me excellent feedback and advice about my manuscript all along the way. Barbara Bernstein, at Hampton Press, has always been a source of enthusiasm and support. Robin Weisberg (copyeditor) and Mariann Hutlak (page layout and prepress) were immensely helpful in preparing this book for publication, and I thank them very much for their hard work. Most especially, Jeff Courtright has been a joy to work with on our many projects, including the extension of ideas from this book and our other work that are central to our next book, which also is being published by Hampton Press.

Others of special note are people with whom I discussed in some way matters related to this book, including ideas that relate to it but may be developed or under development elsewhere. Those people include especially Carl Botan, Peggy Brønn, George Cheney, Harry Cherkinian, Kathy Collins, Melissa Di Motto, Dennis Ganster, Barb Hernandez, Øyvind Ihlen, Larry Kerber, Andy King, Ann Knabe, Ed Lechtzin, Larry Long, John Luecke, Vilma Luoma-aho, Gary Myers, Bonnie Neff, Norm Neuman, David Richardson, Anne Rodriguez, Martha Saunders, Maureen Schriner, Jack Selzer, Alvie Smith, Ben-Piet Venter, Susan Waters, Kay Weaver, Bob Wess, and those who participated in my sessions at PRSA, IPR, NCA, ICA, and other conferences and seminars. I also want to thank the students in my undergraduate and graduate classes that I had the privilege to lead over the years. I learn much from them and am grateful to them for their indulgence in and discussion of my and others' ideas.

Finally, the appendices in this volume are identical to those included in my dissertation, and I am grateful for the permission given to me to use the material in them. I also am grateful to Parlor Press for granting permission to reprint significant portions of my chapter in the book, *Kenneth Burke and His Circles* (2008). I also wish to thank Taylor & Francis for granting permission to reprint my article, "Implications on the Practice and Study of Kenneth Burke's Idea of a 'Public Relations Counsel with a Heart,'" published in *Communication Quarterly* (2004). Both works were derived from my original dissertation and tailored for these occasions.

How can we possibly make them better next time? But we always do and I have come to recognize that we always can just so long as we are willing to pay the price which progress always exacts. That price is not in money alone—that is the easiest part—but in skill as measured by experience and ability, in imagination that visualizes what might be possible and—let us not forget—in long hours of hard work and many discouragements to be overcome. Those are the factors which determine the progress of the future, not only of General Motors but of each of us severally and of all of us collectively. There are no short cuts no matter who does the planning.

—Alfred P. Sloan, Jr. in collaboration with Boyden Sparkes
(1940, p. 191)

1

INTRODUCTION: PUBLIC RELATIONS CONTEXTS

Organizational discourse has been addressed as either a rhetorical or an organizational phenomenon. "Discourse" refers to instances of texts that include both their form and content, not the more restricted sense of discourse as utterances or speech acts. What is lacking is a grounded theory of corporate discourse that integrates rhetorical and organizational theory. The best way to accomplish this objective is to study a particular case of an organization faced with managing a situation that cuts to the core of its business and its relationship with its publics and stakeholders. Organizational communication has been studied as rhetorical in nature at least in terms of crisis and issue management (e.g., Heath, 1997; Seeger, Sellnow, & Ulmer, 1998; Sellnow, 1993; Ware & Linkugel, 1973; D. Williams & Tredaway, 1992), corporate speakers (e.g., Botan, 1994; Cheney, 1992; Hearit, 1996; Matthews, 1995; Seeger, 1994b), corporate culture (e.g., M. H. Brown & McMillan, 1991; Pacanowsky & O'Donnell-Trujillo, 1982, 1983), and public relations (e.g., Cheney & Vibbert, 1987; Elwood, 1995a; Grunig, 1992; Hoover, 1997; Toth & Heath, 1992). Within the context of organization theory, corporate discourse is typically addressed as part of the general communication activity that occurs among members of an organization (e.g., Katz & Kahn, 1966; Morgan, 1986; Weick, 1979b, 1995; Zucker, 1987). When taken together, this research shows that corporate discourse is both rhetorical and organizational, but individual studies shy away from uniting the two orientations and presenting a way to theorize about, criticize, and even plan organizational discourse.

This volume uses a combination of rhetorical and organizational theories as a lens through which to view a particular case of public relations. Anchored in dramatistic criticism, this volume uses a case study to test a theory-driven method for analyzing public relations discourse, deriving a model for the public relations discourse process, and prescribing an approach for proactive, strategic planning. The analytical method integrates Kenneth Burke's rhetorical theory and dramatistic critical method with Karl Weick's theory of organizing. The case analyzed here is that of General Motors Corporation's (GM) management of the issue of alleged defects in the fuel systems of its 1973 to 1987 full-size C/K pickup trucks.

Using Burke's and Weick's theories can help practitioners, students, and researchers make sense of the demands of and plans for public relations efforts. Tompkins (1987) hinted at the similarities between Burke and Weick as he asked, "Does not the following sound Weickian? 'Perception must be grounded in enactment, by participation in some local role, so that the understanding of the total order is reached through this partial involvement' (Burke, 1969b, p. 195). Or should I instead have asked: Doesn't Weick's stress on enactment now sound Burkean?" (p. 86). The purpose of this study is not to take a stand on the case that is central to this project, but to analyze the GM C/K pickup case through both rhetorical and organizational orientations and, thereby, learn more about the discourse and practice of public relations.

At the heart of this volume is a qualitative analysis that applies the Burke–Weick synthesis to the contexts and texts GM officials enacted as they handled the C/K pickup issue. This analysis demonstrates the workability of a critical method for practical application by public relations practitioners and researchers, outlines lessons learned from the case and the method's application to it, develops a model of and program for public relations, and proposes opportunities for further research. This chapter describes the nature of this volume by stating the thesis and research questions, providing justification for the volume, and reviewing pertinent literature in the areas of Burkean and Weickian scholarship on organizational discourse and public relations.

THESIS AND RESEARCH QUESTIONS

An analysis of organizational discourse should address both rhetorical and organizational elements, because people in organizations communicate with one another about aspects of a given environment and frequently cocreate discourse that unifies their enactments. In Smudde (1991), I explained and modeled the document development process in organizations, and key in that process is that professional communicators work collaboratively with others inside and, sometimes, outside their organizations to create discourse. In the case of GM's C/K truck issue and in general, public relations, as organizing activity about enacted environments, functions dramatistically and features symbolic action to inspire cooperation between an organization and its publics.

In tune with this thesis, public relations aims to establish identification between an organization and its publics and stakeholders (i.e., to see themselves in their respective relationships with one another, the organization, and a matter at hand). Public relations echoes enacted environments that can be explained in terms of Burke's rhetoric of rebirth (he used the term *logology* for this idea) and is the outgrowth of certain motives germane to the sensemaking process that can be isolated through pentadic analysis of the literal drama of what is going on. The management of symbols is at the heart of corporate rhetoric and public relations (Cheney & Vibbert, 1987). Corporate rhetoric, as the "management of multiple identities" (Cheney, 1991), is part of the organizing process and functions dramatistically within the context of social order. For example, corporate speakers participate dramatistically in the process of organizing and publicly report on how people made sense of an equivocal environment.

Burke's method for rhetorical analysis—dramatism—and Weick's theory of organizing work well together because of the balance they provide one another in the analysis of public relations. Ultimately, this project answers three questions related to its thesis: (a) Based on the application of the analytical method, how successful was GM's public relations in managing the issue? (b) What does the case study of GM's C/K pickup trucks teach us about the practice of public relations? (c) How effective is the combination of Burke's rhetorical theory and Weick's theory of organizing as a critical method for translating the case into its rhetorical and organizational aspects? Answers to these questions and the surrounding analysis would provide good sense of the simultaneously rhetorical and organizational nature of public relations. Ultimately, a prospective program for public relations is proposed as this book's final chapter as a first step in applying theory to practice.

PROJECT JUSTIFICATION

This volume makes an important contribution to what we know about public relations based on three important points: (a) scholarship on the case is limited to two articles (Hearit, 1996; Ulmer, 1999) that address only one episode of it, few communication textbooks (see Cutlip, Center, & Broom, 1994; Jaksa & Pritchard, 1994; Seeger, 1997a; Seitel, 1998) that limit the case to a critique of journalistic or ethical responsibility, and a dissertation (Burns, 1997) that looks at the case as an example of white-collar crime to allegedly conceal safety problems from the public; (b) the scholarship on public relations treats public relations as either a rhetorical or an organizational phenomenon, not both simultaneously; and (c) both theoretical and practical issues are addressed and grounded in a case study that has broad implications.

A key contribution of this work is its synthesizing theories of rhetoric and organizations—those of Burke and Weick, respectively—into a single philosophical framework and a practical method for analysis and action. This convergence of Burke and Weick into a single analytical system has never been done before. This study also makes four other unique and important scholarly contributions. First, public relations is defined anew and emphasizes, unlike other definitions, the context of symbolic action that is borne of organizing behavior. Next, public relations discourse genres are specifically outlined and pragmatically defined, which serves as an important reference point in this study and for future scholarship and practice in public relations. Third, texts for both internal and external publics are used in the case study about GM's C/K pickups, which has rarely been done in previous research. Finally, a unique program for conducting public relations action is given that draws from the case study and this project's theoretical foundation.

With such a shallow pool of scholarly work done on the C/K pickup case, this project continues the conversation about it and applies major theoretical orientations to analyze it, derive lessons from it, and form a system for understanding and conducting public relations as a simultaneously dramatistic and organizing function. Focused case studies are reasonable critical approaches that have yielded insightful research about organizational communication. Indeed, valuable research using one or more case studies has been done, as I show in the literature review, that has built our knowledge about the nature of organizational discourse, particularly public relations. For this study, the quantity of cases for analysis is not as important as the quality of the analysis about the case chosen for study. This volume does not seek to take sides on the C/K pickup issue, where doing so would not add knowledge about the simultaneous rhetorical and organizational nature of public relations. This volume does add to the knowledge about the case, the practice of public relations, and the theories employed.

The case of alleged fuel-system defects in GM's 1973–1987 C/K pickups is important because of its far-reaching affects among many groups of people and its wide application of corporate discourse to both external and internal audiences. The allegations and federal government investigation came on the heels of the struggling company's record losses of $24 billion in 1991; a tumultuous and total change among its chairman, top corporate leaders, and board of directors; being the high-cost producer of the auto industry; many plant closings and downsized workforce; and residual criticism about producing "cookie-cutter" vehicles (see General Motors Corporation, 1992; Ingrassia & White, 1995; Keller, 1993; Levin, 1989). All of these factors worked against GM's ability to inspire a high level of confidence in the company and its products among its employees, retirees, dealers, stockholders, and suppliers; investors and industry analysts; government leaders; news media; and consumers. The C/K truck issue became an important opportunity for GM to aggressively reestablish its credibility, image, and reputation through its symbolic action about enacted environments. Indeed, the issue can be viewed as a drama, in the Burkean sense, because all discourse is dramatic. "In equating 'dramatic' with 'dialectic,' we automatically have also our perspective for the analysis of history, which is a 'dramatic' process, involving dialectical oppositions. And if we keep this always in mind, we are reminded that every document bequeathed us by history must be treated as a *strategy for encompassing a situation*" (Burke, 1973, p. 109).

Past cases of automobile defects are always in the background when new ones emerge. Some of the most notorious include the 1969 Chevrolet Corvair, which Ralph Nader (1965) addressed in his book, *Unsafe at Any Speed* (also cf. White, 1969). There was the 1972 Ford Pinto, which burst into flames if hit at high speeds in the rear, where the gasoline tank was mounted (Strobel, 1980). In both of these cases, the vehicles were discontinued after their respective manufacturers finished building the models for that year. Other cases of defects—for example Ford Bronco II rollovers (Darin, 1995), Firestone tires and Ford Explorers (Blaney, Benoit, & Brazeal, 2002), Chrysler minivans' defective liftgate latches and failures of its Ultradrive transmissions (Stertz, 1991), Audi 5000-S sudden acceleration (Strnad, 1987), Mercedes-Benz's A-class rollover (Ihlen, 2002a), and Suzuki Samurai sudden deceleration (Kiley, 1988)—are part of the recent history of automobiles in America (see Public Citizen, 1995). The C/K pickup case stands in relation to these and other lesser known cases, but not necessarily among them, because (as is shown) neither the National Highway Traffic Safety Administration (NHTSA) nor state courts ruled that the trucks had any defect.

Because of my "insider" status on this case, having been an employee of GM during the period of the case, there is a risk of bias in my analysis.[1] Having been an insider at GM is more advantageous than not. It works for me, because GM was my employer during most of the case's 6-year history (i.e., 1992–1998). I participated in the communication of messages about the C/K pickup issue to certain GM publics, was a member of GM's internal audience receiving corporate texts, and observed external and internal audiences' reactions to corporate messages. On another level, my insider status works because when I was a member of GM's worldwide corporate communications staff, I experienced the communications processes and policies at GM in place during the case's history, had reasonable access to GM's resources, talked with key GM officials about the issue, and collected sufficient data about the case. The result is insights that outsiders could not formulate and, especially, deeper analysis about how GM officials handled the case and the broader implications to public relations in general.

Although bias may or may not be a significant issue to some readers, there are other criteria beyond bias to consider, according to Hodder (1994): the coherence of the arguments, the correspondence between the data (texts) and the analysis, and the fruitfulness of the study as it takes research in a new direction, develops a new line of inquiry, and establishes a new perspective on the subject. On these terms, my connections with GM are assets, not liabilities, for this volume, and the study is well worth pursuing on these grounds and those already mentioned. Moreover, the theoretical principles and research findings, presented in a review of literature, shows a richness in the knowledge base about rhetoric, organizations, and public relations that pertains to this project.

LITERATURE REVIEW

Tompkins (1987) observed that "organizational theory is but an extension of the classical concerns of rhetorical theory. Moreover, the recent turns toward culture and symbolism are consistent with the 'new rhetoric' of symbolic action" (p. 86). Because of this intersection among rhetorical theory, organizational theory, and organizational communication, these three areas of scholarship are relevant to this project. Specifically, this study employs contemporary theory and research about public relations, Burkean analyses about corporate discourse, and Weickian scholarship about organizational communication. Here is a review of some of the applicable literature in these three areas.

Contemporary Public Relations Theory and Research

Public relations is a subject area in which scholars and practitioners alike have been working hard over the last few decades to develop a stronger body of theoretical research. The common complaint among public relations researchers in both academe and industry is that more formal research that is based on theory and tempered with practical experience is necessary to help people understand the role and value of public relations in organizations and to make it legitimate as a viable and attractive subject for research and a respectable discipline in its own right. Pavlik (1987) observed that

> [m]ost research on public relations is either applied or basic.... *Applied research* is designed to solve problems [and follows the two tracks of (1) strategic research, which is used primarily for developing campaigns or programs, and (2) evaluation research, which primarily concerns the

effectiveness of public relations programs]. *Basic research* is designed to build theory about the PR [public relations] process. . . . A third major research theme encompasses what we call introspective research . . . [which] represents studies that look inwardly at the profession. (pp. 22-23)

This taxonomy is a useful way to review the literature on public relations theory and practice.[2]

Applied Research Much of the applied research on public relations concerns programs and campaigns and can be divided between strategic and evaluative research. Excellent examples of applied strategic research are reports published by The Conference Board. These reports address broad concerns of business leaders and communicators—how to unite business strategies with communications objectives and manage the business of corporate communications (Brothers & Gallo, 1992; Garone, 1995; Troy, 1993). Other Conference Board reports also address particular activities, like strengthening employee communications (Ainspan & Dell, 2000; McNelly, 1996; Troy, 1988) and investor communications (Brancato, 2004). Other research on public relations planning explains strategies for managing crises (Birch, 1994; Fink, 1986; Gonzalez-Herrero & Pratt, 1995; Lauterborn, 1996; Mitroff, Harrington, & Gai, 1996; Seeger, 2006), handling public perceptions of litigation (Lukaszewski, 1995, 1996), prescribing ways to improve the quality of public relations programs (Heath, Leth, & Nathan, 1994), and explaining the tactics for performing various public relations functions (e.g., Beard, 2001; Croft, 2006; Cutlip et al., 1994; Saffir, 1993; Wilcox, Ault, & Agee, 1996).

Applied evaluative research includes case studies that look back on how organizations managed a particular issue, event, or crisis. Indeed, much of this vein of literature concerns crisis management. Farrell and Goodnight (1981) studied the accident at Three Mile Island for the "root metaphors" that guided communication practices among employees at the facility, and found that "accidental rhetoric" confounded those people's ability to deal communicatively with the crisis. D. Williams and Tredaway (1992), in their analysis of the Exxon Valdez incident, observed that crises occur when an organization is in a situation marked by a sense of urgency, close observation by the media, and interruption of normal business operations that may result in lost revenue or credibility. They defined what effective crisis communication is (and by extension issue communication and public relations) and identified two criteria necessary for successful crisis communication—respond to a situation with a proactive stance and restore or maintain the public confidence. Sellnow (1993) also examined the Exxon *Valdez* case but from the vantage point of scientific argument. He argued that discourse conventions about "scientific ethos" tend to dictate how an organization defends its products, procedures, and conduct during a crisis.

Weick (1988, 1996) examined the systematic communication behaviors of people in organizations facing crises, and he explained the enactment process that can bring about crises or avoid them. He contended that crisis situations are often paradoxical—that to understand why a crisis occurred, one must take action, but that very action "affects events that can make things worse" (Weick, 1988, p. 306). The risk of making things worse is far better than letting things go unattended. The enactment process results in an understanding of events, situations, and explanations about how to handle enacted environments. Sensemaking activity is at the heart of environments that lead up to crises, and it is equally part of the management of crises and, in a proactive sense, the prevention of crises in the first place (Weick, 1988). Weick (1996) provided a prescription for heading off and handling surprise situations that calls for organizational leaders to "develop resilient groups that are capable of four things: improvisation [i.e., creativity under pressure to bring order out of chaos], wisdom [i.e., thriving on the synchronous growth of ignorance and knowledge about situations, since the more people learn, the more questions arise], respectful interactions [i.e., trust, honesty and self-respect are upheld by participants and fuel the group's work], and communication [i.e., open and candid discussion about what is going on and what can be done]" (pp. 147-148).

Seeger (1986), in his analysis of the Challenger explosion, and Seeger and Bolz (1991), in their case study of Union Carbide's handling of the disaster in Bhopal, India, demonstrated how crises proceed along three stages—pre-crisis (i.e., flaws are allowed to go unchecked), crisis (i.e., a "trigger event" occurs and threats to the organization arise as people rush to make sense of the problem to limit the damage to the organization's image and legitimacy by fully disclosing details about causes, effects, responsibility, damage repair and future avoidance), and post-crisis (i.e., immediacy of the crisis subsides and the organization resumes "near-normal functioning"). Seeger et al. (1998) refined this view by defining crisis as "a specific, unexpected, and nonroutine event or series of events that create high levels of uncertainty and threaten or are perceived to threaten an organization's high-priority goals" (p. 233). With their extensive review of research on organizational crisis, Seeger et al. emphasized that all crises exhibit threats to an organization, short response times to inquiries about why the crisis happened and what will be the next steps toward making things better, and surprise that the crises happened at all and will have to be handled differently from routine decisions.

Benoit and Brinson (1994) studied crises that befell two well-known corporations, AT&T and Dow Corning. They enacted a rhetorical criticism of AT&T's public statement—in the form of a full-page newspaper advertisement—as an attempt to rebuild its image after blaming low-level workers for the interruption of long-distance service in New York City in September 1991. In the area of how organizations manage publicity about product defects, Brinson and Benoit (1996) studied Dow Corning's handling of its breast implant crisis. The researchers examined the image-repair strategies the company used to fend off criticism about the implants' safety, that only after the company took responsibility for the problem and promised to correct it did the criticism and attacks subside. This case, Brinson and Benoit argued, demonstrates the rhetorical viability of image restoration discourse when trying to maintain an organization's image during a crisis.

In these cases, corporate speakers were in the spotlight, and research on the influence of these people treats both the general characteristics of their role and the characters who take on the role. One topic germane to this research area is corporate advocacy, which basically centers on the idea that selected individuals represent their organizations in a public dialogue about contentious issues, with the goal to gain greater support for and influence from one's organization and its messages than any others involved. In her discussion about the practice of corporate advocacy, Hoover (1997) argued that "Advocacy messages may be delivered by individuals, perhaps corporate spokespersons who are part of the organization and identified by the public as such, or surrogates who can come to be identified through repetition of visual imagery through the mass media" (p. 6).

Seeger (1994a) proposed a simpler view of a corporate speaker as someone who, acting as an organization's representative, "discusses the organization's role and responsibility in society in broad terms while at the same time defending, justifying, and legitimizing the organization's actions" (p. 16). Seeger's (1994a, 1997b) focus on Lee Iacocca, former chairman of Chrysler Corporation, provides special insights about this highly visible leader and corporate rhetor. Seeger described the importance Iacocca placed on enacting the environment through the writing process and delivering messages, which includes "careful organization, preparation, audience analysis, use of direct language, and the need to be personable" (Seeger, 1994a, p. 21). Botan (1994) pointed out that Iacocca "sees his own function as identifying [i.e., discovering] issues and using communication to get others to join in attacking them (p. 30). Such an approach is consistent with Kay's (1994) observation that Iacocca employed an "advocacy style . . . that merges the demands of a national debate model [i.e., examining stock issues on the literal level and providing the necessary proofs] with the expectations of a model in which symbolism dominates decision making and persuasion [i.e., examining stock issues on a symbolic-iconic level and advancing the necessary proofs]. In short, Iacocca's speeches bridge the world of reason and the world of symbols" (p. 119).

In a similar vein, Matthews (1995) explained that Bart Giamatti, the late commissioner of Major League Baseball, "was appointed Commissioner by the *owners* of the twenty-six baseball franchises, not by the fans . . . [and]

was expected to present the views of baseball management" (p. 283). Giamatti managed these multiple identities in his statement to the press about Pete Rose's lifetime ban from baseball. That statement describes the conclusions of an investigation into Rose's gambling on the game, but most important, it stresses "integrity, professionalism, fairness, and responsibility [so eloquently that] Giamatti was able to align himself with the values held dearly by all loyal fans . . . [and share in] a sense of community between his audience and himself" (Matthews, 1995, pp. 283-284).

Such alignment with multiple audiences is a common goal for corporate speakers. Cheney (1991) asserted that a corporate speaker is "confined largely to the alternative(s) 'seen' or associated with his or her personal targets of identification [i.e., the process by which identity is 'appropriated'], in seeking to do 'what's best' for the organization" (p. 19). Cheney (1992) further argued that the net effect of corporate rhetoric is that "the individual or self is to some degree decentered through self-definition and self-diffusion in corporate symbols, images, [and] messages" (p. 176). Corporate rhetors, then, tend to personalize their organizations' images, because "some corporate messages become identified with individuals and those individual speakers become the embodiment of organizations" (Cheney, 1992, p. 178).

Applying a generic approach about corporate apologia, Hearit (1996) reviewed GM's aggressive argumentative strategy in a corporate speaker's rebuttal to *Dateline NBC*'s story about the alleged dangers of GM's C/K pickups. GM's approach, he argued, was to issue a "counter-kategoria that directly challenges the ethics of the media institution that acts as the accuser"; whereas, GM was able to claim to have been the damaged party and victimized by NBC (p. 236). Ultimately, GM's masterful use of this strategy serves as an example of how counter-kategoria "can be an important resource in challenging inaccurate and/or misleading media coverage" (p. 246). Ulmer (1999) also analyzed GM's news conference about the *Dateline* exposé. His analysis was driven by free-speech issues for organizations and highlights key communication elements by officials from both NBC and GM. Like Hearit, Ulmer concluded that GM was both within its free-speech rights and successful in exercising them to "substantially disputing the accuracy of the charges" (p. 166). Both Ulmer's and Hearit's work provide implications for other organizations to successfully defend themselves publicly.

Pratt (1997) discussed a parallel case to GM's as he analyzed ABC News' November 2, 1992, televised report about unsanitary food-handling practices at Food Lion Inc. supermarkets on its *PrimeTime Live* news magazine. To do this exposé, ABC News producers and staffers falsified documents to obtain jobs at Food Lion and, once on the job, used hidden microphones and video cameras to get the story they wanted. The segment included interviews with current and former Food Lion employees. Food Lion argued vigorously in public against ABC News. The supermarket even gave its employees a videotape of its response to share with other people. In federal court, as the company sued ABC News, Food Lion argued that ABC defrauded it by (a) filing falsified employment histories, "engaging in invasive deception," (b) making the company pay for new employee training and wages, and (c) trespassing on company property (Pratt, 1997). Unlike GM, Food Lion did not question the report's accuracy, and ABC News applied its First Amendment rights in its news gathering. Nevertheless, a jury found ABC guilty of fraud and awarded Food Lion $1,402 to cover expenses and $5.5 million in punitive damages (Pratt, 1997).

Basic Research A significant amount of scholarship has been published that builds the foundation for public relations theory. Cheney's work on rhetorical identification (which is addressed later in a review of Burkean scholarship) contributes basic research that possesses a depth of analysis and covers a breadth of issues about the theory and practice of public relations. Several important books have collected some of the basic research on public relations that focuses on its rhetorical nature. Botan and Hazleton's (1989, 2006) *Public Relations Theory* and *Public Relations Theory II* establishes a strong foundation for building public relations theory and gives examples of various theoretical perspectives (e.g., game theory, persuasion, and psychology) as lenses through which to view public relations. In Courtright and Smudde (2007), *Power and Public Relations,* we investigated the multiple dimensions of power that lead to misunderstandings of it and opportunities to harness it effectively and ethically within the field of public relations. Moss, Vercic, and Warnaby (2000) collect a wide range of perspectives on public relations, especially from European viewpoints. L'Etang and Pieczka (2006), in their *Public Relations: Critical Debates and Contemporary Practice*, provides one of the most wide-ranging views of public relations that focuses on "traditional" and "nontraditional" topics about practice areas and issues. Elwood's (1995a) *Public Relations Inquiry as Rhetorical Criticism* is an exceptionally well-focused use of rhetorical criticism as a method of analysis for individual cases and for theory building. Heath's (1994) *Management of Corporate Communications* takes a multidimensional look at corporate communications as both an organizational and, primarily, a rhetorical phenomenon. And Toth and Heath's (1992) *Rhetorical and Critical Approaches to Public Relations* emphasizes the rhetorical nature of public relations and demonstrates how rhetorical orientations can serve as frameworks for analysis.

These books stress that public relations is a rhetorical endeavor, and much of their contents include case studies of particular public relations programs, issues, or crises. For example, Miller (1989) examined the nature of persuasion in public relations; that effective persuasion involves changing, fostering, or reinforcing attitudes and behaviors, and doing so through appeals to both reason and emotion. Using a model of persuasion that integrates several behavioral and cognitive approaches to human behavior, Hamilton (1989) developed and tested a questionnaire about public relations projects that practitioners may use to find out how effective their projects are and aid in future planning.

Taking a somewhat broader look at public relations, Toth (1992) argued that critics be open to and clearly define different perspectives through which they view public relations and do so in ways that inspire more dialogue about it, not stifle it. Heath (1992a) addressed the kind of mediator-critic role that public relations plays in balancing the social, political, economic, and personal forces between an organization's symbolic action and its stakeholders. Heath (1992b) took this approach a step further when he described several critical perspectives for public relations, specifically organizational persona, the need to respond to dissent, standards of truth and knowledge, good reasons behind organizational narratives, and multiple orientations on issues.

In his longer treatment of corporate communication, Heath (1994) thoroughly examined organizational communication, generally, and public relations, specifically, through several orientations simultaneously. He used systems theory and Weick's (1969, 1979b) theory of enactment to explain information processing and Pfeffer's (1981) ideas about enacting zones of shared meanings and beliefs among organizational groups as a means to understand boundary spanning (cf. Aldrich & Herker, 1977; Cheney & Vibbert, 1987; Springston & Leichty, 1994). Heath also employed Burke's concepts of dramatism, symbolic action, and identification; Fisher's narrative paradigm; and Bormann's fantasy theme analysis to explain the rhetorical dynamics—the drama—behind communicative activity among employees.

Work growing out of the International Association of Business Communicators' (IABC) 7-year study of public relations professionals around the world has helped define excellence in interorganizational communication. The principal publications from this study are Grunig's (1992) *Excellence in Public Relations and Communications Management*, which lays out the theoretical basis and the research program for the study, and Dozier, Grunig, Grunig's (1995) *Manager's Guide to Excellence in Public Relations and Communications Management*, which takes the study's findings and sets forth a program for public relations activities founded on a core of knowledge about communication, shared expectations with management about communication, and a supportive organizational culture. Through this IABC-sponsored project, "excellent" public relations basically means the organizational function practices two-way symmetrical communication, contributes to and aligns its activities with corporate strategic planning; is valued for input during management decision making; and upholds a participative culture by fostering two-way communication through teamwork, openness to new ideas, and involvement of others in communication decision making (Dozier et al., 1995). Toth's (2007) work demonstrates the growth and implications of the excellence perspective in multiple areas of investigation and worldwide application.

A topic traditionally associated with public relations is that of issues management, where the management of messages is at the heart of corporate rhetoric and public relations (Cheney & Vibbert, 1987). Crable and Vibbert (1985) argued that effective issues management can proactively influence an organization's public policy environment. They assert that issues are never solved, but they are resolved, progressing through five levels:

1. potential status (i.e., someone shows interest in an issue and asserts what to do),
2. imminent status (i.e., the issue is accepted by others),
3. current status (i.e., the issue gains public prominence, especially among civic leaders),
4. critical status (i.e., people take sides on the issue), and
5. dormant status (i.e., the issue is presumed dead until someone resurrects it with new ideas to resolve it).

An organization may manage an issue through one of four strategies:

1. reactive strategy (i.e., ride it out until it becomes dormant),
2. adaptive strategy (i.e., openly adjust to changes on an issue through compromise or by accepting alternatives),
3. dynamic strategy (i.e., anticipate changes in the environment and any issues that may emerge), or
4. catalytic strategy (i.e., take a proactive stance to create policy opportunities that generate desirable issues).

Additional research addresses functional aspects of issues management. Heath and Nelson (1986) asserted that issues management is performed by a staff function that identifies and monitors trends in public opinion that might mature into public policy and regulations for corporations and industries. That function is also responsible for developing, executing, and measuring campaigns. Heath (1997) presented an orientation of "strategic issues management" based on the principles for managing public policy resources. In his detailed assessment of what this orientation entails, he fundamentally argued that managing issues strategically for an organization means it must continuously engage in: "(a) strategic [business and communications] planning, (b) constant issue surveillance [across organizational and environmental boundaries], (c) aggressive efforts to ascertain and achieve corporate responsibility [within the community], and (d) willingness to openly, boldly, and collaboratively contest ideas relevant to the marketplace and public policy arena" (p. xiv). Such activity is not just the province of one group dedicated to corporate communications, but the shared responsibility of organizational leaders to foster dialogue and harmonious relationships with its publics (Heath, 1997).

In her examination of the staff function for issue management, Lauzen (1994, 1995a, 1995b) looked specifically at the roles of practitioners, managers, and staffs in managing issues, cutting to the level of people's jobs. Lauzen and Dozier (1994) extended such analyses by arguing that coupling proactive issues management with a participative organizational culture results in an effective approach to enacting complex environments. In related research on social responsibility, L'Etang (1994) examines the links between corporate social responsibility and the role of public relations in strengthening those links ethically. And Bostdorff and Vibbert (1994) used Perelman's concepts of value-centered and epideictic rhetoric to propose strategies for organizational values advocacy programs.

Other theory-building research addresses the definition of public relations (L. Grunig, 1992; Harlow, 1976; Long & Hazelton, 1987), corporate advocacy (Cheney & Dionisopoulos, 1989; Hoover, 1997), models of public relations processes (Gonzalez-Herrero & Pratt, 1996; Leichty & Springston, 1993; VanLeuven, 1989), inter- and intraorganizational roles of practitioners (Aldrich & Herker, 1977; Cheney & Vibbert, 1987; Kreps, 1989), symbolic and behavioral relationships that public relations fosters (Grunig, 1993a; Terry, 2001; Vasquez, 1993), and rhetorical and critical approaches to public relations (Elwood, 1995b; German, 1995). Basic research also has been done on meaning creation between public relations and stakeholders (Heath, 1993; R. Smith, 1993), message design by combining Borman's symbolic convergence theory and Grunig's work on publics (Vasquez, 1993), creating more effective communication during organizational change through face-to-face communication between supervisors and employees (not large employee meetings led by executives) about facts (not values) (Larkin & Larkin, 1994, 1995, 1996a, 1996b; also see D'Aprix, 1982, 1996a; Quirke, 2008), and identifying the effects of public relations on other organizational areas (Grunig, 1993b; Jensen, 1995). Some significant theory-based research has also been done in crisis management (cf. Seeger et al., 1998), specifically on product recalls (Gibson, 1995; Lacey & Llewellyn, 1995), the place of the public relations function in crises (Berg & Robb, 1992; Guth, 1995), legitimation strategies (Allen & Caillouet, 1994), corporate apologia (Hearit, 1994, 1995, 1996; Ware & Linkugel, 1973), corporate advocacy (Heath, 1980; Hoover, 1994, 1997), and argument structures (Hollihan & Riley, 1989; Sellnow, 1993; Sellnow & Ulmer, 1995).

Introspective Research As practitioners primarily look at public relations from their own vantage points, they survey the horizon for the profession (Bovet, 1995; Budd, 2003; Howard, 1995). For example, some see the "globalization" of public relations as technology brings people around the world closer (Fitzpatrick & Whillock, 1993; Hauss, 1995b; Kruckeberg, 1995). Others offer counsel on how best to work with editors, producers, and journalists to help them meet their goals while ethically meeting the needs of an organization (Bailey, 2000; Goldman, 1984; Hannaford, 1986; Howard & Mathews, 2000; Kohl, 2000; MediaMap, 2000a, 2000b). Still others argue that to advance in one's career and the profession itself, practitioners and management alike must successfully handle typical complaints about organizational communication—messages are too complex, messages don't come frequently enough, messages come much too often to make sense of what's going on, messages don't give the information people need, messages don't reflect enough of the members' concerns, messages are hiding the "real" truth, and so on (Filipczak, 1995; Young & Post, 1993).

To stay on top of these demands from constituencies, practitioners should strive for excellence in what they do, from being exceptional writers, listeners, and strategic thinkers to working in their communities—all to bolster their professional edge and gain direct knowledge of what is on people's minds (Corrado, 1993; D'Aprix, 1982, 1996a, 2001; Ferguson, 1999; Hauss, 1995a; Quirke, 2008; Serini, 1994; A. Smith, 1991). Such excellence can be maintained in the profession through standards for professional performance. In this area, surveys have served as the key measure of what constitutes accepted professional standards. In their study to test the theory of public relations excellence advanced by J. Grunig, L. Grunig, Sriramesh, Yi-Hui, and Lyra (1995), Deathridge and Hazleton (1998) found that asymmetrical and symmetrical worldviews of public relations can be measured reliably, resulting in valid predictions of public relations effectiveness from either worldview. Terry (2001), in a qualitative study of lobbyists' fantasy themes about their jobs, revealed they enact technician and manager roles and seven categories of motivations for doing their work.

At an individual or small-group level, defining standards for professional (not functional) public relations excellence becomes very muddy. For example, Toth, Serani, Wright, and Emig (1998) examined the trend in public relations roles in organizations over a 5-year period. They found significant role differences among practitioners in agencies, functional managers, and technicians. Work by Cameron and Sallot (1996), Sallot and Cameron (1997), and Sallot, Cameron, and Weaver-Larisey (1998a, 1998b), in several surveys of different population samples, argue that professional standards are difficult to establish, with wide demographic differences among practitioners and educators, even given cooperative efforts between them. The result is no consensus can be reached on what would make up a coherent body or even a core set of professional standards for the practice of public relations. That consensus is made all the more difficult to achieve because of the gulf between scholars' and professionals' views of the "real-world" practice of public relations. As van Ruler (2005) argued, the gulf is wide precisely because of the different worlds in which practitioners and scholars live.

That gulf can be crossed, he posits, by applying an "integrated" model of public relations professionalism that blends the strengths of several, selected perspectives into one.

Even with this lack of agreement about standards for professional excellence, much recent introspective scholarship argues that practitioners must be business strategists (Budd, 2003; D'Aprix, 1996b, 1997, 2001; Dozier et al., 1995; Ferguson, 1999; Garone, 1995; Gayeski, 1996; Jensen, 1995; Landes, 1997; Ledingham & Bruning, 2000; Lukaszewski, 2001a, 2001b, 2001c, 2008; Oliver, 2007; Potter, 1998; Whitwell & Argenbright, 1998; Williams, 1996). In this vein, the most effective public relations professionals are those who participate in corporate planning, counsel organizational leaders on all communication issues and opportunities, and build relationships among people in other departments and organizations.

Such expertise for the benefit of corporate leaders and their organizations has grown in importance in the "new economy" of electronic commerce (or "e-commerce") conducted over the Internet. For corporate communicators, introspective analysis of what practitioners' can and should do with the World Wide Web has become pervasive. As public relations professionals tuned into the promise and potential of the Internet at the turn of the millennium, Nemec (1999) argued that the proliferation of businesses and business activity on the Internet, including Web technology for organizations' own intranets, has created a significant demand for professional communicators to apply their skills to cyberspace. He stated, "There is such a high demand for people to do communications and PR in the technology space that there aren't enough experienced people to go around" (p. 27). This observation is true today: Companies must not squander the value of the Internet for effective and strategic communications, and they must call on professional communicators to lead the way (Nemec, 1999, p. 26). As Nemec (2000) further asserted, "the interpretation of technology is going to be a critical success factor. In the new century, interpretation is communication. The ability to articulate these interpretations quickly, clearly and accurately will differentiate successful leaders from the rest of the pack" (p. 30).

From books and articles to national conferences and local seminars, public relations on the Web remains a hot topic. Perhaps the definitive work on this area—even still today—is that by Holtz (2002), which thoroughly explored and explained the nature of the Internet and the most effective ways practitioners can use it to advance an organization's message. Holtz observed that the use of the Internet for public relations has sorely and surprisingly lagged behind the every-day business use of it in commercial endeavors. As he said:

> The communications profession lags woefully behind much of the Internet community. However, we are not alone. Most of the profes-

> sional uses of the Net are relatively primitive. The Internet is so new that businesses, unsure of what to do with it, are applying old uses to it. That's not uncommon, since the initial uses of *any* new technology are, in fact, the same things that were done with the *old* technology. (p. 3)

Holtz presented a kind of cookbook for harnessing the power of the Internet and Web technology, where public relations professionals will very soon seize the strategic advantage of the Internet for their communications programs. Holtz (2000) offered ways to spark that next-level thinking by laying out 10 ways to integrate organizations' communications efforts into a cohesive strategy.

There is a bevy of literature (practice-based and theory-based) about online public relations, from e-mail and Web sites to blogs and social media (e.g., Baker, 2000; Fialkow, 2000; Holtz, 2006a, 2006b; Holtz & Hobson, 2007; Kelleher, 2007; Kent, 2008; Middleberg, 2001; Smudde, 2005; Witmer, 2000; Xifra & Huertas, 2008). Ryan (2003) studied more than 100 public relations professionals' attitudes toward the Internet and found them to be both largely competent in and comfortable with the technology. The rubs, however, were teaching others principles of "good" Web sites and obtaining sound training in effective use of the Web for dialogic communication purposes. So the work for public relations practitioners has broadened considerably beyond "traditional" mass media outlets to also include the online world of multiple ways to instantly share information electronically with anyone anywhere. This result also means the immediacy of professional communicators' work has accelerated to Internet speed, which far outpaces the affects of faxes and wire services in getting information to target publics. With such demands and opportunities to "get the word out" *now*, skillful and strategic approaches to public relations will prove to be essential.

Burkean Scholarship on Organizational Communication

The first and only time that Kenneth Burke formally addressed public relations is in his work, *Attitudes Toward History*. In that book, he said that an alternative title for it would be, "Manual of Terms for a Public Relations Council with a Heart" (Burke, 1984a, p. i). We know from Cheney and Vibbert (1987) that public relations in the 1930s, when *Attitudes Toward History* was written and published, "became institutionalized in the large public agencies that arose to meet several environmental challenges [of social order (labor unions), political order (Roosevelt's New Deal), economic order (the Great Depression), and technological order (radio and 'mass culture')]" (p. 169).

Given this context, Burke provided terms in *Attitudes Toward History* that help define the work of publicists (his term for public relations practitioners); that they observe a didactic strategy "by coaching the imagination [of people] in obedience to critical postulates" (Burke, 1984a, p. 75). That is, publicists try to inspire people to analyze their situations critically, spark creative ways to address situations symbolically, and achieve consubstantiality with what is going on in human situations. If one observes various possibilities in a situation, the carrying-out, the "bureaucratizing" of one of them stems from the historic texture surrounding it. Publicists would likely place themselves in a position where they can empower people with humanistic attitudes, motives, and symbols of authority to act for the good of society. In other words, publicists' "natural tendency of [their] symbolic enterprise is towards integration of symbolic superstructures" (Burke, 1984a, p. 184).

Publicists, accordingly, have a significant role in history. Their work moderates the shifts of superstructural symbols for new ones, a perspective that predates and is congruent with Kuhn's (1970) concept of paradigm shifts. As Burke (1984a) said,

> Obedience to reigning symbols of authority is in itself natural and wholesome. The need to reject them is painful and bewildering. . . . [T]hose in possession of the authoritative symbols tend to drive the opposition into a corner, by owning the priests (publicists, educators) who will rebuke the opposition for its disobedience to the reigning symbols. The opposition abandons some of the symbolic ingredients and makes itself 'ready to take over' other symbolic ingredients. (p. 226)

Although publicists attempt to maintain something of the status quo through appropriate frames of acceptance or rejection (perhaps doing so by employing some strategic ambiguity), they also provide some impetus into what ways the reigning symbols may not be completely discarded but somehow revised or "bridged" into newer symbolisms. Again, publicists integrate symbolic superstructures, which also include revisions to them. In Burke's (1984a) terms, "[O]ne must not adopt the polemic, pamphleteering attitude so quickly, unless he [sic] is more interested in winning an argument than in understanding a process" (p. 327).

A publicist is not a positivist who merely reports on social situations, but a humanist whose focus is on inducing cooperation between an organization and its publics. In Burke's view, a publicist's chief interest is to tend to the integrity of and educate people about symbols and symbolic superstructures within the historical context of a society, which would include organizations. In this capacity, a publicist, as a coach of attitudes (Burke, 1984a) or even as a writer of "secular prayers" (Burke, 1984a), "would be a perfectly balanced sub-whole in a perfectly balanced super-whole. He [*sic*] would be the microcosm that matched the macrocosm. He [sic] would define his identity by membership in one single all-inclusive corporation" (Burke, 1984a, p. 253).

Burke's *Attitudes Toward History* represents a shift toward society from the individual, which is the focus of his preceding works, *Counter-statement* and *Permanence and Change*. This shift stresses motivation and action over form (cf. Brock, 1995). This shift also suggests a greater emphasis on rhetorical issues, as Burke argued that "naming" is a way we create our own realities and identify "friendly" and "unfriendly" relationships with other people. Burke's most celebrated expression of his ideas about rhetoric (and his general epistemological and ontological orientation) are given in his definition of humans (Burke, 1989):

> Humans are the
> Symbol-making, symbol-using, symbol-misusing animal
> Inventor of the negative
> Separated from our natural condition
> By instruments of our own making
> Goaded by hierarchy
> Acquiring foreknowledge of death
> And rotten with perfection

Symbol systems place humans in the realm of action—symbolic action—and beyond mere biological motion. For Burke, rhetoric is a function of language "as a symbolic means of inducing cooperation in beings that by nature respond to symbols" (Burke, 1969b, p. 43). This definition expands the traditional notion of rhetoric as persuasion—that rhetoric is an element of symbolic action, which includes persuasion and identification. Identification entails simultaneous unity and division—it is rooted in the inherent division among people because of their physical separateness, and language helps them bridge that condition to become "consubstantial," to find common ground or "substance" (Burke, 1969b).

To Burke (1973), because language is "the dancing of an attitude" and shapes our views of reality, guides our behavior, and generates our motives for our actions, human action could be understood through drama. He developed dramatism as a method to derive a "literal statement about human motivation" (Burke, 1968b). Dramatistic analysis proceeds through the pentad (Burke, 1969a), a cluster analysis of the terms that name the *act* (what was done), *scene* (where it was done), *agent* (who did it), *agency* (how that person did it) and *purpose* (for what reason the person did it). Ratios of these five terms show relationships between them and in which term the greatest attention is placed to discover motivation for the act. Burke's cycle of terms for order (Burke, 1970) is a logological approach that helps us understand the role of symbolic action through order, pollution, guilt, purification through either mortification or victimage, and redemption (Brock, 1995, 1999; Burke, 1970). All together, identification, the pentad, and the terms for order are Burke's tools for rhetorical analysis that may be used individually or in combination to understand symbolic action. (Burke's ideas are treated in more detail in the next chapter.)

Typically, scholars use Burke's ideas from his later works (i.e., those published after and including *A Grammar of Motives*) to study organizational discourse. Tompkins, Fisher, Infante, and Tompkins (1975) used Burke's concepts of identification and mystery to explain organizational processes and communication. They tested people's sensitivity to order in the hierarchy, mystery in the hierarchy, and identification with levels in the hierarchy at a northeastern U.S. university. Tompkins et al. found that, although individuals at lower levels of an hierarchy did not perceive more order than those in upper levels, those same people did perceive greater hierarchical mystery than those in upper levels. These results square with two other findings that all respondents identify more with their own rank in the hierarchy than with other levels, and there is a high inverse relationship between one's identification with hierarchical levels and the degree of perceived mystery in upper hierarchical levels.

Focusing on Burke's notions of guilt and redemption, Foss (1984) investigated Chrysler's bailout by the federal government as a rhetorical act. She asserted that the company was at once trying to redeem itself of guilt for producing poor-quality vehicles, failing to meet the demand for small cars, and having to take a bailout to stay in business. Foss identified 10 major strategies that Chrysler used in its advertising during the years 1978 to 1981 to redeem itself and "retool" its image. She concluded that although Chrysler's ad campaigns should have been successful, the symbolism of the bailout itself undermined the themes of the company's viability and reinforced ideas that the U.S. economy is not totally capitalistic—that if a company is big enough it can get federal assistance, and that Chrysler was not financially strong enough and did not have the products to compete.

By far the most-used concept in scholarship about organizational communication and public relations that relates to Burke is identification. The concept of identification is almost always used independently from his others to explain the dynamics of organizational communication, especially public relations. Adler (1993) explained that there are two categories for scholarship using identification: organizational identification and rhetorical identification. The first category refers to one's "buying in to" and, subsequently, participating socially and productively within an organization. Albert and Whetten (1985) asserted that organizational identity is both a product of one's involvement within an organization and a process as people come to know more about the organization and its members—both of which are possible only through communication. M. E. Brown (1969) used a case study of an industrial organization to examine the factors, both symbolic (e.g., achievement) and pragmatic (e.g., money), that motivate people to behave in certain ways in response to their perceived relationship with the organization. He found that identification "is mediated through symbolic rather than pragmatic motivational states" (p. 354).

In their case study of the Roman Catholic Church and a research-and-development laboratory, Hall and Schneider (1972) studied "the individual and organizational correlates of identification" (p. 341)—tenure, job challenge, self-image, needs, and satisfaction. They concluded that "organizational identification appears to be a process in which some 'right type' of person is most likely to enter an organization (through selection and recruitment) and be ready to identify with it" (p. 349). Rotondi (1975) discussed methodological issues with previous research on organizational identification, issues like defining the concept, choosing the best contexts for study, and clarifying the behavioral responses indicating identification. Rotondi found that organizational identification was "directly related to the general personality variables of social isolation, or insecurity in social relationships, and incompetence, as reflected by inadequate feelings of mastery over the self and the environment" (p. 99). Boyd (2004) analyzed the flawed rhetoric of R. J. Reynolds Tobacco Company in its 1995 advertising campaign against restrictions on tobacco advertising, concluding that the company failed to establish identification between the organization's and the public's views of the issue.

With his numerous publications, Cheney (and his co-authors) is without question the leading scholar of rhetorical identification. As Adler (1993) stated, "so far, Cheney's two studies [Cheney, 1983a, 1991] comprise the only research based on the Burkean concept [of identification] . . ." (p. 24). Indeed, Cheney's (1991) *Rhetoric in Organizational Society* is perhaps the most extensive application of Burke's concept of identification. This work, above all others, serves as a model for the author's research project. Cheney's *Rhetoric* is based on the premise that "organizations are fundamentally rhetorical in nature" (p. ix), and he employed an in-depth analysis, using rhetorical criticism, of a single case (i.e., the U.S. Catholic bishops' 1983 pastoral letter, *The Challenge of Peace*) that has far-reaching significance. His case study "is detailed and extensive so as to account fully for the organizational, rhetorical, and identity-related aspects of a series of events: the development of a historic 'corporate' document" (p. 164). Like Cheney's work, I enact a parallel rhetorical criticism of GM's C/K truck issue for this study that shall have broad implications for practitioners, scholars and students. As Cheney (1991) said, "To understand what is 'beneath' as well as what is 'within' a text . . . one must know the complete history of a corporate 'voice' to understand its message deeply . . . to assess the interplay of individuals, interests groups, and symbols in the study of organizational rhetoric" (p. 164).

In his *Rhetoric in an Organizational Society*, Cheney argued that because the nexus of organizations is communication and is, therefore, rhetorical, the paramount task is the "management of multiple identities" among all of an organization's publics. People enact this rhetorical process, because "[w]e are constantly aligning ourselves with the interests of some persons and distancing ourselves from the interests of other persons" (p. 20). Organizational rhetoric is a process enacted by individuals on behalf of themselves and the collectives with which they are affiliated. In Cheney's scheme, "identity" refers to an individual's or group's sense of who they are in the social order; "identification" refers to the process by which people appropriate an identity; "organization" concerns symbolic and material energies used among people to coordinate their own interests and maintain the collective; and "rhetoric" subsumes both processes of identification and organization to simultaneously balance the unity and division among people both within and without a collective. For organizational rhetoric, "[t]he coordination of identities in expression becomes complicated in proportion to the multiplicity of identities for which and to which a collectivity such as a corporation must speak, including both members and outsiders" (p. 17).

Together with Cheney's other publications and, especially, his collaborative works, he addressed issues principally through a Burkean frame (cf. Tompkins & Cheney, 1993). The issues he (and his co-authors) addresses range from communication ethics (Cheney, 1984; Cheney & Frenette, 1993) and the value of close textual analysis of human communication (Cheney, 1983b, 1988, 1992; Cheney & McMillan, 1990; Christensen & Cheney, 1994), to organizational socialization (Cheney, 1983a; Cheney & Tompkins, 1987; Tompkins & Cheney, 1985) and an organization's relations with its stakeholders (Cheney & Dionisopoulos, 1989; Cheney & Vibbert, 1987). Cheney's research has the depth of analysis and breadth of issues, especially those concerning public relations in particular, that has significant applicability to this project.

Other scholars have used Burke's ideas to make sense of organizational communication. Tompkins (1987) leaned on Burke's idea that the central term for rhetoric is not persuasion but identification, which stresses the cooperation among people achieved through language. For Tompkins, symbolic action is at the heart—it is the substance—of organizations, but the concept of identification has been misunderstood or misapplied by organizational researchers. Tompkins (1984) also probed other rhetorical issues in organizations, again focusing on the symbolic action of people. Schuetz (1997) anchored her analysis of corporate advocacy in Burke's dramatistic idea of "entitlement," which addresses the changes in meaning as people apply their own "cycles of terms" to symbolic action and feature particular words (Burke, 1996a). Schuetz used this idea to frame the general concept of corporate advocacy and define it broadly as "communication strategies used by advocates—stakeholders, managers, members of the labor force, and consumers—to promote and defend their issues, policies, and positions through complex symbolic means within a carefully defined context" (p. 237). As a result, Schuetz dramatistically addressed specific aspects of the symbolic action of corporate advocacy, namely that strategies are acts; advocates are agents; issues, policies and propositions are purposes; symbolic means are agency; contexts are scenes; and motives are teased out from these elements.

In their ambitious work, Cragan and Shields (1995) formalized a theoretical method, based on their earlier research (cf. Cragan & Shields, 1981), for engaging in applied communication research. They developed a three-dimensional matrix of three intersecting planes to guide one's analysis in applied communication research. For Burke's dramatism theory (BDT), those planes are the master analogue plane for the purification ritual (Burke's terms for order), the structural plane of the hexad (Burke's, 1968b, pentad plus attitude), and the evaluation plane of linguistic vantage point, cyclical standing, quality of motivation, and degree of identification. A researcher can use this model to triangulate among the three planes to understand the effects between communication and social order, for example. Cragan and Shields reviewed examples of research that reflects the BDT model and illustrates its ability to explain communication.

Weickian Scholarship about Organizational Communication

Weick's theory of organizing is founded on symbolic action, and he emphasized the dynamic and creative forces of human action as the starting point for organizations and organizational theorizing. The central issue for Weick was not organization as a noun but as a verb—*organizing*. By stressing action, organizing is "a consensually validated grammar for reducing equivocality by means of sensible interlocked behaviors" (Weick, 1979b, p. 3). Thus, organizing is an intersubjective activity where people try to reduce a perceived level of equivocality—the various possible interpretations we may have for a situation taken from a flow of events—through communicative action. Human communication is at the heart of Weick's theory because "objects are inconsequential until they are acted upon and then incorporated retrospectively into events, situations, and explanations" (Weick, 1988). In this way, people follow the recipe: "'How can I know what I think until I see what I say?'" (Weick, 1979b, p. 133). This is sensemaking, and it involves the action of talking retrospectively to people about events (Weick, 1988, p. 307). Sensemaking constitutes a socially constructed "grammar" people use when dealing with the cognitive dissonance created by equivocality.

For Weick, the process of organizing is also evolutionary, stems from human action, and proceeds (with causal linkages and specific rules and cycles) from ecological change through the stages of enactment, selection, and retention. As he summarized it:

> Organizations are presumed to talk to themselves over and over to find out what they are thinking.... The organism or group enacts equivocal raw talk, the talk is viewed retrospectively, sense is made of it, and this sense is then stored as knowledge in the retention process. The aim of each process has been to reduce equivocality and to get some idea of what has occurred. (Weick, 1979b, pp. 133-134)

Organizing is a cognitive, language-based activity among people. It is based on talk, especially double interacts, to reduce equivocality from enacted information by "coordinat[ing] their action for making sense together" (Bantz, 1990, p. 134; Weick's ideas are addressed in more detail in Chap. 2.)

With communication at the core of Weick's theory of organizing, rhetorical implications for organizing run throughout his work, which has made it quite appealing to communication scholars. In a special section of *Communication Studies* in 1989, celebrating the 20th anniversary of the publication of Weick's *The Social Psychology of Organizing*, three scholars, as well as Weick, reflected on the impact of this and the whole of his work. Bantz (1989) demonstrated how Weick's ideas about organizing make up a frame for defining organizational communication as collective action, emphasize cultural processes where meaning is central and intersubjectively created, and view organizing as a "symbolic cultural reality" (p. 238). Putnam (1989) examined the role of negotiation in organizing. She argued that the components of negotiation, bargaining, and conflict are rooted in the process of making sense of equivocal environments along the lines of two "antithetical" positions. The double interacts between members of the opposing parties evolve to understanding and resolution through communication cycles that manage tension and new information. Sproule (1989) explained that Weick's theory of organizing places organizations as dynamic, fluid, and flexible processes of enactments among people that hinge on private human symbolic action and adopt public opinions as corporate themes.

In other works, scholars have used or echoed Weick's concepts when explaining organizational communication. Bantz and Smith (1977) and Kreps (1980) performed separate experiments to verify the explanatory power of Weick's initial model (Weick, 1969) of the organizing process. Bantz and Smith's experiment failed to find empirical support for the relationship between equivocality and behavior cycles (i.e., enactment, selection, and retention). Bantz and Smith concluded that even though Weick's theory of organizing has certain advantages for communication researchers, the model suffers from an important difficulty: "Weick narrows the range of relevant variables emphasizing a single variable, equivocality, to the exclusion of others" (p. 183) in the process of organizing. Kreps' (1980) experiment, which sought to correct for certain weaknesses in Bantz and Smith's experiment, concerned people's information-processing behaviors but not the three phases of Weick's model. The results of Kreps' study support Weick's model of organizing—as information equivocality increased, cycles of communication behaviors increased and were statistically and theoretically significant.

Putnam and Sorenson (1982) used Weick's (1979b) refined model as the framework for a study of how people at different levels in an organization use ambiguous information to handle equivocality. They found that people at various levels reduced equivocality differently—workers and foremen added interpretations while managers proposed action steps—and this disparity contributes to misunderstanding and, thereby, represents the key to understanding an organization's sensemaking process. Equivocality and organizing are the focal points to Seeger's (1997a) application of Weick's principles to the study of ethics in organizational communication. Because ethical issues are inherently based on values, "ethical equivocality" results as people enact their individual and often conflicting value systems to interpret those issues in various ways. Communication reduces ethical equivocality, which permeates the organizing process, from individuals to the organization's place in society.

In a complementary application of Weick's model to public relations, Kreps (1989) explained organizational leaders' deep need for timely and accurate information and public relations' vital role in reducing equivocality for leaders and employees. Of particular importance is performance management. Kreps showed how Weick's model strengthens the significant role public relations professionals play when making sure leaders and members are well-informed about the confluence of environmental constraints and internal issues on organizational development. In an extension of this work, Kreps (2007) demonstrated the theoretical and practical applicability of Weick's model so that professionals can better "coordinate efforts (organize) to process equivocal information and direct organizational activities" (p. 28). Kreps presented seven recommendations for public relations organizing and analyzes an example of crisis communication that illustrates the model's workability for the practice and study of public relations.

Smircich and Stubbart (1985) proposed that the concept of "enacted environment" be used in strategic management theory and practice. Their idea is to view the primary role of mangers as the management of meaning and not the management of events. For Smircich and Stubbart, managers enact environments as they "look out into the world to see what is there . . . to access, organize, and evaluate data . . . [in] an intellectual challenge to delineate a strategy that will meet the real demands and real constraints that exist 'out there'" (pp. 725-726). This process of enacting environments is the root of strategic management, "because these enactment processes form the invisible foundations supporting strategic choice" (p. 734).

Weick's theory has also been useful in examining aspects of organizational culture. Larkey and Morrill (1995) employed concepts about the symbolicity of organizations that are consistent with Weick's in an analysis of organizational commitment. Larkey and Morrill leaned on the concept of identification articulated by Cheney (and his co-authors) and asserted in Weickian terms that organizational commitment is a symbolic process of sensemaking germane to an organization's culture that "pays serious attention to the meanings that bind people together with each other and their organizations, as well as push them apart" (p. 199). In related research, Everett (1994) argued that the link between enactment and organizational adaptation is the foundation for organizational evolution, which itself grows out from enacted environments.

Pacanowski and O'Donnell-Trujillo (1982) argued for a nontraditional, process approach to studying organizational culture by defining organizations as "the interlocked actions of collectivity" (p. 122) and laying out a program that focuses on a series of "indicators and displayers of organizational sense-making" (p. 124). A year later, Pacanowski and O'Donnell-Trujillo (1983) again argued that the research about organizational culture overemphasizes structural aspects and neglects the processural aspects through which the structures are created. With the view that organizational communication is cultural performance, they propose a method for integrating process thinking into research about organizational culture. M. H. Brown and McMillan (1991), with a postmodern view of culture as text, assert that close textual analysis of organizations is possible because organizational cultures are the products of their symbols, texts and subtexts among all members of a collective in its hierarchy.

CONTENT PREVIEW

There is sufficient scholarship in the three subject areas germane to this study, as the literature review shows, and there are also significant points of crossover in the research among those areas. The most important crossover occurs between the rhetorical and organizational views of corporate discourse. The purpose of this volume is to examine the case of GM's public relations about the C/K pickup issue through a combination of theories of rhetoric and organizations. That combination is the heart of a method to analyze patterns of symbolic action in the organizing of public relations. Having covered the nature of and research history for this study in this chapter, the next step is to establish an analytical method that will be applied to the case.

That method's theoretical foundation synthesizes the work of Burke and Weick, where close textual analysis is guided by a generic approach.

The groundwork for establishing the analytical method is set in the next chapter, which reviews key principles in theories both from Burke and Weick. From this framework about the two theories emerges an analysis of the common ground shared between them. This analysis provides the theoretical basis of the analytical method, including a breakdown of the areas of consubstantiality between Burke and Weick. Integrated with the theoretical orientation for the method is a pragmatic approach for analyzing texts, which establishes a system to analyze public relations texts within discourse genres. Following this presentation of the method, the final section of Chapter 2 describes how the method is used in the analysis of the case.

The case history is traced logologically in Chapter 3, using Burke's "rhetoric of rebirth" tempered with Weick's theory of enactment. Significant events that officials from GM and non-GM organizations bracketed from the environment are highlighted in the curve of the issue's history. This logological examination of GM's C/K pickup issue applies the method to explain the order of things (i.e., the enacted environments) for GM about the C/K truck issue and what GM officials and opponents to GM enacted as the pollutants, guilty parties, and purification strategies on the road to redemption. The case history shows GM's rhetoric of rebirth and how identification was established through published news coverage, studies, and reports about the truck's safety, corporate publications, official statements, and personal interviews to trace the case's history. That discussion also points to the discursive choices that those officials made—primarily GM officials. This chapter, then, establishes the context for the analysis of the public relations texts.

The application of this project's analytical method continues in Chapters 4 and 5. In Chapter 4, a microscopic level of analysis is applied to the case using this project's method. The chapter examines the organizing of GM officials, their efforts to develop key messages about the issue, and form a communication strategy to inspire cooperation with the automaker's publics. Following this examination is an application of the method in a close analysis of a text that is representative of the essential strategy behind the automaker's public relations action.

On a macroscopic level, Chapter 5 applies the method to explore how GM officials enacted the strategies and applied the key messages in PR texts. The chapter focuses on the range of public relations discourse that GM officials created to manage the issue of the safety of C/K pickups' fuel systems among external and internal publics. The macroscopic analysis of PR texts focuses on the evolution of the case through the public relations discourse genres enacted during the case's history. The chapter discusses the actors involved and their roles in the case and, most importantly, applies the analytical method at a high level to explain how GM officials' sensemaking resulted in specific genres of symbolic action about the issue for the company. The combined micro- and macroscopic analyses offer a holistic view of how GM officials made sense of equivocal situations on the C/K pickup issue and enacted texts in strategic ways to inspire cooperation between the automaker and its publics.

Chapter 6 answers this volume's three research questions and evaluates both the case and the analytical method. That evaluation consists of judgments about why GM attained redemption (or condemnation) in the C/K pickup case, and that judgment explains why the company was successful (or not) on traditional PR grounds and, especially, on the grounds of this project's method, which goes beyond traditional evaluative criteria. This analysis paves the way for Chapter 7 to set up a proactive program for the dramatistic organizing of public relations, based on lessons learned from the case and implications for future research and practice.

2

DRAMATISTIC ORGANIZING AS METHOD

The analyses of the GM C/K pickup case in Chapters 3, 4, and 5 address rhetorical and organizational elements simultaneously, because it is through symbolic action that organizational members make sense of what is going on around them and enact that sensemaking through symbolic action. Because the breadth of both Burke's and Weick's work is wide, it is important to know what concepts from each theory are emphasized in this volume. This chapter develops the major components to the analytical method and describes how it is applied to the case chosen for this project.

Separate summaries of Burke's and Weick's theories present the method's essential theoretical framework, and these summaries are followed by an analysis of the issues about combining them into a single theoretical orientation. Then, dovetailing from this common ground between Burke and Weick, a framework for textual analysis leans on discourse genres to establish an effective way to apply the theoretical framework to unique categories of public relations texts. Finally, a description of the steps for applying the resulting analytical system to a case example completes the explanation of this project's analytical method.

THEORETICAL FRAMEWORK

Two major features of this project's analytical method are (a) its theoretical framework based on the common ground between Burke's rhetorical theory and critical method and Weick's theory of organizing, and (b) an approach for enacting textual analyses of public relations discourse. The theoretical framework establishes the principles that guide the criticism of the case study, and the approach for textual analysis provides a way to apply those theoretical principles directly to specific kinds of texts germane to the case study. The starting point for this project's analytical method is Burke, which is the primary theoretical orientation.

Burke's Theory of Rhetoric and Tools for Criticism

Burke once said of himself and the critical enterprise: "I think that there has to be a lot of leeway in this business. I see no reason for being authoritarian. . . . The fundamental notion of choice in my scheme is difference" (cited in Chesebro, 1992, p. 365). The fact that Burke created an open system—one that welcomes others' views that are similar and different, converging and diverging—allows it to grow beyond what he originally set forth. As Chesebro argued, "To remain viable, a system of analysis must be an 'open system,' responding to changing human conditions and adapting to shifting attitudes, beliefs, and actions. In this regard, even Burke's system of analysis must undergo transformation if it is to remain receptive to ever-changing human dynamics" (p. 364). During the 70-plus years of Burke's writings, he, other critics, and surrounding circumstances helped to reshape and extend his system. The breadth of application and appeal to those in many fields other than rhetoric (e.g., organizational communication [see Cheney, 1983b, 1991; Tompkins, 1984, 1987], feminism [see Condit, 1992; Japp, 1999], and sociology [see Duncan 1968, 1989; Gusfield, 1989]) demonstrates the importance that critics have placed on Burke's ideas and critical method. Perhaps the three most important elements of Burke's rhetorical system are the nature of rhetoric, dramatism, and terms for order.

The cornerstone for Burke (1989) is that "Humans are the /symbol-making, symbol-using, symbol-misusing animal" (p. 263). Symbol systems (i.e., language) place humans in the realm of action—symbolic action—and beyond mere biological motion. Accordingly, symbolic action "is the basis of all human knowing, and all knowing is constrained by the principles of that capacity" (Gregg, 1978, p. 13). Symbolic action may take any form and is rhetorical; whereas, Burke says that rhetoric "is rooted in an essential function of language itself . . . the use of language as a symbolic means of inducing cooperation in beings that by nature respond to symbols" (Burke, 1969b, p. 43).[3] In this way, Burke expands the traditional notion of rhetoric as persuasion—that rhetoric is posterior to symbolic action. For Burke, the central term for rhetoric is not persuasion but *identification*, which emphasizes the common ground people share. Yet because people are inherently separate from one another, identification also entails division simultaneously with that sense of unity. To manage that division, people use language to "alternately be focused on the 'oneness' or the 'separation' [of people from one another]" (Brock, 1995, p. 15). Either focus means people seek common ground, or "substance," which is "the context for the communication or the key to the speaker's attitudes" (Brock, 1990, p. 191).

When people unite within a context they are said to be "consubstantial" (Burke, 1969b, p. 21). Identification, or "consubstantiality," between people results when the content of one's statement appeals to someone through its *form*, that is, a discourse pattern that "gratifies the needs which it creates [in someone]" (Burke, 1968a, p. 138). The forming of discourse

> involves action, from those fundamental principles of symbolic forming that are covert, primal acts of the mind through the acting of principles and ideas in repetitive, progressive movement, to the summing up act of perceiving the forming structure which encompasses all. At each level, the action includes inducement to participate; to participate is to act in terms of building expectancies and to be gratified by the fulfillment provided. The inducement . . . is rhetorical; invitation to action involves critical and evaluative faculties at every level and is therefore partisan in stance and tone. (Gregg, 1978, p. 10)

In this way, rhetoric becomes "equipment for living," because it helps us make sense of things when we name or define them, and rhetoric represents a creative strategy for dealing with or solving problems within situations (Foss, Foss, & Trapp, 1991, p. 177).

The language we use shapes our views of reality (or "frames of reference"), guides our behavior, and generates our motives for our actions. For example, the symbolic action of naming, this "symbolic tinkering," stands as one's "vast symbolic synthesis, a rationale of imaginative and conceptual imagery that 'locates' the various aspects of experience. This symbolism guides social purpose: it provides one with 'cues' as to what he [sic] should try to get, how he [sic] should try to get it, and how he [sic] should 'resign himself' [sic] to a renunciation of the things he [sic] can't get" (Burke 1984a, p. 179). Consequently, social components tend to drive one toward acceptance, rejection, or passivity of different symbolisms that may be emphasized. Such actions are extensions of an overarching symbolic frame in human situations. So language is the "dancing of an attitude" as we react not to a thing itself, but to the symbols we create for the thing (Burke, 1973, p. 9).

To Burke, human behavior (action) could be understood as drama, and he developed dramatism as "a method of analysis and a corresponding critique of terminology designed to show that the most direct route to the study of human relations and human motives is via a methodical inquiry into cycles or clusters of terms and their functions" (Burke, 1968b, p. 445). Dramatism is a methodology that provides a literal statement about human motivation, not one based on a metaphor of a drama, because language performs a literal function; whereas, "we must look at language to see what reality means" (Foss et al., 1991, p. 183).

Burke prescribed the pentad, a type of "cluster analysis," for discourse that can be used to discover motives in symbolic action. It is, as Gregg (1978) pointed out, "A calculus for charting the rhetoric of form" (p. 12). Burke (1969a) described the pentad:

> In a rounded statement about motives, you must have some word that names the *act* (names what took place, in thought or deed), and another that names the *scene* (the background of the act, the situation in which it occurred); also, you must indicate what person or kind of person (*agent*) performed the act, what means or instruments he [*sic*] used (*agency*), and the *purpose*. . . . [A]ny complete statement about motives will offer some kind of answers to these five questions: what was done (act), when or where it was done (scene), who did it (agent), how he [*sic*] did it (agency), and why (purpose). (p. xv)

Dramatism takes "act" as "the terministic center from which many related considerations can be shown to radiate . . ." (Burke, 1968b, p. 445) when acts, scenes, agents, agencies, and purposes are clustered into "ratios." Ratios (20 in all) show relationships between pentadic elements. For example, an act–agent ratio focuses on the affect of acts on individuals according to their nature; a scene–act ratio examines what kind of act is required within a specific scene. Ratios help us discover "which term in the pentad receives the greatest attention by the rhetor and thus suggests in what term to look for the motivation of the act" (Foss et al., 1991, p. 187).

As symbol-using beings, we are also "goaded by hierarchy," which grows out from an inherent aspect of language: the negative. Humans invented the negative, because "in using language, we must recognize that a word for a thing is not that thing" (Foss et al., 1991, p. 190). The use of a term implies its opposite—order implies disorder, unity implies division, acceptance implies rejection, and action implies motion—and the "terministic screens" (Burke, 1966b, p. 45) we use suggest the order we place on things. Commandments, which reflect a sense of order, are meant to govern the actions of people and result in the imposition of a hierarchy, where people and things are divided along arbitrary classifications (i.e., "bureaucratization"). Such classes are imbued with relative levels of power, where those closer to the top of the hierarchy are further removed from and exercise greater power than those below them. To move beyond the mystery one feels about others at higher and lower levels in a hierarchy, individuals seek perfection within it and do so in their situations according to the ideal professed by the person(s) at the top.

According to Burke, humans possess the ability to accept or reject their situations and attempts to symbolize them. Acceptance is a positive response to a situation, hierarchical position, or the hierarchy itself, and rejection is a negative response allowed by language. When someone rejects social order, thereby polluting it, the result is guilt, which "is inherent in society—class conflict is inherent in hierarchy. Guilt compels purification [i.e., one's being absolved of guilt by others] through either mortification (self-sacrifice) or victimage (scapegoating), both of which lead to redemption [or a symbolic rebirth of the person who rejected the hierarchy]" (Wilder, 1989, p. xii). This dramatistic view of social order describes Burke's (1970) "terms for order," his rhetoric of rebirth, that is grounded in the human invention of language.

Taken individually, Burke's tools for dramatistic criticism—identification, the pentad, and terms for order—allow critics to see deeply into the motives behind symbolic action and do so in specific ways. If taken together, those same tools can augment each other's strengths to form a rounded, holistic approach to analyze symbolic action, generally, and organizational discourse, specifically. Human symbolic action is the focus of and, thus, the link among the pentad, identification, and the terms for order. As Brock (1995, 1999) explained, these tools build on one another and can work together as a system for rhetorical criticism. As levels of order and abstraction increase in symbolic action, "the pentad can be used to establish identification(s) for the terms for order within the nature of pollution, guilt, purification, and redemption" (Brock, 1995, pp. 18-19).

Burke's system allows for critical analysis of individuals and social orders of any kind—it is a system open to others' views and other applications, including analyses of organizational discourse (see Chesebro, 1992). Brock (1995) argued that Burke's tools for rhetorical analysis (i.e., the pentad, identification, and terms for order) can be used together to create greater understanding of the symbolic nature of discourse than if each tool was used alone. Indeed, I have found these tools to be quite useful in my work as a public relations professional. For example, Burke's view of rhetoric is sufficiently broad that it would accommodate special events, crisis and issue communication, corporate speakers, and press conferences as symbolic acts.

Weick's Theory of Organizing

Weick placed communication at the foundation for his systems theory of organizing, and he recognized the dynamic and creative forces of human action as the starting point for organizations and organizational theorizing. The central issue for Weick is not organization as a noun but as a verb—*organizing*. By stressing action, organizing is "a consensually validated grammar for reducing equivocality by means of sensible interlocked behaviors" (Weick, 1979b, p. 3). Organizing involves information about an environment that organizational members enact to make sense of a given situation. Human communication is at the heart of Weick's theory because "objects are inconsequential until they are acted upon and then incorporated retrospectively into events, situations and explanations" (Weick, 1988, p. 307). Here is a summary of Weick's theory of organizing and some important implications for understanding the rhetoric of organizational discourse.

Organizing is an intersubjective activity where people try to reduce a perceived level of equivocality—the various possible interpretations we may have for a situation taken from a flow of events—through communicative action. The point here is not the traditional view that people create a conception of reality then act on it, but quite the reverse: People act first within flows of experience, then try to make sense of that action. In this way, people follow the recipe: "How can I know what I think until I see what I say?" (Weick, 1979b, p. 133). This is sensemaking, and it involves the action of talking retrospectively to people about events (Weick, 1988). Sensemaking constitutes a socially constructed "grammar" people use when dealing with the cognitive dissonance created by equivocality, or "[h]appenings that represent a change, a difference, or a discontinuity from what has been going on, happenings that seem to have more than one meaning" (Weick, 1979b, p. 4).

Reducing equivocality can occur only after "consensual validation"—people agree on what is illusory and what is real (Weick, 1979b), which marks the beginning of a socially developed grammar for organizing. Given this consensus, organization members may reduce equivocality through cycles and assembly rules. Cycles are stable subassemblies of interlocking communication behaviors—reflecting the essence of organizing—between people, or "double interacts," within stable social groups. Being subassemblies, cycles are tightly connected internally but loosely coupled to other cycles. Assembly rules are "inferred recipes" used by influential members to develop a process for all members to "mobilize several double interacts into larger processes that are directed at inputs" (Weick, 1979b, p. 113). A grammar for organizing uses rules for "forming variables and causal linkages into meaningful structures" (Weick, 1979b, pp. 3-4). The conjunction of cycles with assembly rules means that cycles can be systematically "assembled into larger subassemblies in the interest of stabilizing equivocal displays and transforming them into information, enacted environments, and cause maps" (Weick, 1979b, p. 113). Cause maps are a way to make sense of intercycle linkages—to "examine relations in organizations"—and predict the fate of the system by paying special attention to "interdependent variables, causal loops, and the presence or absence of control" (Weick, 1979b, p. 74). Again, the central component throughout cycles is sensemaking communication among people.

Organizing, as a sensemaking activity, is based on the principle that people act first then try to figure it out. The traditional sociocultural model of organizational evolution is Darwinian in its approach, following along three stages through time: Variation in behaviors develop among organizational members, selection of certain behaviors over others is made, and retention of those selected behaviors is asserted as part of the group process (Bantz, 1990). For Weick, the process of organizing is also evolutionary, but stems from human action and proceeds (with causal linkages and specific rules and cycles) from ecological change through the stages of enactment, selection, and retention.

People tend to take smooth flows of experience for granted until some change occurs, since "[i]t is only the occasion of change when attention becomes active" (Weick, 1979b p. 130). These changes—ecological changes—are the "raw materials for sense-making" in an enactable environment (Weick, 1979b, p. 130). Enactment operates at the level of the individual, where someone is guided by preconceptions to "bracket" an event from the flow of experience—to take a sample of that flow for closer inspection (Weick, 1979b). Enactment suggests organizational adaptability and is, then, key to Weick's model, being "the process by which organizational members produce the environments to which they respond" (Everett, 1994, p. 96).

An enacted environment results in and possesses its own kind of equivocality because it is "an orderly, material, social construction that is subject to multiple interpretations" (Weick, 1988, p. 307). If an environment is enacted, there are as many environments as there are enactors ascribing meaning and looking back at past events to shape the future from the context of the present, to avoid past mistakes and capitalize on past successes. Selection entails a group process of sorting out which enactments make the most sense. Here communication (and rhetoric) is paramount as people build consensus about what enactments are acceptable and why, thereby imposing meaning on enactments.

During the retention process, the group identifies which enactments are acceptable—worth keeping in the collective's memory—for future organizing and sensemaking. Retained enactments bridge organizing and the environment over time, determining an organization's adaptation to its surroundings (Weick, 1979b, p. 136). In summary,

> Organizations are presumed to talk to themselves over and over to find out what they are thinking.... The organism or group enacts equivocal raw talk, the talk is viewed retrospectively, sense is made of it, and this sense is then stored as knowledge in the retention process. The aim of each process has been to reduce equivocality and to get some idea of what has occurred. (Weick, 1979b, pp. 133-134)

Organizing is a cognitive, language-based activity among people. It is based on talk, especially double interacts, to reduce equivocality from enacted information by "coordinat[ing] their action for making sense together" (Bantz, 1990, p. 134). In Weick's theory, organizing is an intersubjective activity among people to reduce perceived levels of equivocality, which means that communication is the *raison d'être* for organizations. Although Weick did not address it in rhetorical terms, organizing can be viewed as a rhetorical process among people that involves retrospective structuring about events and actions from the environment. Weick's theory can be used, for example, to explain the interpersonal communication (i.e., double interacts) between organizational members in one group/department and members of another group, organization, or external public. Weick's theory can also be used to account for the strategies of organizing, for example, as people argue about which enactments should be selected and, later, which ones should be retained for organizational memory. In this regard, sensemaking can be viewed as a rhetorical process among people that involves retrospective structuring about events and actions from the flows of experience.

Consubstantial Areas between the Theories

Taken together, Burke's rhetorical theory and critical method and Weick's theory of organizing can be used to explain the processes of public relations. For example, Burke's orientation can explain the "big picture" of human symbolicity, and Weick's theory can examine specific instances of human communication during organizing. Specifically, Burke tends to focus on people's patterns of interaction, stress hierarchy, and lack a formal organizational angle. Weick's theory addresses communication strategies, emphasizes loosely coupled systems, and lacks a rhetorical orientation. The blending of these apparent opposites creates an analytical method that balances both perspectives, based on their common ground, through which to view the rhetorical and organizational nature of public relations.

Organizing, according to Weick, is an intersubjective activity where people try to reduce perceived levels of equivocality through communicative action. Dramatism, as defined by Burke, is a methodology that provides critical insight about human motivation and symbolic action, adding that structure to Weick's theory. When taken together, Burke's and Weick's theories can explain the development of discourse from public relations activity. Amid the points of intersection between the two theories, two principal areas of overlap explain how the two theories fit together to make up an analytical method: their loci of communication and their senses of order.

Loci of Communication Even though both theories have their genesis in human communication, ultimately Burke emphasized the individual in symbolic action and Weick privileges the group. For Burke, symbolic action begins with the individual and has implications for people acting in social groups. He explained that identification echoes social order (congruent with the rhetoric of rebirth) and includes:

> one's material and mental ways of placing oneself as a person in groups and movements; one's ways of sharing vicariously in the role of leader or spokesman; formation and change of allegiance; the rituals of suicide, parricide, and prolicide; the vesting and divesting of insignia, the modes of initiation and purification that are involved in the response to allegiance and change of allegiance; [and] the part necessarily played by groups in the expectancies of the individual. . . . (Burke, 1973, p. 227)

This perspective parallels Weick's idea of sensemaking—the core to the process of organizing—and entails a social construction of perspectives, or frames of reference, about what is going on. People first bracket events from the flow of experience individually, but then people talk to one another to make sense of those and prior enactments and select appropriate enactments for the current situation and for retention. As Weick (1995) explained, "Sensemaking begins with a sensemaker. . . . The trap is that sensemaker is singular and no individual ever acts like a single sensemaker. . . . Sensemaking is never solitary because what a person does internally is contingent on others" (pp. 18, 40). Weick's point is that sensemaking is an intersubjective process where people consensually arrive at what is plausible, coherent, reasonable, acceptable, and credible (Weick, 1995).

Although Burke's and Weick's respective loci of communication differ, they can be viewed as complementary. That is, Burke's dramatistic method can help Weick's theory of organizing account for individuals acting in groups. Given that people act within a larger social context, each person within a group is an autonomous symbol user, who makes discursive choices for given situations. Burke's dramatistic method allows a critic to focus on one person and his or her symbolic action. Since that symbolic action, as Cheney (1983b) posited, tends to be persuasive in nature and targeted for an organization's publics, "persuasion is inherent in the process of *organizing*, as Kenneth Burke implies in offering the term 'Administrative Rhetoric'" (p. 144). Administrative rhetoric is "a theory of persuasive devices which have a directly rhetorical aspect, yet include operations not confined to sheerly verbal expression" (Burke, 1966a, p. 301). Whether verbal or not, people can decide what discourse type to use and how to frame the message from one occasion to the next based on socially constructed rules.

Organizing rules for selection and retention (Weick, 1979b) affect communication choices and, by implication, the kind of discourse people enact. Here, Burkean rhetoric and Weickian organizing recognize the important role of conventions for discursive action, and when used together, the two theories extend each other's orientation, especially that of Weick's vis-à-vis Burke's. The keys are Burke's idea of form and Weick's concept of recipes. For Burke (1968a), "form is the creation of an appetite in the mind of the auditor, and the adequate satisfying of that appetite" (p. 31) by reflecting certain discursive patterns—progressive forms (i.e., fulfilling expectations in new ways), repetitive forms (i.e., consistently reusing concepts in new ways), conventional forms (i.e., upholding conventions for recognized discourse from poetry to memos), and simple forms (i.e., using "metaphor, paradox, disclosure, reversal, contraction, expansion, bathos, apostrophe, series, [and] chiasmus") (Reuckert, 1982, p. 23). For Weick (1979b), recipes are "the means to generate structures that have the characteristics you want.... Adapted for organizing, the question becomes: given our need for a sensible enacted environment, how do we produce it?" (pp. 46-47). For both Burke and Weick, the concepts of form and recipes are consubstantial because they can be applied to the creative processes, social dimensions, and discourse structures behind communication.

For example, although someone may act as the representative of an organization or a document was published by and about an organization, organizational discourse is the sum of the many people's enactments shared, selected, and retained according to organizing recipes during the sensemaking process. In the case of a technical document, like an annual report, the document's development process (see Smudde, 1991) includes writers, editors, photographers, graphic designers, management, and legal counsel. These people made sense of their enactments about the organization's performance during the previous year, projected these enactments in particular frames of reference, and followed recipes to enact one discourse type that would induce cooperation between the organization and its publics, especially stockholders and investors.

Rhetorical choices about the form, content, and even frame of reference for enactments are the object of the creative process of sensemaking, which are in tune with Weick's idea of organizing grammars. When describing Burke's view of the creative process, Rueckert (1982) effectively reflects Weickian organizing, saying that process "starts with experience, moves to the abstracting of essences from experience, thence to the translation to that essence into some kind of progressive form, and then to the bodying forth of that form" (p. 170). Because communication is the nexus of organizing, the sensemaking recipes people use necessarily include those related to enacting certain frames of reference and particular kinds of texts, from reports and e-mail to speeches and press releases, that advance the selection and retention of enactments.

Senses of Order Burke professed an unquestioning adherence to hierarchy, and Weick upheld a socially constructed grammar for organizing among loosely coupled groups. For Burke, "the ordering of man [sic] is ineluctable and ubiquitous. . . . [T]hat hierarchical stratification is inherent in man's [sic] ability to use language for the purpose of abstracting categories and in his [sic] propensity for 'systematic thought'" (Tompkins et al., 1975). The bureaucratic division among people results in "mystery," which is the corresponding condition that arises as those at the top become mysterious to those in lower layers of a hierarchy, and vice versa (Burke, 1984b; Tompkins, et al., 1975). The influence of mystery is both positive and negative on organizational communication. According to Tompkins et al., on the one hand, "with its properties of glamour and magic, [mystery] serves to induce cooperative action, but [on the other hand] it also inhibits the criticism of those at the top by those at the bottom" (p. 136). But are organizations truly so rigidly hierarchical? The answer is some are and some aren't so much.

Large organizations like GM, McDonald's, or the U.S. Postal Service tend to organize along complex hierarchies, whereas smaller organizations like grocery stores, auto dealerships, or local places of religious worship are simpler. Nevertheless, the common denominator is, as Burke observed, that people enact some order as well as, as Weick argued, a concomitant grammar for organizing. This is where Weick's social constructivism of organizations counterbalances Burke's deep sensitivity to order. According to Sproule (1989), Weick demonstrated that organizations are "really less fixed than many managers would think. An organization is always in flux, changing through the process of enactment as people constantly modify the institutional landscape through their actions" (p. 260). That modification is a response to the equivocal, uncertain environment in which people find themselves when organizing. What equivocality is to Weick is, thus, on par with what ambiguity is to Burke. The response to the environment is symbolic action to reduce equivocality/ambiguity through organizing behaviors. That symbolic action involves interpretation of what is going on so that appropriate events with which identification is significant can be selected and retained for further organizing action.

As described earlier, Weick viewed organizing as the result of people engaging in loosely coupled systems, or "cycles," according to socially constructed "recipes" that govern behavior (see Weick, 1979a). Such a process is a function of both an individual's own symbolic action during enactment, a group's symbolic action during sensemaking, and both together. People bridge the divisions or loose couplings among each other within the order of organizations through identification and may adopt, as Burke (1984a) prescribed, one of three frames of reference about their situations: a frame of acceptance about the *status quo* of enacted environments and retained enactments (i.e., to do their duty in organizing); or a frame of rejection, which is to enact alternative environments in response to those enacted or retained within the *status quo* (e.g., corporate restructuring [see Smudde, 1993] or labor strikes); or a frame of passivity, which is to enact environments that are neither those that are accepted nor those rejected by others. Frames of reference and enacted environments are congruent with each other, because both establish contexts, even perspectives about what is going on that people share, select, and retain when organizing (see Weick, 1995). In this way, Burke's sensitivity to hierarchy (and rhetorical emphasis) balances with Weick's idea of loose coupling (and the centrality of communication). In combination, Burke and Weick, then, apply well to the variably complex structures of organizations and the orientations of individuals who seek identification with one another.

The paradox within Burke's notion of identification—it involves simultaneous unity and division bridged through symbolic action—has direct implications on organizing and, particularly, in the naming of situations. Cheney and Tompkins (1987) argued that identification in organizations "is a process closely tied to identity [i.e., what is commonly taken as representative of a person or group], both linguistically and conceptually," and linked to individual and group commitment. Identity, identification, and commitment, then, are the result of socially constructed symbolic action when people organize, and this process view of organizational identification is in line with Weick's ideas of enactment and sensemaking. As Weick (1988) stated, "enactment involves both a process, enactment, and a product, an enacted environment" (p. 307). Indeed, enactment entails one's recognition that something has polluted the order of things, and subsequent activity will focus on reestablishing identification and creating order anew in an evolutionary way. Larkey and Morrill (1995) argued that organizational identification involves symbolic action among people within and across hierarchical groups that

> emerges from daily and informal interactions between individual actors in organizations over what it means to be an organizational member [see Weick's notions of raw talk and consensual validation in the process of sensemaking]. . . . It is through such interactions, particularly between rank-and-file members and managers, that individual actors co-create overlapping identities and ultimately to a lesser or greater degree create the shared symbolic systems ("cultures") which enable individual actors working in concert to become the organization [i.e., participate in the process of organizing]. (p. 198)

One's use of language hinges on his or her motives to induce cooperation, to establish identification with others. Identification entails a simultaneous unity and division among people who use symbols (language) to seek

Dramatistic Organizing as Method 43

common ground, or "substance," with others (Brock, 1990, p. 191). As symbol users, we are guided by a sense of order—"goaded by hierarchy" (Burke, 1989)—and we possess the ability to accept or reject situations and attempts to symbolize them (Burke, 1970). Acceptance is a positive response to an existing order. Rejection is a negative response allowed by language (i.e., using a term always implies its opposite). When the order of things is polluted, one's rejection of the old ways creates feelings of guilt and compels purification to attain redemption, all of which is concomitant with a rhetoric of rebirth.

Implicit in Burke's idea of order, as he worked out his "cycle of terms for 'order'" (Burke, 1970, pp. 183-196), is paradox, which involves not permanent division between teministic opposites, but "a blending of opposites" (Brock, 1985, p. 95). In this way, if Burke's adherence to hierarchy represents one pole of organizational structure and Weick's idea that people organize across loosely coupled cycles represents the other pole, they actually blend together as one would imply the other. This paradox suggests a more symbolically holistic view of organizations that are fundamentally hierarchical but tempered by loosely coupled systems of people making sense of their enacted environments. So, the reality of organizing is paradoxical, because it is simultaneously symbolic and situational.

Charting the Consubstantiality The critical orientation of both theories together represents a means between the two relative extremes of Burke's rhetorical theory and Weick's theory of organizing. Indeed, this rhetorical and organizational consubstantiality drives the analytical method, which promises to be a viable critical orientation for making sense of and enacting public relations discourse. As a result of the preceding analysis, Table 2.1 shows how the two theories complement each other terministically and conceptually.

These two theories, when used together, balance one another and give a critic a flexible approach to analyze public relations. Specifically, public relations discourse is the product of symbolic action about present and past (i.e., selected and retained) enacted environments to induce cooperation between an organization and its publics. These environments can be enacted dramatistically vis-à-vis the pentad (to discover the motives that lie behind symbolic action) and terms for order (to understand the historical progression of events from enacted environments) guided by Burke's concept of identification and Weick's ideas about sensemaking.

The combination of Burke's and Weick's theories is flexible because it allows a critic to strike an appropriate balance between the rhetorical *and* the organizational. A critic, then, may garner more explanatory power about organizations and organizational discourse by tempering Burke's dramatistic method with Weick's theory of organizing, and vice versa, than by using either theory alone. In this way, Burke's and Weick's ideas may be much less

TABLE 2.1. Complementary Terms and Unifying Concepts Between Kenneth Burke and Karl Weick.

BURKEAN TERMS	WEICKIAN TERMS	UNIFYING CONCEPTS
Symbolic action	Communication	Language structures thinking
Individuals	Groups	Social dimensionality
Form	Recipes	Conventions for discursive action (discourse genres)
Identification	Sensemaking	Rhetoric; intersubjectivity
Ambiguity	Equivocality	Interpretation of actions and events
Pentad (dramatism)	Cause maps (organizing)	Human action and motivation
Terms for order	Enactment	Evolution of human activity
Frames of reference	Enacted environments	Context; perspective
Hierarchy	Loose coupling	Order is inherent
System created	Systems theory	Systems orientation

divergent than they are tangent when it comes to understanding organizational discourse. Indeed, the theories are consubstantial, and applying this theoretical framework to actual texts leans on their common ground about discursive action. Rounding out the method, then, is a pragmatic approach for textual analysis based on discourse genres for public relations.

FRAMEWORK FOR TEXTUAL ANALYSIS

The theoretical framework would not be complete without a way to apply it to artifacts of public relations. What is needed is an approach that allows a critic to flex the muscle of the unified concepts between Burke and Weick on particular texts. A critic must be able to address how corporate officials used language to structure thinking in an organizational society and for target publics through particular, accepted kinds of discourse. A critic would also be able to find how such rhetorical action reflects reasons why people did what they did within particular contexts and how things for an organization systematically evolve over time into new ways of thinking and acting. And a critic should be able to use all this analysis to evaluate completed public relations activities and plan for future public relations organizing to induce cooperation between an organization and its publics. The key to selecting a framework for textual analysis that complements this project's theoretical framework and gives a critic ample explanatory power is the idea that "all language use is a matter of making discourse. The making of discourse depends on differences between speaker and listener, or writer and reader. As certain discourses become more deeply embedded in the social functioning of groups, these discourses become conventionalized; they become recognized as *genres* which serve functional purposes in communication" (Grabe & Kaplan, 1996, p. 136; italics added). Again, discourse concerns instances of texts in both form and content.

When people think of public relations, they tend to think about the kinds of things that public relations practitioners do—the symbolic action of those corporate officials. That activity, of course, involves the use of language to create specific discourse forms about enacted environments to induce cooperation between an organization and its publics. This ability to conceive of public relations texts as unique categories of communication (i.e., organizational communication) is possible through a generic approach, which is the final, essential part of this project's analytical method. Such categorization of texts is possible, because

> [g]enres are constituted through an examination of actual instances of discourse. They are inductive generalizations, not dialectically apprehended noumenal forms. One can deduce from a genre that given rhetorical acts should exhibit particular conventions, but one cannot deductively produce the genre itself. (Fisher, 1980, p. 291)

A generic approach

> aims at understanding rhetorical practice over time by discerning recurrent patterns that reflect the rules that practitioners follow.... [Those] rules outline the parameters within which symbolic action will express the rhetor's motives, will be acknowledged by the audience as a form or recognized as a convention for expressing intention, and will be capable of satisfying audience expectations. (Campbell & Jamieson, 1986, p. 295)

This approach to generic analysis "aims to illuminate rather than classify" (Swales, 1990, p. 43). So we can think of public relations texts as fitting specific genres of discourse that can be studied for their rhetorical and social dimensions, for as Burke (1973) said, "to guide our observations about the form itself [of some discourse type], we seek to discover the functions which the structure serves. This takes us into a discussion of purpose, strategy, [and] the symbolic act" (p. 101).

There is a large community that upholds conventions about enacting PR discourse for external and internal audiences. Such social agreement about texts gets at the heart of discourse genre. As Swales (1990) asserted,

The [communicative] purposes [of a genre] are recognized by the expert members of the parent discourse community, and thereby constitute the rationale for the genre. This rationale shapes the schematic structure of the discourse and influences and constrains choice of content and style. ... In addition to purpose, exemplars of a genre exhibit various patterns of similarity in terms of structure, style, content and intended audience. (p. 58)

Organizations like the Public Relations Society of America (PRSA) and the IABC were created to further the profession of public relations/corporate communications and help practitioners master that organizational function and the discourse they are charged to create. University programs in public relations; textbooks and handbooks (e.g., Bivins, 1999; Caywood, 1997; Cutlip et al., 1994; Dilenschneider, 1996; Lesly, 1998; Newsom & Carrell, 1997; Simon & Zappala, 1996; Walton, 1996; Wilcox, Ault, & Agee, 1996; Wilcox, Nolte, & Jackson, 1996); companies like Lawrence Ragan Communications that are dedicated to publishing and holding conferences for and about public relations; scholars and experts who research, publish, teach, and speak about PR; and practitioners themselves as employees of organizations or independent consultants all uphold and influence what is understood as and expected from public relations discourse. Moreover, people from the news media and other organizational functions and disciplines (e.g., marketing, sales, research, personnel, law) also participate in PR discourse that is enacted for any given purpose. With this broad community of people, the genres of public relations discourse are institutionalized, but they also allow people to adapt them to specific organizational needs and communication situations. Like Burke (1973) observed, "when you begin to consider the situations behind the tactics of expression, you will find tactics that organize a work technically [i.e., structural affects] because they organize it emotionally [i.e., psychological affects]" (p. 92).

Research on discourse genres shows them to be purposive, contextual, and flexible (see Herrington & Moran, 2005). Fortunately, genres (including those in public relations) are sufficiently stable over time that they can be learned, applied, studied, and perfected. Significant changes in discourse genres, when they do occur, follow along Burke's sensibilities about order (or, alternatively, Kuhn's [1970] perspective of paradigm shifts or Foucault's [1972] concept of epistemes).

The review of literature in Chapter 1 covered the nature, activity, and central issues of public relations. That review showed limited generic analyses, like apologia (see Hearit, 1994, 1995, 1996; Ware & Linkugel, 1973), have been used as critical orientations to study specific corporate texts. Textbooks and handbooks address public relations discourse in terms of the available channels or media (e.g., events, teleconferences, publications, exhibits, closed-circuit television) through which messages may be communicated to given audiences, which suits the didactic nature of these resources. Many of these sources also give operational descriptions of the kinds of public relations writing practitioners create, emphasizing content and style tempered with process issues about creating them. These orientations, however, are rather linear and relegate the significance of the texts to that of mere products of one's work chosen for projects in areas like media relations, employee communications, investor relations, and so on.

More to the point, this linear orientation eschews addressing exemplars of public relations texts that can be used to define them within categories of discourse and applied in ways that add knowledge about their rhetorical and organizational significance. Indeed, no scholarship has been advanced that formally presents "the textual features and their implicit exigence" (Cross, 1993, p. 142) of public relations discourse genres. Even the larger PR discourse community as described earlier—and of which I am a member—primarily upholds learned conventions (i.e., master-to-apprentice learning in the classroom and especially on the job, and "back-end" learning from one's practice in another profession, like journalism or law, and working with public relations documents daily) for specific kinds of public relations texts. So what kinds of discourse are included in public relations that exhibit certain patterns of similarity? That genre set includes and is not limited to the following (also listed in Table 2.2):

TABLE 2.2. Representative Genre Set for Public Relations Discourse.

Prepared statements	Press conferences	Newsletters
Press releases	Press kits	Video news programs
Media advisories	Interviews	Corporate reports
Video news releases	Articles	Corporate image pieces
Photo news releases	White papers	Pitch letters
Audio news releases	Case studies	Pitch calls
Fact sheets	Speeches	Posters
Backgrounders	Meetings	Conversations
Tip sheets	Advertorials	Podcasts
Matte releases	Satellite media tours	Magazines
Wikis	Biographical statements	Flyers
FAQs	Public service announcements	Blogs
Written correspondence		

- Prepared statements comment on a specific, contentious subject emerging on the public stage. A statement may be attributed to a named corporate spokesperson or official or to the organization itself.
- Press releases are written and issued over a third-party "wire service" (e.g., PR Newswire, Business Wire, etc.) to announce breaking news in sufficient detail, like a significant event, issue, achievement, or major action taken by an organization or specific members of it. Press releases also include information about whom to contact on the announcement.
- Media advisories (sometimes called "media alerts") are sent to the news media to announce an event that is scheduled in the near future and to persuade editors and journalists to attend it. The notice outlines details in concise statements about who is involved or hosting the event, what the big news is that will come out of it, why the event and the news from it is important, where the event will be held, when it is scheduled, how people can get more information about the event and any other aspect related to it, what is slated for the event's program, what the general attendance policy (if any) is, and any historical background that may apply about the people, hosting organization(s), or event.
- Video news releases (VNRs) are short, videotaped productions of an organization's news that mimics television news segments, including voice-over commentary, b-roll of pertinent scenes for the story, and on-screen interviews with a corporate spokesperson, recognized public figures, or other people as appropriate. Times are announced with media advisories for television news organizations to record a VNR from a satellite broadcast or to download a VNR from an Internet Web site using specialized software (e.g., RealVideo or QuickTime). A script for the VNR is usually made available for news outlets' use.
- Photo news releases (PNRs) consist mainly of a photograph of a specific, unique subject that visually captures the interest of editors or reporters and "tells the story" by itself. PNRs include short captions about the photographed subject and cite whom to contact.
- Audio new releases (ANRs) are specific recorded announcements on audiotape about timely subjects produced for radio broadcast. Content is usually focused on a particular issue (e.g., rising prescription drug prices and proposed government cutbacks on Medicare coverage) and targeted at one segment of the population (e.g., retired and elderly Americans), including those who are not demographically part of that segment but are sym-

pathetic toward it. Tapes are typically sent to radio stations in target markets for specified air times.
- Matte releases (also spelled "mat" or "MAT" releases) are complete and concise print-news stories written by public relations professionals then laid out and possibly written by an organization like NAPS (North American Precis Syndicate), PR Newswire, NewsUSA and others, which distribute these stories free (similar to news releases) to news organizations, according to the client's target audiences. The content of these "prefabricated," camera-ready news stories generally concerns consumer-oriented matters that are not anchored in time (i.e., they are "evergreen"), and feature an organization and its product or service as part of the story.
- Fact sheets succinctly present only important facts (i.e., who, what, where, when, why, how, how much, etc.) in context about a complex subject that an organization faces.
- Flyers (also referred to as "leaflets") can be thought of as a minimalist version of a fact sheet. Printed on one side of a single sheet of paper, a flyer presents only the plainest facts about its subject—what, who, where, when, why and how—within a utilitarian and pleasing page design, possibly including tear-off features with contact information, for example.
- Posters are highly visual promotional documents, with verbal content being integrated within the overall aesthetic design. Because of their artistic nature, posters' verbal content may focus on only selected facts about a subject (who, what, where, when, why *or* how), such as a brand, event, or a single product, and do so chiefly through visual design.
- Backgrounders specifically define an issue, then comprehensively and concisely present it without editorializing. The main purpose is to fill in the gaps in other public relations discourse, like press releases or statements, and prescribe action to take on the issue.
- FAQs ("frequently asked questions") are lists of anticipated questions target audiences might have and appropriate answers prepared in advance, usually to supplement an announcement or other PR discourse, to elucidate interrelated issues of some subject.
- Biographical statements describe relevant experience and background of selected people who are cited experts or spokespeople on an issue.
- Tip sheets are very simplified fact sheets that are meant to present a kind of verbal "thumbnail Sketch" with the most basic of background information about a subject.

- Press conferences (sometimes called "press briefings" or "news conferences") are held by organization spokespeople to personally present an official view of things (e.g., announcements or breaking news), and, if permitted, address questions and concerns that journalists would have about a subject or issue.
- Satellite media tours primarily function as a way for public relations professionals to "virtually" gather people (i.e., journalists) from a vast geographical area all at once without those people having to come to the site of a PR opportunity. The featured event of an SMT is hosted live at a given location (studio or on site anywhere) by the subject organization and broadcast via satellite link (including web-based transmission) to target people.
- Press kits (may be referred to as "communication packages") contain several documents and other support material (e.g., photos, graphics, computer discs of special files) pertaining to a subject in one folder for easy handling by journalists and other interested parties.
- Interviews that are arranged for an organizational official to comment on something for a mass media outlet, typically television, radio, or print news, that has broad, timely news appeal.
- Articles are written by or ghostwritten for organizational leaders or authored by third-party "experts" to advance specific messages on an issue to readers of selected publications. Such articles can be published as bylined pieces to develop a particular thesis or advance an opinion (e.g., "letters to editors" or "op-ed" essays) in response to a specific issue raised in a periodical or the public at large.
- White papers treat a subject "objectively" by presenting a favorable balance of the issues upheld by an organization and are of interest to target publics. White papers reflect a level of and rely on research and analysis like that applied in scholarly work.
- Case studies sufficiently and concisely describe individual customers' application and benefits of an organization's product or service. These short stories demonstrate measurable results, personal experiences, and positive support about an organization and what it offered for the featured customer.
- Speeches or presentations are written by or ghostwritten (whole or in part) for organizational leaders to address key topics for specific public-speaking occasions
- Meetings are groups of people who gather to address some matter of importance. Meetings range in size from very small (e.g.,

team meetings) to very large (e.g., shareholder meetings). They typically are convened at predetermined places and times, and follow a set agenda of interest to all stakeholders involved. Other discourse genres may be used with them.

- Public service announcements (PSA) assert informative, concise, and compelling statements that are of interest to the general population and are advanced over mass media channels to assert an organization's interest in the public welfare on specific subjects.
- Advertorials are paid editorials (rather than traditional opinions written independently by a publication's editor) that advance an organization's messages on specific subjects.
- Newsletters provide specific audiences (e.g., a company's employees, a professional organization's members, or a special interest group's supporters) with brief journalistic coverage in text, photos, and illustrations of organizational performance, happenings, issues, people, and other topics of interest.
- Video news programs dynamically cover, like newsletters, an organization's news, announcements, environmental influences, and other topics for its members. These programs resemble local television news programs, as they have one or two people as the "anchors," prerecorded news segments (perhaps with a field reporter covering a story), and other features common to broadcast news.
- Corporate reports (e.g., annual reports and public interest reports) recount details about an organization's position, policies, and performance, usually over a period of time (i.e., a calendar or fiscal year) and on particular subjects.
- Corporate image pieces (e.g., brochures, Web sites, advertisements) are meant to convey a very limited number of key messages about an organization in specific, effective ways (e.g., sales-oriented language and ample visuals as part of an overall graphic design) that fulfill the communicative purposes and fit a selected medium.
- Pitch letters are meant to persuade news outlets' editors or reporters that a particular story is compelling and worth covering in specific ways that should appeal to their audiences. These letters typically have included with them other documents (e.g., press releases, fact sheets, or articles) presented in a package or press kit.
- Pitch calls are placed by telephone to garner interest among editors and reporters about a particular story and the news appeal it

will have on audiences. Such calls often precede and follow the sending of material information related to the story idea being pitched.
- Written correspondence is prepared in advance (i.e., form letters) to consistently send key messages on one popular issue to individuals, or prepared as needed to address individuals' specific concerns or to fulfill particular communication purposes for PR assignments.
- Conversations (telephone, face-to-face, or real-time video conference calls) take place with representatives of stakeholder groups to comment on an issue, answer specific questions on an issue, arrange personal interviews with corporate leaders or experts, or done to fulfill some other ad hoc purpose.
- Magazines are periodic publications organizations may use that reflect much of the characteristics of mainstream printed magazines. Like those in the mainstream, magazines used for public relations efforts include cover, feature and sidebar stories. They also may include summaries of "breaking" news of interest to the organization and other content.
- Weblogs (i.e., also called "blogs") are single Web sites created and maintained by one or more people who want to post text entries and photos/graphics about topics important to them on some broad subject(s).
- Podcasts are single audio or video files created and maintained on unique Web sites (like a blog) by one or more people who produce episodes of content for people to download to their computers and listen to.
- Wikis (pronounced "wee-keys") are simple websites that are open to anyone who would like to post information that pertains to the content and purpose of a given wiki. The word, "wiki," is Hawaiian for "quickly," which refers to how quickly and easily they can be created and maintained with information from anyone who wants to add it. In this way wikis do not have restrictions on content or organization, but they do possess technology to track exactly who posted or revised what and when.

All of these categories of public relations discourse reflect and correlate with the theoretical framework primarily because, according to Table 2.1, they derive from conventions for discursive action that are upheld by members of the large community of people in the field of public relations (and other disciplines) in both industry and the academy. These people use language intersubjectively to structure their thinking about the ways things are for an organization. Then, the social process of creating any PR discourse type is governed by contextual cues about the order of things reflected in the text itself, which is shared among diverse publics to induce cooperation with them. As Killingsworth and Gilbertson (1992) observed, "In selecting appropriate genres, writers model appropriate actions. They tell the [audience] something about the action implicit in the [discourse] and something about how they want the [audience] to respond. . . . Genres are shorthand codes for describing typical kinds of communal actions" (pp. 73, 87). The categories of PR discourse, then, are major genres of public relations that practitioners create and on which the theoretical model can be applied in generic analyses of public relations organizing (cf. Miller, 1984).

Because discourse conventions for PR are so broadly upheld, these discourse categories can be said to fit what Orlikowski and Yates (1994) called "communication genres," which serve as *institutionalized template[s]* for social action—an organizing structure that shapes the ongoing communicative actions of community members through their use of it. Such genre usage, in turn, reinforces that genre as a distinctive and useful organizing structure for the community" (p. 542, italics added). This insight is particularly important to the case of GM's C/K pickup issue, because GM depended on several kinds of public relations discourse, as did the other players in the drama. Orlikowski and Yates' research explains how people in particular organizational functions (even whole organizations) routinely enact many kinds of discourse. The researchers call this set of discourse types a "genre repertoire," the study of which helps to explain established communicative practices and how activities are organized. Public relations, according to this scheme, comprises institutionalized genres of organizational communication that are distinctive and "characterized by a socially recognized communicative purpose [i.e., being constructed, recognized, and reinforced within a community] and common aspects of form [i.e., the readily observable features of the communication, including structure, medium, and language]" (Orlikowski & Yates 1994, pp. 543, 544).

The forming of discourse involves symbolic action that includes inducement to participate, where the inducement is rhetorical (Gregg, 1978). People choose specific discursive forms because those forms make sense for and convey meaning about enacted environments, and dramatism is well-equipped to help us understand why. As Cathcart (1993) stated,

> The challenge for the modern critic is to grasp the significance of form as the source of meaning in our mass media. . . . [Dramatism insists] that "text" is more than the formal relationship of words with ideas . . . [and] seeks out "text," not just in the verbal narrative, but in all the ways object, event, condition, and relationship are interpreted by receivers. (pp. 304-305)

Dramatistic rhetorical criticism, the heart of this project's method, is rooted in Burke's view of rhetoric as the use of symbols to induce cooperation, based on the concept of identification, and assumes that people act in accordance with motives (Burke, 1969a, 1969b).

METHODOLOGICAL PROGRAM SUMMARIZED

This volume's method examines the practice of public relations and genres of public relations discourse using Burke's three tools for rhetorical criticism and integrating the concepts and terms of Weick's theory of organizing. Dramatism drives the application of this project's method. Weick's ideas complement both the theory and the practice of public relations as the basis for data collection, because public relations texts represent the enactment of this project's overall theoretical framework. The combination of Burke's and Weick's theories, with the generic textual analysis for public relations discourse, makes up this project's method. It is a critical approach to translate that human symbolic action during the process of organizing into its rhetorical and organizational aspects. The steps for applying the method simply include:

1. Describe the case history logologically to understand the rhetorical context for public relations organizing by GM and non-GM officials and the evolution of the issue to restore order for the company.
2. Examine the genres of public relations texts dramatistically to demonstrate the microscopic and macroscopic levels of how GM officials used language to structure public thinking about enacted environments and induce cooperation.
3. Evaluate the successfulness of the public relations organizing in the case, deriving lessons from it, and judge the method as a way for practitioners to plan, create, and analyze public relations discourse.

This volume, like that employed by Cheney (1991) and others cited earlier, uses the qualitative methodology of rhetorical criticism and specifically that of Burke's dramatism. Rhetorical criticism of public relations is an important way to advance knowledge about such discourse, because as Elwood (1995b) said, "rhetoric constitutes the core component of public relations" (p. 12). Indeed, rhetorical criticism gets its strength from three general areas: rhetorical theory, which involves explanations about the use of language; public address, which studies the uses of rhetoric and why those uses were used; and criticism, which applies a theoretical framework as a standard for judgement (Brock, Scott, & Chesebro, 1990). In this regard, rhetorical criticism is a qualitative method for analyzing human symbolic action in any context, and the use of dramatism as this project's primary orientation is appropriate.

The point to rhetorical criticism is to move beyond a visceral response to something and into an informed understanding about it, whether the artifact is a speech, news story, poem, bumper sticker, social movement, or nonverbal behavior. This critical impulse is both an epistemological response (to come to know or understand something) and a scientific response (to want to know how something is). So, a rhetorical criticism of the case of GM officials' management of the C/K truck issue will yield a systematic analysis of GM's public relations organizing, and by applying the generic approach to PR, make sense of GM public relations texts in macroscopic and microscopic ways. With rhetorical criticism as the general orientation, the three steps to this project's analytical method make up a systematic approach to analyze the case.

Describing the Case Logologically

The first step is to understand the symbolic action of the case chronologically. Events, associated symbolic action, and reigning environmental characteristics within the case's history are described using historical documents and accounts to give context to the people, actions, and motives in the case. Special attention must be given to points in the chronology of events that reveal the logological progression of order, pollution, guilt, purification, and redemption, and as logology is the nexus of this step, these terms serve to organize the case's history. Such a revelation simultaneously describes the establishment of identification between a group and its publics and a rhetoric of rebirth for the actors in the case who achieved redemption. That rhetoric can be traced graphically as a cycle of terms for order that relate to those on both sides of the case under study.

As much as the logology of the case also represents an evolution from order to redemption, the case's description must also reflect the organizing processes of those involved in it. This dimension adds the organizational perspective to the rhetoric of rebirth, which further defines the logological context of the case. Finally, as rhetorical criticism is the general orientation for this project's method, interpretations of the symbolic actions would serve to bridge events, actions, and environments to yield a cohesive account of the case.

Analyze the Case's Public Relations Texts

The second step in the method involves close analysis of texts from the case. Chapters 4 and 5 feature separate and complementary levels of analysis. Together, both chapters make up an application of the Burke–Weick synthesis that is operationalized through the structure of public relations organizing and discourse genres. On a microscopic level, textual analysis begins by looking at the organizing process of the GM officials involved in the case, because that group enacted the texts to be analyzed within a flow of particular events. From the range of genres enacted by those officials, one text is examined very closely as it is representative of the group's organizing and the lot of texts in the case.

To systematically analyze the texts on a macroscopic level, they are grouped according to discourse genres germane to the case. The macroscopic analysis of the texts are addressed in reference to a key turning point in the case's history that is a watershed for the organization that attains redemption. Specifically, texts are examined for differences in them that were enacted before and those enacted after that turning point. The genres are described and interpreted using Burke's pentad, which would reveal strategies to induce cooperation between an organization and its publics. Such an analysis would explain the content, context, and organizing processes of texts from the vantage points of the scene, act, agent, agency, and purpose reflected in them.

Evaluate the Case and Method

The final step in the analytical method is to evaluate the case and the method itself. This evaluation begins with making judgments about why the organization that attained redemption (or was condemned) was successful (or had failed) on both traditional public relations measures and, more important, in terms of the theoretical framework, primarily that represented by Table 2.1 above. This latter point is crucial because it takes us beyond common explanations of success (or failure) and provides a deeper understanding that could drive more effective communications efforts. This level of analysis would yield a way to formulate a public relations program based on lessons derived from the case. Finally, the method would be assessed for its limitations and strengths, from which next steps for public relations practitioners and researchers would be outlined.

3

LOGOLOGICAL DESCRIPTION OF THE CASE

The case of GM's 1973-1987 pickups effectively spans 6 years—from 1992 to 1998—and there is an ever-present possibility that the issue could again take the public stage, if someone places enough importance on it and gains sufficient support from other people and groups (see Crable & Vibbert, 1985). With this case's long evolution, Burke's (1970) terms for order, which is his logological tool for tracing out history terministically, can help us understand the context, even the drama, of the public relations organizing by GM and non-GM officials. Logology is an analytical method of "words about words" (Burke, 1970, p. 1)—"a purely empirical study of symbolic action" (Burke, 1966b, p. 47)—that we can use in this case study to look at the verbal nature of public relations to establish "fruitful analogies between the two realms" (Burke, 1970, p. 1).

Burke's cycle of terms for order, which is central to his "rhetoric of rebirth" (Rueckert, 1982), comes from the idea that humans are "goaded by hierarchy" (Burke, 1989), which is a condition that derives from creation stories at the heart of many world cultures that describe humanity's fall from grace (see Frazer, 1922). When people reject an hierarchical system (i.e., the order of things), they do so because it's been polluted and, therefore, feel guilt. Purification from that guilt is possible through either mortification (self-sacrifice) or victimage (scapegoating), either of which leads to redemption and a new order (Burke, 1970).

In the case of GM's 1973-1987 C/K pickups, there are two principal parties engaging in symbolic action in opposition to each other: GM officials and independent (non-GM) groups' officials.[4] In a Burkean way, the two sides confront each other, "each beset with anxiety . . . each is apparently in acute need of blaming all its many troubles on the other, wanting to feel certain that, if the other and its tendencies were but eliminated, all governmental discord (all the Disorder that goes with Order) would be eliminated" (Burke, 1970, p. 4). Accordingly, there is a cycle of terms for order for the C/K pickup issue, which is presented in Fig. 3.1 and is adapted from Burke's (1970) graphic representation of his terms for order.

In general, the case is one of competing dramas about how order became polluted and what steps will be taken and by whom to achieve redemption. The non-GM groups felt that a defective fuel-tank design for GM's 1973-1987 C/K pickup trucks (the pollution) undermined their designation as safe vehicles (the order of things). These non-GM groups wanted GM to be held accountable for the defect and stand up and publicly proclaim its responsibility for the defects (purify itself through mortification). Then GM would have to fix every 1973-1987 C/K pickup on the road (achieve redemption). For GM, however, the non-GM groups' assertion that any defect existed made them guilty of polluting the order of things for its safe pickups. To make things right again for the automaker and its customers (purification), the opposing groups would receive the blame for the charade (victimage), and the C/K pickup designs would be vindicated (achieving redemption for GM). The following discussion of the case history, which highlights the salient events that pertain to its logological progression, demonstrates the C/K pickup issue's rhetoric of rebirth traced in Fig. 3.1.

ORDER

For both groups, the order of things was stable for GM's 1973-1987 C/K pickups. Very simply, there was nothing wrong with the trucks, and they were accepted generally as safe vehicles. Prior to their manufacture and sale, GM staff researched, designed, and tested the trucks, resulting in a robust design that met or exceeded government safety standards and consumer expectations for safety, affordability, and high-performing full-size pickups. After being purchased by consumers, GM engaged in the usual activities with its franchised dealers to help individual customers with any problems, like regular maintenance, worn or damaged parts, and repairs done according to company-issued special service bulletins that are common in the automobile industry.

Consumers as Final Arbiter

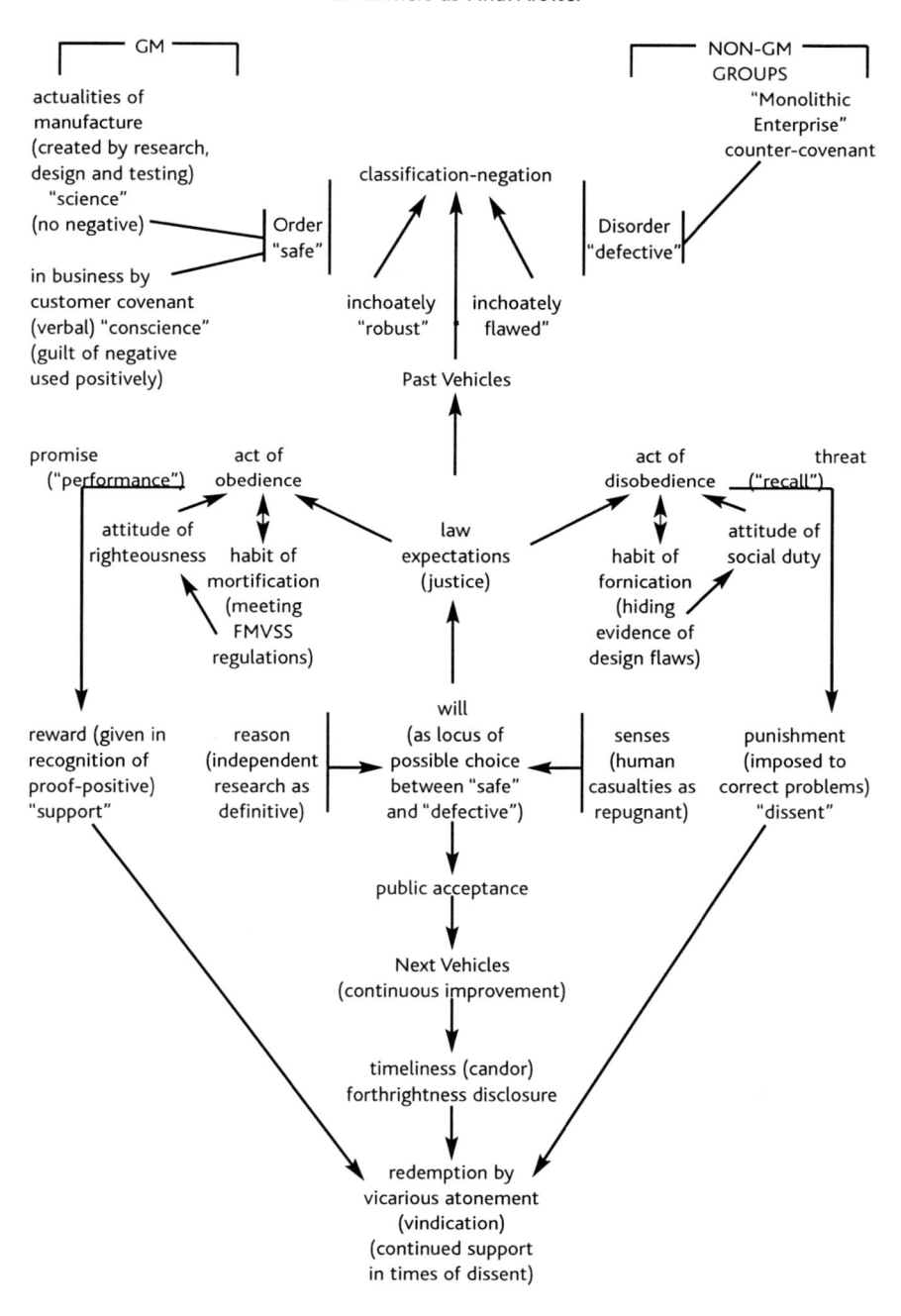

```
         GM                                          NON-GM
                                                     GROUPS
actualities of                                       "Monolithic
manufacture                                          Enterprise"
(created by research,                                counter-covenant
design and testing)        classification-negation
  "science"
(no negative)       Order  ↑  ↑  ↑     Disorder
                    "safe"               "defective"
in business by
customer covenant
(verbal) "conscience"    inchoately  inchoately
(guilt of negative        "robust"    "flawed"
used positively)
                            Past Vehicles

promise           act of                    act of          threat
("performance")   obedience                 disobedience    ("recall")
      attitude of      ↕                        ↕      attitude of
      righteousness  habit of      law        habit of    social duty
                     mortification expectations fornication
                     (meeting     (justice)   (hiding
                     FMVSS                     evidence of
                     regulations)              design flaws)

                              will
reward (given in   reason    (as locus of  senses      punishment
recognition of    (independent possible choice (human    (imposed to
proof-positive)   research as  between "safe" casualties as correct problems)
"support"         definitive)  and "defective") repugnant)   "dissent"

                        public acceptance
                              ↓
                         Next Vehicles
                      (continuous improvement)
                              ↓
                        timeliness (candor)
                      forthrightness disclosure
                              ↓
                         redemption by
                       vicarious atonement
                          (vindication)
                       (continued support
                        in times of dissent)
```

FIGURE 3.1. Cycle of terms for order present in the C/K pickup issue.

POLLUTION

For this order of safety there existed a disorder, upheld by non-GM groups, that the C/K pickups possessed an inherent defect resulting from a flawed design for the trucks' fuel systems. The order of things for GM's 1973-1987 C/K pickups became polluted when the safety of GM pickups' fuel systems were labeled defective (i.e., the alleged excessive vulnerability of fuel tanks to rupture and explode in crashes), and the federal government was asked to become involved to force the automaker to fix the problem on all of these trucks on the road. Specifically, on August 14, 1992, the Center for Automotive Safety (CAS), a Washington consumer group, and Public Citizen, "a nonprofit public interest law group" (Public Citizen, 1995), filed a recall petition with the National Highway Traffic Safety Administration (NHTSA) to recall GM's full-size C/K pickups (9.6 million of them) built and sold between 1973 and 1987.

The reason for the recall was an alleged potential defect in the design of the vehicles' fuel system ("Feds want," 1992). CAS reported that the matter required more study for three main reasons: (a) "[t]he death rate for GM trucks in all types of crashes—and especially in crashes involving fires—is higher than that for Ford and Chrysler models"; (b) "at least 248 people have died in the trucks appears to be credible"; and (c) "[a]gency investigators need more time to scrutinize more than 70,000 pages of material submitted by GM, Ford, Chrysler and other parties" ("Feds want," 1992). The allegations put GM officials on the defensive, as they reacted to the groups' claims by asserting their sense of order. GM's public response on August 14 to the recall petition stated simply:

> GM believes, [sic] that its full-size pickups, both current and former models, meet the safety needs of GM's customers. All GM vehicles including our full-size pickups continue to meet or exceed all Federal Motor Vehicle Safety Standards, including the specific requirement applicable to fuel system integrity. (General Motors, 1995, p. 1)

The fundamental issue to those in NHTSA, Public Citizen, and CAS (and plaintiffs' attorneys as the issue grew in importance) was whether the trucks' "side-saddle" fuel tanks, which are mounted on the outside of the frame rails (see Figure 3.2), are more vulnerable to puncture and fire in a crash than fuel tanks that are mounted between the frame rails ("Feds want," 1992).

An 8-year statute of limitations on recalls meant that the oldest trucks that would be covered by a recall were those built from 1984 to 1987. That is, if GM were found in violation of the Federal Motor Vehicle Safety Standard (FMVSS) 301, which governs the design and performance of fuel systems, it "would be legally obligated to recall perhaps about 200,000 of the 9.2-million 1973-87 C/Ks built" and face "the threat of lawsuits every time one of those trucks is involved in a fiery, side-impact crash" ("The C/K battle," 1994). The agency contended that, as long as the trucks remained on the road over the next 20 years, another 32 people would die ("The C/K battle," 1994).

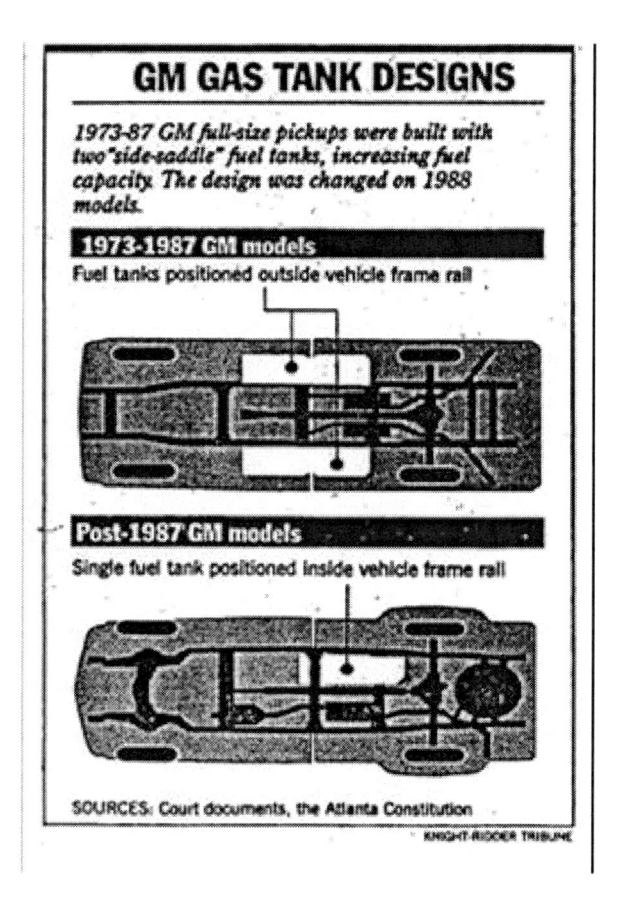

FIGURE 3.2. Comparison between full-size C/K pickup truck designs, 1973-1987 models and thereafter (Weiser, 1993).

GUILT

With the pollution came a kind of guilt—one that is borne of both sides' responsibility to thoroughly argue their cases in public. Here began a long argumentative tug of war about which of the two camps should be assigned guilt for polluting the order of things. In the first half of this phase, the basic arguments about where guilt lies on either side of the issue became increasingly visible in the public as federal investigation, litigation, and news coverage grew. In the second half, the dialectic of guilt became more pronounced as factual evidence, especially from GM officials, was applied vigorously to support empirical arguments about the pickups' safety.

Based on the report from the OAS and Public Citizen, NHTSA agreed at the outset of this phase that more "engineering analysis" of the truck's design was warranted, began investigating the safety of the fuel systems, and issued a formal information request to GM. The automaker disputed the administration's findings and submitted a detailed report on October 9, 1992, of independent research that showed "[GM's] 1973-1987 pickups had lower fatality rates than rival trucks in side-impact collisions" ("GM says," 1992). But in a November 10 letter to GM, NHTSA asked the company to "'clarify' the statistical analysis it had submitted" ("GM says," 1992), and stressed that the investigation itself does not indicate that the agency determined that a safety-related defect exists in the vehicles. GM argued that there was no defect in the fuel system design, because it met—even exceeded—current federal safety standards and those in place at the time of the trucks' production (General Motors, 1995, p. 1). NHTSA conceded this point but felt that bigger issues in the public interest about vehicle safety took precedent.

The first class-action lawsuits were filed in Autumn 1992, and GM was already facing about 120 liability lawsuits across the country. Those suits alleged that the fuel systems were unsafe on C/K pickups built between 1973 and 1987 ("NBC admits," 1993). The first liability lawsuit brought against GM for an allegedly defective fuel system design in a 1987 C/K pickup was that filed by the family of a veteran supervisor at GM's Arlington, Texas, assembly plant. He died in a fire in his pickup "caused by a drunk driver who crossed the median on a divided highway and sideswiped [the pickup]" (General Motors, 1995, p. 1). The case, *Zelenuk v. GM*, was settled out of court in February 1992, and all 50,000-plus documents reflecting the design, manufacture, and testing of the fuel systems were sealed by the court. GM announced on October 5, 1992, that it would release these documents to the public in response to criticism, led by Public Citizen, that the company was more interested in maintaining confidentiality than on the issue of safety (General Motors, 1995). One month later, GM released documents from the

Zelenuk v. GM case to "interested parties and made available to the public and news media in Dallas" (General Motors, 1995, p. 2).

The most notorious case was that brought against GM in Atlanta, Georgia, by the parents of Shannon Moseley, who was struck on the driver's side of his C/K pickup by another vehicle traveling at 70 miles an hour and died as a result of a fire that engulfed the truck. Like the Zelenuk case, the driver of the car that hit Moseley was legally drunk, with a blood-alcohol level of 0.28% immediately after the accident, and sustained only minor injuries (Moran, 1993, pp. 70-71; "NBC admits," 1993). The trial began on January 4, 1993, in Birmingham, Alabama, because the accident occurred in that state. Both litigants were placed under a gag order until the case was decided, which was on February 4, 1993. GM also faced at least two class-action lawsuits by C/K truck owners who wanted compensation because, the litigants contended, the vehicles were defective or were worth less ("The C/K battle," 1994).

Media coverage grew as GM faced increasing litigation and wrangled with NHTSA, the CAS, and Public Citizen over the trucks' safety. The NBC was producing a story to air on its television news magazine, *Dateline NBC*, and contacted GM officials as part of the story's development. Public awareness and response to the C/K pickup issue grew tremendously with the *Dateline* report, which aired on November 17, 1992.

The television news magazine's report, entitled "Waiting to Explode," represents a critical episode in the C/K truck issue for GM, since as Lechtzin (personal communication, August 25, 1997) explained, "[the issue] didn't really catch public attention until *Dateline* in November of '92." The report focused on the controversy about whether GM's 1973-1987 C/K pickups have a defective design with their side-saddle fuel tanks. The program segment about the C/K trucks was described by an independent report on NBC's conduct in producing it:

> The GM truck segment was the first story [Robert] Read produced for *Dateline*. The story was Read's idea.... Read's proposal to produce the GM segment was discussed in early September with at least [Jeff] Diamond [executive producer of *Dateline*], [David] Rummel [senior producer of *Dateline*], [Marc] Rosenwasser [senior supervising producer for *Dateline*] and [Jerry] Tully [editorial producer for *Dateline*], and was approved by Diamond. [Michele] Gillen [*Dateline* correspondent] was assigned as correspondent and an expense budget of $54,000 was approved. Some eight weeks later, on November 17, 1992, the segment was broadcast.
>
> The GM truck segment was called "Waiting to Explode?" It reported on allegations about the safety of certain GM C/K pick-up trucks manufactured between 1973 and 1987. The allegations were that the trucks were prone to catch fire in side-impact collisions because of their

gas tanks—which were mounted side-saddle outside the frame of the truck—had a tendency to rupture on impact. The segment lasted fifteen minutes and included interviews with families who had lost children in truck fires, plaintiffs' lawyers, auto safety consultants, and GM representatives. The segment also included videotape of accident scenes, television commercials for GM trucks, crash tests of trucks by GM and NHTSA, and "unscientific crash demonstrations" conducted for *Dateline*. (Warren & Kaden, 1993, pp. 15-16)

Although the segment ran for 15 minutes and addressed much of the controversy about the pickups, the 56 seconds that were devoted to crash tests of two C/K pickups ultimately proved to be NBC's undoing and the turning point of the issue for GM.

In the meantime, GM worked on clarifying for NHTSA the original statistical analysis it provided the agency on October 9. Three days after the *Dateline* exposé, NHTSA and GM officials met to discuss the findings of an independent research firm, Failure Analysis Associates (FaAA), contracted by GM, which analyzed how well the C/K pickups and other vehicles conformed to FMVSS 301. GM issued a statement on December 2, 1992 about the meeting and the research firm's findings, which show that "the rate of post-collision fires has been essentially the same for 1973-1987 GM, Ford and Dodge pickups.... The facts show that post-collision fires do occur in all vehicles—albeit with extreme rarity—at nearly identical rates in side impacts and all impacts regardless of fuel tank location [i.e., either inside or outside the frame rails]" (General Motors, 1995, pp. 1, 2).

News outlets the next day reported a NHTSA official saying that the agency was going to recommend an investigation of the pickups. GM issued a statement in response to these stories that restated the findings of the FaAA report and asserted:

We are not aware that the NHTSA has reached any decision in this matter. We've been advised that the agency may announce its decision on December 14.... If, indeed there is an investigation—given the facts—the only rational conclusion can be that there is no safety-related defect. Given that, a costly, distracting, and time-consuming investigation at this critical time for the agency, the industry, the economy and our company could not be in the best interest of the public. This petition should be denied. (General Motors, 1992)

Five days later, on December 8, 1992, NHTSA announced it would begin investigating the 1973-1987 Chevrolet and GMC C/K pickups for "a safety defect related to the danger of fires following side impact [sic] crashes" (General Motors, 1995, p. 2). GM's response that day to NHTSA's announcement stated, "We welcome the agency's decision because it will move the fact-finding process away from the sensationalized, wildly exaggerated charges of the last few weeks. . . . [T]he initiation of a formal NHTSA investigation, based upon fact and sound engineering, statistical and related science, and the directly relevant federal safety standard, is desirable" (General Motors, 1995, p. 2). Along with this statement, GM included a one-page fact sheet, entitled "Facts You Should Know about the GM Pickup Truck Controversy," which summarized the findings of GM and independent researchers. (See Appendix A for a reprint of GM's December 8, 1992 statement and samples of other PR genres used in this case.)

As the assignment of guilt was worked out in this phase, GM continually demonstrated that it was cooperating with federal authorities and that the fundamental performance and safety of the C/K pickups is sound. The non-GM groups continued to assert that GM had not been as forthright as it should have been in sharing information about the pickups' design and that the automaker made poor decisions about building the trucks with the fuel tanks mounted in dangerous areas along the outside of the frame rails. This dialectic of guilt culminated in the second half of the guilt phase, which featured increased use of empirical evidence and greater involvement of more publics.

During this period of heightened public awareness about alleged problems with the 1973-1987 C/K pickups, officials from both GM and non-GM groups began calling for purification by leaning heavily on factual evidence. The arguments sought to show why (in GM's view) the pickups' performance is sound and the design is safe; and (in the non-GM groups' view) the trucks should be recalled because of a design defect that makes the pickups unsafe. That is, GM sought purification through victimage—that the non-GM groups be held accountable for polluting the order of things about the trucks and the company. On the other hand, the non-GM groups sought purification through mortification—that GM admit that its trucks' fuel system design was dangerously flawed and fix it in every operating model to forestall any further loss of life.

The dynamics in this latter part of the guilt phase center on each camp asserting not only where guilt lies with the opposition, but especially directing those arguments at specific publics that can influence others' opinions and adding greater force with quantitative facts to back them up. Purification, then, would surely be granted to the camp that was seen as being more credible and believable by consumers and other publics, like employees, stockholders, the news media, civic leaders, and the industry. The other group would be assigned guilt for polluting the order. Guilt and purification, then, in this phase are dialectical, where attention shifts between the two until they are resolved.

At this point, the personal side of the issue became more prominent for GM, because owners of the vehicles and critics started to voice their personal concerns about the safety and monetary value of the trucks. Many owners wrote to GM to express these concerns or opinions related to the C/K pickups. To manage the responses to the large number of pickup owners' letters, GM officials developed its first discourse for direct contact with individuals: a standard reply letter to truck owners who wrote to GM. In two pages, that letter detailed the findings of independent researchers and years of real-world performance data about the trucks. GM also addressed its 1.5-million stockholders with a similar letter that reassured them of the truck's safety and the company's drive to quell the issue forthrightly and expediently.

GM officials had been managing the issue reactively in the public arena by issuing statements (and counter statements) about its antagonists' (i.e., NHTSA, the CAS, Public Citizen, plaintiffs' lawyers, courts of law, adversarial pundits, etc.) assertions to the press over electronic channels, like news-wire services. The letter to C/K pickup owners was to be sent only by designated communications officials at GM and the two marketing divisions for the pickups—Chevrolet and GMC Truck (Lechtzin, 1992), which would give the company greater ability in tracking correspondence and assuring consistent messages. The two-and-a-half-page letter argues against the credibility of news reports, asserts that critics (primarily lawyers' groups and their hired safety experts) are misleading the public, and claims that the fuel system is not defective, showing statistical evidence about the trucks' and other vehicles' fuel system performances.

For nearly 3 months after the *Dateline NBC* story aired, GM sought to obtain the trucks from NBC used in the *Dateline* story, but the show's producer wrote in a letter that the vehicles were destroyed. Through a tip from a journalist that the tests were rigged, from the help and depositions of witnesses to *Dateline*'s crash test, and from GM's own investigation of the surrounding area of the crash-test site in Indiana to collect evidence and the very vehicles used in the tests, GM officials enacted an environment that the *Dateline NBC* report was based on purposely rigged crash tests and, on February 8, 1993, filed a defamation lawsuit against NBC for fraud. That suit stated specifically that "NBC knowingly and purposely rigged two car-truck crashed [sic] with remotely detonated incendiary devices to attempt to cause vehicle fires to fraudulently characterize GM's 1973-1987 full-size pickup trucks as being prone to post-collision fuel-fed fires" (General Motors, 1995, p. 3).

GM officials also staged a press conference on February 8, 1993, for a corporate speaker, GM Executive Vice President and General Counsel Harry J. Pearce, to publicly report on that enacted environment as defined in the defamation suit (Lechtzin, 1993). This event was attended by almost

200 representatives of the news media. Pearce conducted the session that included exhibits of the trucks used in *Dateline*'s report, video excerpts of the program, enhanced photographs of parts of the report to show how the tests were rigged, results of analyses about the pickup's safety, and a complete kit of information, including copies of photographs and statistical analyses and statements about the program. Copies of that kit were sent to all GM communications offices to help manage the issue for employees.

PURIFICATION

As a result of GM's recognizance work and its corporate speaker's presentation about the enacted environment surrounding the unethical *Dateline NBC* story, NBC management recanted the story and apologized on the air the next evening, February 9, 1993 (see Hearit, 1996). The next morning, GM released a transcript of that apology and its response. News reports for days and weeks to follow covered NBC's improper reporting and the aggressive redemptive strategy GM people enacted to bolster the company's image and reputation. An important result of this episode was that it called into serious question journalistic coverage of the issue (and similar ones; see Pratt, 1997) and implied that all publics carefully assess what anyone other than GM says about the pickups. GM was starting down the road to purification.

Just 4 days before GM's press conference about the *Dateline NBC* program, the jury in the *Moseley v. GM* trial in Atlanta delivered its verdict: $4.5 million in compensatory damages awarded to the Moseley family and $101 million in punitive damages against GM.[5] In fact, GM could not hold its press conference or talk about the issue publicly until the trial was completed. The CAS took the opportunity on February 16, 1993, to stage a news conference with jurors to celebrate the verdict and reallege that GM shredded documents. GM rebutted by saying it would appoint an independent counsel to investigate the matter (General Motors, 1995).

GM officials also took the opportunity presented by this episode to enhance the company's internal communications. On February 11, 1993, the fledgling employee news program, *GM This Week*, aired a story about the *Dateline NBC* episode over the company's satellite network for all of its locations. The videotaped program, which was produced once a week, followed developments in the C/K truck issue until the program was canceled in 1997 and was an important outlet of information about the issue for employees in GM and its subsidiaries. *GM This Week* continually reinforced key messages about the C/K issue and specific developments as they occurred. The program occasionally featured interviews with GM officials, dealers, employees, and customers when covering the issue.

In March 1993, GM published "a special report on the safety performance of [its] C/K pickup trucks" (O'Neill, 1993) entitled *GM Focus: Special Report* (General Motors, 1993a). It is designed as a full-color, tabloid-size newsletter that recounted the coverage of the issue by *Dateline NBC* (and news media in general) and "real-world" data about the trucks' safety performance. (Although it is labeled as volume 1, number 1, it is the only issue of its kind that has been published.) *GM Focus* was mailed to every employee and retiree and distributed in large quantities to all GM locations, including subsidiaries and GM dealerships. The objective was to "educate our employes [sic] and other stakeholders so they can be effective ambassadors for GM. What they say about this issue and how they say it can have a dramatic affect on the public's perception" (O'Neill, 1993). In fact, employees could share copies of the report with people they knew who were interested in the issue.

From April 1993 to December 1994, GM and the NHTSA wrangled over recalling the allegedly defective C/K pickups. Even though the agency's own investigators concluded that no recall was warranted, given that real-word performance of the trucks "'does not suggest any significant increased risk of fires'" (*Detroit News*, April 28, 1993), NHTSA asked GM in April to voluntarily recall the vehicles. GM rejected the request, providing the agency with a 1.5-inch thick document to that affect (General Motors, 1995). On October 17, 1994, Frederico Peña, U.S. Department of Transportation secretary, acted on his own and announced that a safety defect existed in GM 1973-1984 C/K pickups and that a "final decision on whether to proceed with a government-ordered recall or to close the investigation would be made after a public meeting scheduled for December 6" (General Motors, 1995, p. 8). GM countered the announcement by saying Peña's decision was unjustified, citing the data from independent researchers and "real-word" surveys of the trucks' performance. At this point, according to Lechtzin (personal communication, August 25, 1997), the GM strategy shifted from a reactive mode:

> From *Dateline* until October 17, '94, we were in maintenance, figuring that the government was actually going to drop the case. Three or four times we had good information that they were going to drop it. Peña, being a politician . . . October 17 he says recall them for no reason—has no right to do it. He steps completely out of bounds, at which point, from a public relations standpoint, we went very active.

Media reports about Peña's action asserted that Peña was motivated by political concerns, not the facts as demonstrated by the agency's own and independent investigations. On November 3, 1994, members of the U.S. Congress—Rep. Bob Carr (D-MI), who was then chairman of the House Appropriations Subcommittee on Transportation, and Representative John

Dingell (D-MI), who was then chairman of the House Committee on Energy and Commerce—led the call for and launched investigations into these claims about Peña. The chief executives of the Big Three—Chrysler Chairman and CEO Robert Eaton, Ford Chairman and CEO Alex Trotman, and GM President and CEO John Smith—signed a letter to then U.S. President Bill Clinton to "address the intolerable state of regulatory uncertainty that will otherwise result from Secretary Peña's decision" (Eaton, Trotman, & Smith, 1994). GM also filed suit in U.S. District Court in Detroit challenging Peña's legal authority to order a recall of the pickups.

An investigation of Peña's actions surrounding his personal decision to recall the pickups revealed in late November 1994 that, although he acted "within the scope of his authority and discretion," Peña had a pattern of continually overruling NHTSA technical staff who urged closing the investigation based on its findings that the trucks pose no unreasonable risk (General Motors, 1995), thus vindicating the trucks' safety and fuel-tank design. This episode marks the final purification of GM. On December 2, Peña announced that GM and NHTSA reached a settlement to close the investigation: The company would fund more than $51-million worth of research and development on auto safety over 5 years, and the federal agency would drop its investigation and a proposed recall of the pickups (Auto safety groups). The CAS and Public Citizen tried to advance an argument of bias against one member working on the GM/Department of Justice (DOJ) settlement who owned GM stock, but the point was dismissed as "a publicity stunt" by the DOJ (General Motors, 1995).

While this episode between GM and NHTSA was playing out, the automaker was fighting 36 class-action lawsuits. In July 1993, GM reached a settlement with attorneys in the class that the company would send to each of 5 million owners of 1973-1987 C/K pickups a voucher good toward $1,000 off any new GM vehicle, except electric cars and Saturns—a move that was upheld by several state supreme courts ("GM pickup settlement," 1996). Legal challenges were advanced in those states where the class actions were filed, but the judges in each state eventually approved the settlement (General Motors, 1995). The last judgment approving the settlement was tendered on December 20, 1996, in Louisiana State Court (General Motors, 1996). However, appeals were filed by several parties, delaying the distribution of the certificates (Zagaroli, 1997). And in a reversal of the most notorious case brought against GM for the safety of the pickups' fuel systems, the Georgia Court of Appeals, on June 13, 1994, unanimously overturned the $105.2 million verdict against GM in the Moseley case and sent it back for a retrial. Reasons cited were numerous procedural errors in the trial, including improper admissions and exclusions of evidence. Media reports called this event a major victory for GM that could forestall a recall (General Motors, 1995, p. 6; *GM This Week*, June 16, 1994).

Chapter 3

REDEMPTION

The public relations activity about GM's 1973-1987 pickups waned considerably since the agreement between GM and NHTSA, the approval of the class-action settlement, and the overturned verdict in the Moseley case, all of which effectively spelled redemption for GM by vindicating the trucks.[6] The non-GM groups (excluding NHTSA) denounced GM's agreement with NHTSA and the class-action settlement, and continued their campaign against the trucks, especially regarding litigation. Indeed, public coverage of the issue focuses on pending litigation against GM, but has had almost no affect on GM's redemption. In fact, daily tracking of public opinion conducted by an independent research company for General Motors shows overwhelmingly that people were aware of the C/K pickup issue in the news, but they felt the company was "going the right direction" on the issue, and it had no affect on the monetary value of C/K pickups of all model years (General Motors, 1994; see Appendix B). There also was a concomitant reduction in the public's awareness of the C/K issue, especially after the class-action settlements with C/K pickup truck owners. Only when Peña announced his plan to investigate the trucks against the recommendation of NHTSA researchers, did people become more aware, but only marginally so.

For example, in October 1997, the CAS and Public Citizen sought to mark the 25th anniversary of GM's 1973-1987 C/K pickups' debut. CAS Director Clarence Ditlow issued a statement about "the Rolling Firebombs" that gave the tally of deaths in fire crashes, money paid in settlements, fuel-fed fire lawsuits and GM profits over the 25-year period (Center for Automotive Safety, 1997). A GM spokesman responded by contesting Ditlow's claims about lethal defects in the trucks' design and saying, "the actual performance of these vehicles demonstrates that you're at less of a risk of serious injury riding in one of them [any of the 1973-87 C/K pickups] than most other vehicles on the road" (Zagaroli, 1997; also see Olson, 1993a, 1993b). The scene that Ditlow tried to create made little impact on the news media or the issue.

In one of the remaining lawsuits regarding the C/K pickups' fuel system design, the case of *McGee v. General Motors*, filed in the Broward County, Florida circuit court, GM's alleged suppression of evidence again arose. At the center of the suit was whether Kenneth Starr, counsel with Kirkland and Ellis in Washington, DC, and acting on GM's behalf in C/K pickup litigation in 1994 and 1995 along with GM attorneys, knowingly suppressed evidence of perjury. The perjury charge alleged that a GM engineer (who testified under oath in numerous trials) changed his story that he could not remember why and for whom in GM he calculated the costs of auto fuel-fed fire-related fatalities to the company and that GM attorneys knew and had documentation about (i.e., an interview with the engineer and memos about him changing his story) why he made the analysis (Hammond & Larsen, 1998; Larsen & Hammond, 1998). Ultimately, in February 1998, the circuit court judge determined that the documents, which Starr and GM said did not exist or were protected by attorney–client privilege, were not privileged and ordered their release. The effects of this release of information included the possibility of opening of prior cases brought against GM (Larsen & Hammond, 1998); however, no prior cases were opened for retrial because of this information release. On May 18, 1998, the jury in the *McGee v. GM* case "delivered a $33 million judgment against the corporation for a fuel-tank fire that killed two people" (Larsen, 1998, p. 1). A GM statement about the verdict said "the jury was obscured in their analysis by improper evidentiary rulings throughout the trial," and the company appealed the decision (Larsen, 1998, p. 6).

With this case's long evolution, Burke's (1970) terms for order, which is his logological tool for tracing out history terministically, can help us understand the context, even the drama, of the public relations organizing by GM and non-GM officials. A logological view of the case helps explain the verbal nature of GM public relations organizing to establish "fruitful analogies between the two realms" of symbolic action and the process of organizing (Burke, 1970, p. 1).

In the case of GM's 1973-1987 C/K pickups, there are two principal parties engaging in symbolic action in opposition to each other: General Motors officials and independent consumer and automotive safety groups' officials. In a Burkean way, the two sides confront each other, "each beset with anxiety . . . each is apparently in acute need of blaming all its many troubles on the other, wanting to feel certain that, if the other and its tendencies were but eliminated, all governmental discord (all the Disorder that goes with Order) would be eliminated" (Burke, 1970, p. 4). Fig. 3.3 simplifies the dynamism of the case shown in Fig. 3.1 and more pragmatically shows the logological evolution of the case along four discreet phases. In general, the case is one of competing dramas about how order became polluted and what steps will be taken and by whom to achieve redemption.

As Fig. 3.3 shows, the non-GM groups felt that a defective fuel-tank design for GM's 1973-1987 C/K pickup trucks (the pollution) undermined their designation as safe vehicles (the order of things). These non-GM groups wanted GM to be held accountable for the defect and stand up and publicly proclaim its responsibility for the defects (purify itself through mortification). Then GM would have to fix every 1973-1987 C/K pickup on the road (achieve redemption). But that's not how things worked out. GM showed the non-GM groups' assertion that any defect existed made them guilty of polluting the order of things for its safe pickups. To make things right again for the automaker and its customers (purification), the opposing groups received the blame for the charade (victimage), and the C/K pickup designs were vindicated, achieving redemption for GM.

PHASE 1: Order	PHASE 2: Pollution & Assignment of Guilt	PHASE 3: Purification	PHASE 4: Redemption
General Motor's 1973–1987 C/K pickups sold under the brands of Chevrolet and GMC Truck were considered safe and without defects.	"Consumer safety" groups labeled the pickups "defective." These groups and GM argued where guilt lies; the groups said GM pickups had defective fuel systems, and GM argued the safety groups targeted a problem that doesn't exist.	GM increasingly secured public approval over opponents' arguments. GM used multiple discourse types, often featuring independent experts and third-party analyses that the pickups were safe. The revelation that *Dateline NBC*'s report fabricated vehicle fires placed GM as a victim and gave GM benefit of the doubt. Opponents' experts were seen as having suspect motives.	Several events, including the NHTSA calling off its investigation of the pickups, led to the vindication of the pickups as safe and GM as respectable. Media coverage waned considerably and opponents slipped into a kind of obscurity. A new order for GM, its pickups, auto industry, and auto safety critics emerges.

FIGURE 3.3. The logological evolution of the case.

Since the issue's beginning, GM was made the scapegoat but could not get a hearing about the safety of its 1973-1987 C/K pickups. Its only forum was the public stage. After NBC aired its evening television news magazine, *Dateline NBC*, GM officials were able to shift the guilt, first, to NBC for its biased and unethical reporting and, later, to the federal government by establishing a new drama that replaced the one about NBC. This latter drama ultimately saw its climax in the settlement with the federal government and falling action to redemption for the automaker thereafter.

Multiple PR discourse genres were a big part of the swat team's strategy to achieve redemption by being less reactive and very proactive (Lechtzin, personal communication, August 25, 1997) in the post-*Dateline* phase. The team was notably aggressive and proactive concerning major milestone events, like Peña's decision to recall the pickups against the recommendations of NHTSA's own analysts, the Alabama appeals court decision to overturn the verdict in the *Moseley v. GM* suit, the agreement between GM and the NHTSA that stopped the investigations of the pickups, and the class-action settlement providing owners of C/K pickups built between 1973 and 1987 with coupons for $1,000 off a new GM vehicle—all of which helped to vindicate the pickups and GM.

The detailed logological analysis of the case in this chapter shows that GM's internal and external publics slowly and increasingly identified with the company's position, and they especially did so at particular points in the issue when significant events favored GM. When certain publics, primarily those in the "GM family," were invited to participate and information about the issue resonated more on their terms, identification appears to have become stronger. The general public came to identify with GM's position on the C/K pickup issue as third parties supported GM, news organizations and the federal government agreed with GM's empirical data about the pickups' safety, groups opposing GM lost credibility and favor with the news media, and GM family members enacted the issue's drama with friends, neighbors, and others on a personal level.

QUANTITATIVE CORROBORATION OF THE LOGOLOGICAL ANALYSIS

Feedback is essential about whether the PR discourse is having the effects that are specified in the communications plan. That feedback is rarely volunteered from target publics and must be obtained systematically. In the case study, GM officials constantly monitored the environment and how their texts and key messages were being received and used by the automaker's various publics. (See Appendix B for example measurements.) GM officials tracked public opinion daily, and the tracking of public opinions was conducted by an independent research company, Wirthlin Worldwide, for GM.[7] The studies show overwhelmingly (see Appendix B for graphic representation of results) that people were aware of the C/K pickup issue in the news, they felt the company was "going in the right direction" on the issue, and it had no affect on the monetary value of C/K pickups of all model years (General Motors, 1994). There was also a concomitant reduction in the public's awareness of the C/K issue, especially after the class action settlements with C/K pickup truck owners. Only when Peña announced his plan to investigate the trucks against the recommendation of NHTSA researchers did people become more aware, but only marginally so.

This case study's longitudinal, logological analysis of the C/K pickup issue with GM's Voice of the Public (VOP) survey program blends the qualitative and quantitative analyses of two independent studies of the C/K pickup issue and is a unique opportunity to corroborate an unusually specific and comprehensive data set documenting public attitudes and communications effectiveness. The VOP survey program was conducted continuously from September 1992 to November 1994, which makes the tracking of public attitude changes in response to news coverage possible during what essentially is the first 2 years of the issue. Internal financial metrics were considered for this report, but because they were determined to be not as useful for this case as the VOP survey information, they have not been applied here. The analysis reported in this case study follows two steps:

1. The case can be best understood in its salient parts, as defined by the four discrete phases of the case's history.
2. Results from GM's detailed reputation-measurement survey that encompass the case's entire time period are applied and have been segmented into the four-phase case history to analyze how public opinion (and the opinions of key segments) changed.

The quantitative analysis can be thought of in terms of a model of communications impact. That model would say events and communications affect public awareness, attitudes and behaviors in a logical sequence that can be measured over time. This model has particular relevance to this case study, because it gives a way to apply quantitative results from GM's surveys with the qualitative, rhetorical analysis of the entire issue presented above. The communications-impact model simply works as follows. When people are exposed to an event or communication, they first become aware of it. That awareness stimulates people to make sense of it in ways that are meaningful to them as individuals, which means they adopt a particular attitude toward the event or communication. Then, based on what they think and feel about the event or communication, they take (or don't take) action on it. Certain measures can be taken to capture attitudes more directly related to the events/communications, and thereby rule out the influence of other forces. The final results gleaned from those measurements, then, indicate an extent to which individual events or communication efforts directly influence people's attitudes about them and the action they took.

The complex context and prolonged duration of the C/K pickup issue means that both positive and negative forces were very much part of its history and would, consequently, influence each measurement. Measurements taken during the course of the issue would account for variables that capture elements both close to the action and less directly tied to it, forces that are external to the specific events or communication activities on which we are focused, and the connection between attitudes and behaviors. Three key variables—awareness, attitudes and perceptions of GM—were addressed by metrics from the VOP survey. The specific variables are:

- *Awareness* about various kinds of news relevant to the issue, including awareness of news about GM in any respect; trucks and what companies are involved; and positive or negative news and characterization of specific news as "positive" or "negative" for GM.
- *Attitudes* associated specifically with events and news beginning after the development of interest, where these attitudes cover whether awareness of the news affected one's opinion of GM, one's consideration of GM products, or one's perceptions of media fairness as positive, negative, or neutral.
- *Perceptions* of GM, that measure the following: "short-term" effects on image, which asks whether respondents believe the company is currently heading in the "right direction or on the wrong track"; longer term effects on the company's overall image; the perception of GM commitment to safety; and people's consideration of purchasing a GM vehicle

There also was separate analysis of actual sales of GM vehicles. This analysis was done to juxtapose the apparent effects of public communications and news coverage about the C/K pickup issue on vehicle sales. That comparison offered no conclusive evidence that shows a direct causal relationship between what happened over the course of the issue and people's buying decisions. There are too many intervening factors to see any relationship, and that in the time frame involved, the forces at work pulled in opposite directions. Nevertheless, GM's sales remained strong during the 6 years of the C/K/ pickup issue, as shown in the company's annual reports for each of those years.

To examine the outcomes of events and communications related to the C/K pickup issue, measures of the three key variables defined above are described within the historical context of each of four phases for the issue shown in Fig. 3.3.

Phase 1 (Order; Prior to August 1992)

This period is categorized as *neutral* relative to the truck issue. There were no particular events to raise visibility about any matter of the 1973-1987 C/K pickups. Other news dominates the public's recall of GM in the news. GM was recovering from the effects of plant closings, layoffs, and a major financial loss. Financial performance of the company was improving slightly, but market share was continuing its long decline.

- *Awareness*. As a baseline measurement for this case analysis, 10% to 20% of the public was aware of GM in the media, which is used here as a "normal" level of awareness that is compared to the awareness levels measured in later phases.
- *Attitudes* tied to events. Not measured, as no events on the issue had occurred.
- *Perceptions* of GM. The short-term image measure (right track/wrong direction) showed mixed results, with slightly more consumers indicating they saw the company as "on the right track." Although the company had taken some hits for other problems earlier in the year, by mid-year there had been a significant upturn on this measure.

Phase 2 (Pollution of order and assignment of guilt; August 1992 to February 8, 1993)

This period features predominantly *negative* events, including a consumer product recall request, *Dateline NBC*'s exposé on the pickup's fuel-system design, NHTSA's inquiry into the trucks' safety, and the *Mosley v. GM* liability trial news coverage. In general, news media coverage is characterized as cynical about GM, its integrity and its products (not just the C/K trucks).

- *Awareness*. Consciousness of GM in the news jumped sharply through this period. Also, by December 1992 consumer awareness of a truck "problem" had reached a significant level (46%). Most of those aware of news about a truck problem (78%) associated the problem with GM.

- *Attitudes* tied to events. Those mentioning they heard about GM in the news said the coverage was negative. Among those who associated the truck problem with GM, 46% indicated it made them feel less favorable toward GM. Of those aware of the C/K pickup problem, 26% indicated it made them less likely to consider a GM vehicle if they were shopping.
- *Perceptions* of GM. There was a sharp drop in GM's "right direction" measure beginning in August and continuing through the end of the year. Positive mentions of product characteristics declined and negative mentions increased. But there was no measured change in overall perceptions of GM, no measured decline in GM purchase intent, and a slight decline in GM truck purchase intent.

Phase 3 (Purification; February 9, 1993 to December 10, 1996)

A prolonged period of "purification," where GM eventually came out ahead of its critics and was ultimately seen to have proven its case about the C/K pickups through very compelling and strategic communications in many different kinds of public relations discourse—often suffused with empirical evidence and expert opinions—that were directed at multiple audiences inside and outside the company. This phase of the case can be explored better by examining the characteristics of three critical periods of time within the phase.

Phase 3, Period 1 (February 9, 1993 to April 1993). The events and media coverage during this period are characterized as *mixed* with both negatives and positives. Prominent events in this period include the *Moseley v. GM* verdict against the automaker, which was more of a negative; GM's press conference about the *Dateline NBC* exposé and lawsuit against NBC for a defamatory and biased report, both of which were seen as positive; NBC's on-air apology, which was also seen as positive; GM's hiring of former FBI head William Webster to investigate was positive; and NHTSA's request for an investigation into whether a product recall was warranted was seen as negative. Immediately after GM's press conference about *Dateline NBC*'s report, the news media as a whole began to be somewhat apologetic and more self-critical about its newsgathering and reporting practices, using the unfair coverage of GM and its products as a primary example of the need to improve.

- *Awareness.* By February 1993 the steep jump in awareness of the truck issue peaked in the 75% range.

- *Attitudes* tied to events. There was a significant decline in the proportion of the public who said their awareness of the truck events made them feel less favorable toward GM, though still 25% of the public agreed with that. However, in new measures taken soon after GM's press conference, more than 50% of the public agreed that the media had misrepresented the issue and had been unfair to GM.
- *Perceptions* of GM. GM's right direction/wrong track measures reversed direction and became more positive. Overall favorability ratings remained constant. Overall purchase intent stayed constant, although there was a further drop in purchase intent of GM trucks.

Phase 3, Period 2 (May 1993 to June 1993). Initially still a mixed news environment, with GM's refusal of the NHTSA request beginning the period. Overall, the media was less focused on GM, and the tenor of coverage became more *positive* toward GM.

- *Awareness.* Recall of GM in the news and recall of the truck issue began to fall off, dropping from more than 75%.
- *Attitudes* tied to events. Nearly 66% of those who were aware of the truck issue continued to agree that the media had misrepresented GM concerning the problem.
- *Perceptions* of GM. GM's "right direction" numbers took a dip immediately after the recall refusal, but they steadied quickly and moved up throughout the period. Positive attributions for product traits increased sharply as negatives declined. Positive perceptions toward GM and GM truck-purchase intent both increased slightly.

Phase 3, Period 3 (July 1993 to December 1993). The news environment continued to grow more *positive* for GM and stayed there.

- *Awareness.* Awareness of GM in the news and the truck episode continued to decline, although it still remained above 50%.
- *Attitudes* tied to events. Still about 25% of the public felt more negative toward GM as a result of this event.
- *Perceptions* of GM. GM's "right direction" numbers continued upward to highs above those in 1992 prior to the truck events. Overall image of the firm also continued the improvement first observed in May. This was the final period for the VOP survey.

Phase 4 (Redemption; December 1996 and beyond)

The overall news environment is "neutral" on the issue, especially as it nearly fades out of all coverage. Awareness was not measured but is believed to have returned to more "normal" levels. Attitudes tied to events were also not measured, but the presence of GM in the news is a regular occurrence and would presumably have some effect on people, but not to the levels seen in the C/K issue. And perceptions of GM were not measured as in the VOP, but other opinion surveys have shown largely positive associations with GM.

In summary, the VOP measures show a number of important things. Baseline levels of awareness and attitudes tied to events and perceptions of GM in Phase 1 shot up dramatically in Phases 2 and 3, which would be expected for a high-profile issue affecting the world's No. 1 automaker. Attitudes about GM's role in the events moved sharply negative in Phase 2, during which negative forces were more dominant, then those attitudes gradually began to move consistently more positive in Phase 3. Awareness of the events peaked in Phase 3, Period 1, when GM moved its communications into high gear. This movement was possible because the gag order in the *Moseley v. GM* litigation provided GM officials with about 2 months in which they engaged in virtually uninterrupted, intensive communications planning so they could launch a strong, public counteroffensive on the issue, using *Dateline NBC* as the catalyst. This kind of respite from the fray of the issue was a luxury and is rare in issue or crisis management situations. The overall swing of news from negative to positive in Phase 3 was reflected in short-term perceptions of GM, with a sharp dip in the second period, followed by a steady improvement that began and stabilized in the third time period. Longer-term perceptions of GM and purchase intent showed similar but more moderate down-then-up trends. Effects on sales were most difficult to measure, because they were influenced by many other forces; however, a potential dip early in 1993 appeared to be stifled.

EPILOGUE: AN "ILL-DEFINED" ISSUE

This issue was unlike other high-profile product-safety crises, including those that befell Pepsi (syringes in cans) and Tylenol (poison added to bottles) that proved to be cases where people tampered with the products. Companies with product-tampering crises tend to follow defined plans of action to manage the situation (Seeger et al., 1998, whereas the C/K case was not a matter of product tampering and was "ill-defined" (Lechtzin, personal communication, August 25, 1997) in that no established crisis plan could help company officials manage the issue. GM does have crisis plans for certain crises, like:

> a fire in a plant, a worker gets killed—who do you notify, what do you do, how do you handle it, et cetera. That's a purely defined . . . situation. This [the C/K pickup issue] was an ill-defined situation where you never knew who the players were, where they were coming from, and what you could even begin to control. . . . Those are real textbook cases [i.e., Pepsi and Tylenol] on how to handle product tampering—how to be prepared for product tampering. They don't know exactly where it's going to happen, when it's going to happen, or exactly how it's going to happen, but you have all the material and all the people ready to go to talk about your process and how it's impossible. (Lechtzin, personal communication, August 25, 1997)

GM officials began managing the C/K pickup issue with a "reactive" strategy, then moved to a "proactive" one when the environment was right (Lechtzin, personal communication, August 25, 1997). Every day during the case's history, certain GM officials monitored an highly equivocal environment in which events came any time from any of these parties on any aspect. These events became the subjects for particular genres of public relations discourse that addressed the drama of the issue within the context of enacted environments. The exchange of public relations discourse from GM to selected groups and the public (legal activity tends to dominate the case history) reveals the company's public relations approach for managing the drama and makes up the substance of the case for this research project. In the next two chapters, the critical method will be applied to the public relations discourse genres of this case at microscopic and macroscopic levels, further illuminating the simultaneously rhetorical and organizational nature of public relations.

4

MICROSCOPIC TEXTUAL ANALYSIS OF THE CASE

The case of how GM officials managed the issue of fuel-system safety for the company's full-size C/K pickups sold between 1973 and 1987 spans nearly 6 years, from early 1992 to 1998. Although there were many players in the drama of the case, as Chapter 3 demonstrates, the focus of this project is the public relations organizing by GM officials about the issue and their resulting symbolic action to induce cooperation with the company's publics. As GM's sensemakers, those officials had the responsibility to respond to dissent about the trucks' safety and balance the various political, social, business, and personal forces between the company and its publics (see Heath, 1992b). This responsibility naturally befits the realm of corporate public relations, as covered in Chapter 1, and it assumes a high level of competence in the genres of public relations discourse, outlined in Chapter 2, that GM officials enacted to manage the issue inside and outside the company.

This and the next chapter presents further application of the analytical method on GM public relations texts that were at the heart of the case's history described in Chapter 3. In this chapter, the central concern is the general strategy GM officials employed to advance key messages on the issue and gain support from the public. To do this, the officials working on the case exhibited certain behaviors in their organizing processes. They also labored to distill from an equivocal environment a particular set of messages that they felt would influence people's thinking on the issue, no matter how long it would last. This chapter addresses the case's strategic character by overviewing GM officials' organizing of the issue, laying out the key messages for communications with internal and external publics, and presenting a close textual analysis of a highly representative text from the case that embodies many aspects of GM official's public relations action during the case history.

A microscopic analysis of a representative text from the case is necessary, because it illustrates the essential strategy behind GM officials' public relations actions, which all derive from the same analysis of the issue. The selected text, which is a press conference conducted by a single corporate speaker, is as much emblematic of the case writ large as it is definitive of particular aspects of it. More important, the representative text lends itself to a detailed enactment of the calculus of the analytic method on this project's subject. The application of the method on a representative text "possess[es] systematically interrelated structure, while at the same time allowing for the discussion of human affairs and the placement of cultural expressions" (Burke, 1969a, p. 60). In other words, the representative text demonstrates the workability of the Burke–Weick synthesis to explain how public relations officials use language in specific discourse types to induce cooperation between an organization and its publics.

ORGANIZING THE ISSUE

A small group of communications, legal, and engineering professionals in GM was empowered by GM CEO and President John F. "Jack" Smith, Jr. to enact the environment surrounding the safety of the C/K pickups. As Lechtzin (1993), then director of GM's legal and safety issues, recalled, "The multipronged attack on the trucks' safety prompted something that now seems so simple but is not practiced in many organizations: We formed a 'swat' team that eliminated traditional bureaucratic boundaries so we could react quickly and without constant direction from management. At its core were Mr. [William J.] O'Neill [then director of public affairs for GM's North American Operations] and I from PR, three attorneys and two engineers" (p. 4).

In the beginning of the issue, as Lechtzin (personal communication, August 25, 1997) explained, the GM swat team was

> ... in pure crisis reactionary mode. No one would listen to us. ... All we were doing was reacting day by day, hour by hour to events that were coming from eighteen different directions. From *Dateline* until October 17, '94, we were in maintenance, figuring that the government was actually going to drop the case. Three or four times we had good information that they were going to drop it. Peña, being a politician . . . says recall them for no reason—has no right to do it. He steps complete-

ly out of bounds, at which point, from a public relations standpoint, we went very active.

Through it all, the sensemaking swat team was organizing to make order out of chaos. The team was able to do this because it was a cohesive group, sharing leadership responsibilities for managing the issue and depending on the special expertise of each member. It avoided "group think" (Janis, 1972) by tapping into multiple information sources internally and externally, critically examining information sources, thriving on both supportive and contrary views, and expeditiously advancing well-formed responses to inquiries or allegations (Lechtzin, 1993, personal communication, August 25, 1997). In short, these seven individuals were the primary sensemakers for the company, reducing equivocality through consensual validation on the C/K truck issue and news media reports. For example, when it came to the highly visible event of the *Dateline NBC* report, which is explored in detail later, the swat team made sense of the evidence, eyewitness accounts of the crash tests, and NBC's actions "to do what was correct" to frame the issue within context and publicly defend GM's integrity and the reputation of its products (Lechtzin, 1993).

The swat team of sensemakers selected and retained enactments that indicated a polluted order for GM, and they formed discourse to manage GM's multiple identities and induce cooperation among its publics:

> Basically we reported to Harry [Pearce, then GM's general counsel]. Harry kept Jack [Smith] and the Board [of Directors] informed about what we were doing. We didn't have to hold committee meetings and write reports, and go up the ladder and all the rest. And that, in any organization, is the only way to handle a crisis. You can't handle a crisis by committee. (Lechtzin, 1997)

The GM swat team had been successful in containing media coverage of the trucks' alleged safety defects in several important ways. GM officials openly disclosed the company's cooperation with NHTSA and frequently released public relations texts about events related to the issue. GM officials also released updates about NHTSA's investigation of or pending litigation about GM's 1973-1987 C/K pickups. And even with the gag order placed on the two parties in the *Moseley v. GM* trial, GM officials used that "quiet period" to amass more information and build their case for the pickups' safety that would prevail against opposing groups and, ultimately, lead to GM's redemption. Because NHTSA had not yet reached a final decision on whether to recommend a voluntary recall of the trucks to repair the alleged defect, such containment was something GM officials wanted to sustain.

KEY MESSAGES

The purview of this swat team was to orchestrate all external and internal communication about the C/K pickup issue, where Lechtzin was the lead public relations official for GM and "the only source of public information" on the issue (Lechtzin, personal communication, August 25, 1997). According to Lechtzin, the swat team recognized three levels of confrontation:

> One was the peer, almost behind the scenes confrontation and maneuvering (that's as good a word as any) between us and the government, and that was going on. Then you had the plaintiff bar coming at us constantly. And then you had the PR side, the public, and . . . the media, and our job was to control that piece of it so that it did not overwhelm or cause politicians to do something that we didn't want them to do. Basically, we were working to keep as much heat off NHTSA and the regulators as possible. And they can say all they want that there's nothing wrong with these trucks and there's no reason to recall them, but if public pressure becomes high enough, that's the way government works, that's the way government agencies work. And our job was not so much corporate reputation as to keep the heat off the government. (Lechtzin, personal communication, August 25, 1997)

To be successful in this public relations organizing, the GM swat team asserted and backed up certain key messages consistently, compellingly, and appropriately for given enactments throughout the issue's history. Those messages (gleaned from the data listed in Appendix C) were as follows:

- The automaker genuinely cares about passenger safety and tested the pickups' fuel-system design—as it does for every GM vehicle—very thoroughly, the results of which showed superb performance.
- GM has a long history of and strong reputation for conducting credible research, design, engineering, and testing for every vehicle before it goes on to manufacture then sale to the public.
- GM is cooperating fully with NHTSA's investigation, providing large volumes of documentation about the pickups for the agency's and the public's scrutiny.
- The 1973–1987 C/K pickups meet or exceed applicable FMVSS standards, and the government cannot punish a company for making improvements to its products over time.
- Continuously improving products over time with new and better technology is a natural and essential part of the automobile

business to meet customers' changing needs and enhance vehicles' performance beyond that of previous models and competitors' products. (This idea is referred to as "the principle of continuous improvement.")
- Scientific facts from tests conducted by independent, third-party safety analysts and the federal government show conclusively that the C/K pickups' fuel-system design is safe and free of defects.
- The pickups are as safe or safer than other manufacturers' comparable full-size pickups with varying fuel-system designs and many passenger cars, according to 20 years worth of states' highway accident data.
- The motives and statements of the opposing groups are inherently suspect, because they are predominantly supported by plaintiffs' attorneys, who have vested interests in litigation against the company.

These key messages served the swat team well in its organizing process, which included making sense of certain enactments about the pickups and, when appropriate, reporting publicly on enacted environments in ways that advanced GM's position and induced cooperation with targeted publics. In this way, enacted environments defined the context for public relations discourse that the swat team created and the drama in which the agents in the C/K pickup drama acted.

Having the environment well understood and these key messages in hand were critical to developing a communication strategy, then executing it through PR discourse that would influence people's thinking on the C/K pickup issue. For example, when NHTSA requested additional information in late 1992 from GM while the agency's investigation of the pickups was already in progress, GM officials created a lengthy statement that explained how that additional information was gathered. That statement included empirical data about the safety of the pickups as gathered by the third-party research firm, FaAA, and a brief summary of the firm's credentials is given. The statement outlines key findings of FaAA's report, which were "available to the public since mid-October [1992]" and show:

> [T]he rate of post-collision fires has been essentially the same for 1973-1987 GM, Ford and Dodge pickups. . . . A person's chance of being killed in a side impact has been essentially the same in a GM, Ford or Dodge pickup (0.196 per 10,000 registered vehicle years for GM; 0.199 for Ford; and 0.191 for Dodge), but in a fatal side collision in which a fire occurred, however, the GM rate has been 0.019 per 10,000 registered vehicle years. The Ford rate has been 0.007 and the Dodge 0.005. Every

statistic above remains true when the new comparisons are made. (1992, December 2)

On the face of them, the significance of the accident statistics appear very small, but there is a gap between GM's chance for a fatal side collision with a fire and that of either Ford or Dodge full-size pickups. Specifically, the GM rate for such an occurrence for every 10,000 registered vehicle years (0.019) is higher than those of Ford (0.007) and Dodge (0.005). NHTSA researchers initially argued that there was a significant difference between the statistics for GM and its two main competitors' trucks. GM officials, however, consistently asserted the difference was not significant, without citing tests for statistical significance. Interestingly, neither NHTSA nor GM ever debated this point of statistical significance in public.

The point dissolves during the course of the issue as GM officials continually shifted public attention to third-party research and evidence about the C/K pickups' safety over many years. The shift tends to tout other safety statistics, where the C/K pickups are not in a position worse than its competitors. That backing showed that the 1973-1987 C/K pickups have the least amount of risk of being killed when compared to competing full-size pickups and many other vehicles. The point about the statistical gap and its significance disappears altogether later in the issue's drama as Peña himself appears to be a political pawn, relegating much of what he stood for and ever said to be inconsequential. This scene with Peña plays into GM's hand that the objective performance is sound and personal agendas of groups opposing the automaker are the true motivation for a recall.

Closely related to this motivation appears to be an attitude of opposing groups that GM is a monolithic enterprise that is uncaring and impersonal. Indeed, "the mainstream press seemingly views every statement by the government or big business as half-truth or bald-face lie. As the distance widens between top executives, the press has a pervasive feeling that they are being manipulated by spokespeople, spinmeisters and public relations professionals" (Bailey, 2000, p. 20). The cornerstone discourse that turns this image around for GM, crystallizes the key messages about the issue in one text, and reflects an aggressive communications strategy is a press conference featuring a GM senior executive.

A REPRESENTATIVE TEXT

The scene on Monday, February 8, 1993, was "a packed house of more than 150 print journalists and 25 camera crews in the hastily converted showroom of the GM building in Detroit," and the corporate speaker was Harry

Pearce, then executive vice president and GM's general counsel (Lechtzin, 1993, p. 4). Speaking on behalf of GM and as a representative of those in the GM organization and its stakeholders, Pearce enacted a "trial-lawyer's summation" (Lechtzin, 1993, p. 8)[8] of the case against NBC for its journalistic misconduct in producing the "grossly unfair and inaccurate reporting" about GM C/K pickups (General Motors, 1993b, p. 4). His purpose was to publicly "end the sensationalism and distortions appearing in the mass media so that a dispassionate and objective consideration can be given to these vehicles" (General Motors, 1993b, p. 3).

Pearce's role was to enact, through a frame of rejection, a critical analysis of the enacted environment and inspire people to see anew the *Dateline* report as an unethical and immoral symbolic act against the people and organization of GM. Ultimately, the press conference served as a public forum for GM to dramatically shift guilt for the issue and demonstrate the safety of its pickups by, primarily, showing the lengths someone (in this episode, NBC news staff and consultants) must go to make the fuel system fail. Key to this strategy was highlighting empirical data about the pickups' exceptional safety record as documented by state and federal agencies.

To assemble all the support material and logistical aspects of the 2-hour press conference, the sensemaking swat team worked with people from GM's Indianapolis Truck Plant, Chevrolet Creative Services, GM Photographic, and GM's security people. "There were some different kinds of things that were put out for different audiences, like there were communication packages for GM editors, [a] letter to stockholders, the newsletter—the special edition newsletter . . . [and] independent articles made slight, right afterward" (Lechtzin, personal communication, August 25, 1997). The event was broadcast via satellite to all of GM's dealers in North America and to all GM locations, and it was carried by all radio and television stations (General Motors, 1993b, p. 2).

As a result of *Dateline*'s November 17, 1992 broadcast, as Pearce stated, GM "fac[ed] a poisoned environment spawned by the cheap, dishonest sensationalism of NBC's *Dateline* program entitled, Waiting to Explode, and its aftermath" (General Motors, 1993b, p. 2). *Dateline* personnel were motivated to ensure that fire would occur upon the impact of a car into the truck's fuel tanks. And Pearce successfully demonstrated that motivation. In dramatistic terms, Pearce's remarks frequently reflect a scene–act ratio to illustrate that the broad elements of the scene—the agents who staged the crash tests; the agencies of the model rockets, the remote electronic transmitter to ignite the rockets, the duct tape to fasten the rockets to the fuel tanks, and so on; and the act of the crash tests themselves—could only have produced the deceptive demonstration of a defect in the pickups' fuel system.

On behalf of those in GM, Pearce argued that the guilty party for polluting the order of both the pickups' safety reputation and, especially, "good journalism" was *Dateline NBC* personnel and their news-gathering consultants, who assured GM that they would produce a fair and balanced story. Lechtzin (1993) recounted that "Dateline [*sic*] producer Robert Read asked if we would cooperate in on-camera interviews because he wanted a fair and balanced review of the issue" (p. 4). The swat team worked with *Dateline* producers to hold interviews with a GM safety expert (Lechtzin, 1993), and after 4 hours of interviews, almost 3 hours of which were taped, "49 seconds of the GM engineer ended up in the *Dateline* program. The rest ended up on the cutting room floor, along with the truth" (General Motors, 1993b, p. 9). Those GM officials also tried to obtain the vehicles for analysis, which NBC said did not exist, but a GM attorney found easily in a junk yard near the crash site. As Pearce said, "we took NBC at its word. . . . That's not a mistake I'm going to make again" (General Motors, 1993b, p. 11).

To further assert where guilt lies, Pearce advanced an argument about harm to GM by announcing, "GM filed a defamation case in Marion county, Indiana, against NBC and TISA, The Institute for Safety Analysis [which helped NBC to conduct the crash tests for the story], seeking compensatory damages and punitive damages based upon the outrageous misrepresentation and conscious deception contained in its November 17th, 1992 edition of *Dateline*, asserting a safety defect in GM's 1973 through 1987 C/K pickup trucks" (General Motors, 1993b, p. 3). Throughout the media briefing, Pearce employed an agent–purpose ratio, as he asserted how much and how often NBC people specifically behaved unethically and uncooperatively to protect themselves and their company. Remember that such an instance already occurred regarding NBC's unwillingness to give GM the trucks used in the crash tests.

Another example of the agent–purpose ratio is Pearce's assertion that NBC producers were motivated to conceal the manner in which the truck fire started. Pearce reviewed for the audience the details of photographs that showed smoke coming from model rocket engines, which had been taped to the fuel tanks of the C/K trucks to ensure that there would be a fire when they were hit by a car during the crash tests. Pearce said, "Did NBC say anything about that smoke to their viewers? Did they even show it to them? No. . . . Did you hear anything about rocket engines during the course of that crash demonstration, anything about open flame being artificially produced beneath our truck, sparks, thermal energy, any intimation of that?" (General Motors, 1993b, p. 19).

For Pearce (and the sensemaking swat team), *Dateline NBC*'s story was just as much an attack on the people of and affiliated with GM as it was on the safety of one of GM's products. He stated:

> I will not allow the good men and women of General Motors and the thousands of independent businesses who sell our products and whose livelihood depends upon our reputation of our products to suffer the

consequences of NBC's irresponsible conduct transmitted via the airwaves throughout this great nation in their November Dateline program. GM has been irreparably damaged and we are going to defend ourselves. (General Motors, 1993b, p. 11)

In this statement, which occurred early in his remarks, Pearce transcended being a decentered self conveying a corporate message. He personalized both the message and the image of GM as he emphasized that the huge company is comprised of thousands of people who care deeply about what they do and those who ultimately benefit from their work.

In line with Cheney's (1992) observation about corporate speakers, the rhetorical effectiveness of Pearce's remarks—as they represent the culmination of the enactment, selection, and retention of the sensemaking swat team—is that his corporate message became identified with GM employees and he became the embodiment of GM. Indeed, identification between Pearce and GM employees would result from the gratification they felt about the form of Pearce's remarks. Because of this formal effect, in dramatistic terms, the emphasis within the context of the scene of the press conference is on the agent–act ratio. That is, Pearce, as the corporate speaker who publicly reported on the environment enacted by the sensemaking symbolic action of the swat team, assumed both symbolically and literally a personal role in representing the people of GM. As that agent, Pearce's act to speak in defense of the company and its stakeholders was natural and most effective as it induced cooperation with NBC to admit its guilt, recant the story, and apologize for its journalistic misconduct. His act also sparked renewed self-analysis among journalists about their craft.[9] Internally to GM, Pearce's work kicked off communication in both print and video media about the C/K truck issue, which further helped employees (and retirees, dealers, and suppliers) to feel better about the integrity of the company and act as credible spokespeople among their family, friends, and neighbors (see General Motors, 1993a, 1993b, 1993c).[10]

THE CORNERSTONE TO REDEMPTION

As a result of the work of GM's swat team, including Pearce's presentation of the enacted environment surrounding the *Dateline NBC* story, NBC management recanted the story and apologized on the air the next evening, February 9, 1993.[11] News reports for days and weeks to follow covered the redemptive strategy GM officials enacted to bolster the company's image and reputation. Within the context of organizing, Pearce engaged in sensemaking and functioned dramatistically to report publicly the enacted environment about the unethical *Dateline NBC* report. The broad response in GM's favor—from NBC's recanting of the story, to articles placing GM and the public as victims of journalistic misconduct, to reports reframing the pickups' safety—indicate successful restructuring of people's thinking on the issue. The swat team was just beginning to induce cooperation with GM's publics, and there was much work left to do.

This single event, with Pearce as GM's corporate speaker, kicked off a larger, more aggressive PR effort that reached internal and external publics. Indeed, the public relations discourse enacted after this event is characterized by many PR discourse genres over the next 5 years that reflect pentadic elements in much simpler ways, allowing the scene (i.e., enacted environments) to dominate while highlighting agents—especially those on whom guilt was assigned—and their actions therein.

Since the issue's beginning, GM was made the scapegoat but could not get a hearing about the safety of its 1973-1987 C/K pickups. Its only forum was the public stage. After NBC aired its evening television news magazine, *Dateline NBC*, GM officials were able to shift the guilt, first, to NBC for its biased and unethical reporting and, later, to the federal government by establishing a new drama that replaced the one about NBC. This latter drama, as Chapter 3 showed, ultimately saw its climax in the settlement with the federal government and falling action to redemption for the automaker thereafter.

The next chapter shows how multiple genres were a big part of the swat team's strategy to achieve redemption by being less reactive and very proactive (Lechtzin, personal communication, August 25, 1997) in the post-*Dateline* phase. The team was notably aggressive and proactive concerning major milestone events, like Peña's decision to recall the pickups against the recommendations of NHTSA's own analysts, the Alabama appeals court decision to overturn the verdict in the *Moseley v. GM* suit, the agreement between GM and the NHTSA that stopped the investigations of the pickups, and the class-action settlement providing owners of C/K pickups built between 1973 and 1987 with coupons for $1,000 off a new GM vehicle—all of which helped to vindicate the pickups and GM.

5

MACROSCOPIC TEXTUAL ANALYSIS OF THE CASE

The genres of public relations discourse were GM officials' responses to the drama as they saw it at particular times. The drama itself was formed by the texts enacted about the issue. This chapter examines a large sample of GM's public relations discourse dramatistically—90 texts for external and internal audiences. (See Appendix C, which is essential to the document references in this chapter, as they refer to texts by genre and by sequential number.) The texts cover the 6-year period that is divided into two simple phases: texts created before *Dateline NBC*'s report and texts created after it. This analysis dovetails from the issue's history traced in Chapter 3 and builds on the microscopic textual analysis in Chapter 4. The result demonstrates the broad use of language by GM officials to structure thinking about the literal drama of the C/K pickup issue to induce cooperation between the company and its various publics.

The turning point of the case was, as described in the preceding two chapters, the *Dateline NBC* report that aired in November 1992, because it affected the course of the issue and especially GM's public relations discourse after it. Indeed, the kind of communication that was enacted before *Dateline* was "completely different" (Lechtzin, personal communication, August 25, 1997) from anything enacted after the report. A short transitional section between these two phases addresses the major segment of the *Dateline NBC* report itself that was important to GM officials who managed the C/K pickup issue.

This chapter presents a macroscopic analysis of the case's evolution through GM officials' PR texts. Like Chapter 4, representative texts of 12 applicable PR genres are analyzed macroscopically through this project's method. (Refer to Appendix A for selected examples.) This chapter shows fundamental differences in the PR discourse enacted before and after the NBC exposé. Specifically, the discourse in the pre-*Dateline NBC* period is characterized as reactive, defensive, and fact-based. Discourse in this period also reflects purposes to downplay the issue and minimize the drama of those involved in it, because there was a limited story to tell. The result is a small number of texts enacted in response to events regarding the embryonic issue. The time between the airing of the *Dateline* report and GM's first discourse in the post-*Dateline* period is "quiet." That is, no one in GM could publicly comment on any aspect of the C/K pickup issue because of the judge's "gag" order in the *Moseley v. GM* case. GM officials used this period to engage in major fact-finding, replanning, and message-refining work on both the *Dateline* report and the issue itself.

Discourse in the post-*Dateline* period reflects motives that are opposite of those in the pre-*Dateline* period. The PR discourse in this final period of the issue is characterized as proactive, authoritative, and empirical. Discourse in this period uses the *Dateline* report to elevate the drama's visibility and importance for GM's benefit—to shift the assignment of guilt to the people attacking the automaker and its products. GM officials achieved this result by structuring people's thinking on the issue by strategically enacting many different texts in multiple genres, directing discourse at several publics at once, and selecting third parties to publicly lend support to the company's cause.

In general, the lens of the Burke–Weick synthesis reveals that GM sensemakers intersubjectively defined the C/K pickup issue facing the company throughout its history. The subsequent kinds of public relations discourse they created befitted the enacted environments (contexts) and those enacted by targeted publics. GM sensemakers engaged in symbolic action through the texts they enacted to structure people's thinking about the issue, induce cooperation between targeted publics and the automaker, and, ultimately, achieve vindication for the pickups. That redemption was possible as GM officials, who were driven by the context of events, enacted dramas about the issue in specific kinds of texts that more closely resembled the dramas enacted by the company's target publics. In this way, the automaker induced cooperation with its publics.

PR DISCOURSE BEFORE *DATELINE NBC*

When the issue about GM's 1973-1987 C/K pickups first emerged in August 1992, the GM swat team managed it through two types of discourse: conversations with journalists and prepared statements on specific topics about the issue. The first category, conversations, is innumerable and undocumented, and therefore, it is not part of this volume. Such conversational discourse, presumably, was used often, as the issue was new and GM officials handled inquiries individually. As the swat team enacted more environments about the issue, its organizing process retained more symbolic action about it; whereas, that team of officials became the central authority on the issue. Swat team members Ed Lechtzin and Bill O'Neill (with support from communication staff when needed) had the special duty of managing internal and external communications about the issue through the range of channels available, from individual to mass. The only other genre GM officials used in this short, pre-*Dateline NBC* phase of the case was that of prepared statements. The swat team retained these and other documents from the case's later phase for the company's historical record of the issue.

CAS and the Public Citizen filed a recall petition with NHTSA in August 1992. This action marks the beginning of the issue, because it moves beyond individual lawsuits brought against the company and formally brings it into the public consciousness. The first lawsuit against GM that involved the pickups was the *Zelenuk v. GM* case. What made this suit instrumental in the history of the C/K pickup issue was that the CAS and plaintiff's attorneys called attention to the judge's ruling in the case that all documents submitted by GM had to be made public. The two groups used this event to foreground their impending recall petition, as the documents submitted in evidence would apply to the claims in that petition. As a result of the raised awareness of the lawsuit, GM public relations officials on the swat team handled media inquiries individually about the judge's ruling. (A GM statement in October 1992 said the documents in the Zelenuk case had been made public, because so much attention was given to GM's attempts to maintain confidentiality rather than focus on the issue of safety.)

When GM officials enacted their very first statement in August 1992 on the C/K pickup issue, the act is a statement of opinion that is attributed to the company. The agency for that act is a prepared formal statement released to the news media over a wire service that responds to the scene at NHTSA with the filing of the recall petition. That statement, released on August 14, 1992, simply reads:

> GM believes, that its full-size pickups, both current and former models, meet the safety needs of GM's customers. All GM vehicles including our full-size pickups continue to meet or exceed all Federal Motor Vehicle Safety Standards, including the specific requirement applicable to fuel system integrity. (B-11, p. 1)

Through a frame of rejection, the purpose for the statement is to assert the fundamental safety of the pickups, which would downplay the claims advanced in the petition. Driving the GM officials in their act is the scene, which dictates that some defensive response be tendered. The scene also motivated other parties, like news media and trial lawyers, to act on it. The statement, then, projects a strong scene–agent ratio between the enacted environment of the trucks' safety being called into question and particular opposing critics advancing claims about the presence of a safety-related defect.

Because the case was in litigation, GM policy was to keep calls with journalists focused on the specifics of the ruling itself and not comment on any other aspect of the case while it was still in litigation. This discursive action befitted the team's desire to defend the company and maintain a low profile for the issue because the drama then was limited to a lawsuit and two opportunistic groups seeking benefits from it. Although the implications of a recall were well understood by the GM swat team and company management, the environment for the emerging issue was not, because there were too many variables—they "never knew who the players were, where they were coming from, and what you could even begin to control" (Lechtzin, personal communication, August 25, 1997). Monitoring the very equivocal environment included watching for any public statements from non-GM groups, news coverage, or other activity that drew attention to the petition itself, the trucks' safety record, and GM conduct.

GM officials issued four statements on November 16, 1992, in response to "a news report on the release of documents [in the Zelenuk case] by General Motors regarding its 1973 through 1987-model light-duty pickup trucks" and allegations about their safety (PS-1). The date these statements were issued is significant, because it is the day before the airing of *Dateline NBC*'s exposé on the pickups. Because GM officials were already aware of the basic content of the report but not what would finally be broadcast, the prepared statements are clearly meant to advance factual data about the pickups' performance and safety, and assert strong arguments about the motives of those opposing GM. The statements, then, emphasize the scene of the debate about the trucks' safety, where participating agents on either side of it act according to their appropriate roles as naysayers.

In this set of four statements released in mid-November 1992, the act was very much the same as that for the very first statement released about the issue but the scene was different. The stated scene was the release of internal documents pursuant to a judge's order in the *Zelenuk v. GM* case in Dallas. But underlying motives for these statements reflect a larger scene about the entire issue that is at risk of going out of control with criticism of the trucks that would be aired on *Dateline NBC* the next day. In this way, GM's own story used a frame of rejection about critics' claims and a frame of acceptance about the trucks' safety to structure people's thinking before the television news magazine would.

The swat team's choices to enact prepared statements (any conversations notwithstanding) were really "standard procedure" when responding to a new issue for external publics. Because the issue was new and limited in scope, the swat team worked behind the scenes to understand the drama and all its elements. The team reactively gave its target publics only what they needed in the form of official assessments about enacted environments. According to Lechtzin (personal communication, August 25, 1997), the environment was very equivocal and it was difficult to anticipate who or what would come on the scene at any time. So structuring people's thinking about the issue through PR texts was also difficult but necessary. The swat team made a strong attempt to do just that the day before *Dateline NBC* aired its report, because the report's final content was unknown. As the case history shows in Chapter 3, there was little affect those texts had on public opinion, and the team had to organize more intensely after the report.

When the very first statement on the issue was released, special-interest groups were emerging on the scene. There were also plaintiffs' attorneys, who assembled class actions against the company alleging safety defects in the C/K pickups' fuel systems. And another prominent group was the news media, as they sought to learn more about a potentially huge recall burden placed on the world's No. 1 automaker. The grandest symbolic act in the C/K drama was that created by NBC in its *Dateline NBC* program.

THE TURNING POINT: *DATELINE NBC'S* REPORT

The *Dateline NBC* exposé, "Waiting to Explode," aired on Wednesday, November 17, 1992, and was summarized in Chapter 3. Of the 15-minute report, 56 seconds focused on a GM official's public attack on the report's truthfulness and, fortuitously, presented a major opportunity to redirect the public's attention on the pickups' real-world performance and the company's dedication to safety. Rather than quoting the entire exposé, the following is a transcription of the critical 56 seconds that gave the GM swat team its greatest boost to manage the issue about the television show's truthfulness and, ultimately, the C/K pickups' safety (Lechtzin, 1993). The segment's transcription is preceded by the introduction of the report by the show's anchors, Stone Phillips and Jane Pauley:

> MR. PHILLIPS: You think of pickup trucks as rough and rugged, designed to take lots of punishment, but the news tonight is that pickups made by General Motors from 1973 to 1987 may have a fatal flaw, a gas tank in the wrong place. Top safety experts say it's already claimed more than 300 lives.
>
> MS. PAULEY: If true, that would dwarf the problem with the infamous Ford Pinto, and the 1970's Pinto fires claimed 27 lives and led to a mas-

sive recall. Now there are serious questions whether the GM pickup should be recalled. General Motors denies there is a fatal flaw. Watch Michele Gillen's investigation and you decide. . . .

MS. GILLENS [sic]: To see for ourselves what might happen in a side impact crash, Dateline NBC hired The Institute for Safety Analysis to conduct two unscientific crash demonstrations. In our demonstration, unlike GM tests, the fuel tanks were filled with real gasoline.

In one crash, at about 40 miles per hour, there was no leakage and no fire, but in the other, at around 30 miles per hour, look what happened: At impact, a small hole was punctured in the tank. According to our experts, the pressure of the collision and the crushing of the gas tank forced gasoline to spew from the gas cap. The fuel then erupted into flames when ignited by the impact in the car's headlight.

The pickup's tank did not split wide open. If it had, the fire would have been much larger. (General Motors, 1993c, pp. 7-8)

Because the television report featured GM C/K pickups, the company sought in vain to obtain from NBC the trucks used in the crash tests—the show's producer wrote in a letter to GM's director of public affairs for North American Operations that the vehicles were destroyed. As Warren and Kaden (1993), who conducted an independent investigation and prepared a final analysis about the *Dateline NBC* exposé, stated:

First, as GM stepped up its protests and made more persistent requests for the test material, the Dateline producer mistakenly thought the complaints were abating. Without consulting either the reviewing attorney or anyone else, the producer told GM the trucks had been junked and were unavailable. That was misleading. Second, when GM learned about the igniters and threatened to bring suit for defamation, NBC personnel failed to mount a sufficient investigation into the facts and thus made the initial decision to defend the whole story without having an adequate understanding of the facts concerning the demonstrations. (p. 7)

Immediately after receiving a tip in early January 1993 from a journalist who heard that *Dateline*'s tests were rigged, a GM attorney traveled to the site of the crash tests and the surrounding area and found "a fireman, an off-duty sheriff's deputy, an off-duty Indiana state trooper, a girlfriend of one of the firemen, video, and still photographs," and a day later found both trucks and both cars used to strike them in the crash tests (Lechtzin, 1993).

GM officials had to refrain from issuing any formal public statement about the report and what they discovered, because the company was under a gag order from Alabama's state supreme court while the *Moseley v. GM* case was in litigation. Indeed, the company could not publicly address any aspect of the C/K pickup issue. Nevertheless, with this "quiet" period in the issue's history, the swat team turned all its attention toward amassing evidence and building a case that would conclusively demonstrate to the public not only that the report was false and misleading, but also that the trucks do indeed have a safe fuel-system design. The PR officials on the swat team also formulated a comprehensive communications strategy to win broad-based support for GM's messages—to induce cooperation on the issue between the company and its internal and external publics.

PR DISCOURSE AFTER *DATELINE NBC*

From GM officials' recognizance work and communications organizing, the swat team enacted an environment about *Dateline NBC*'s report. The public relations discourse after the *Dateline* report is markedly different than what preceded it, reflecting an aggressive attitude toward managing the issue. This orientation stands in sharp contrast to the reactive character of the texts in the pre-*Dateline* period. The team staged a press conference for a corporate speaker to publicly report on that enacted environment to induce cooperation with the news media and general public. With the *Moseley v. GM* case decided on February 7, 1993, and the gag order lifted, GM officials chose the next day for its first public comment in months—in the form of a press conference—about the C/K pickup issue, and the subject was the *Dateline NBC* report, which dovetailed into topics upheld by other stakeholders. The result was a holistic and dramatistically complex response by a corporate speaker to the entire issue, focusing on the news magazine's report and using it as a way to address the web of contentions in the C/K pickup issue.

Press Conference

As Chapter 4 showed, the press conference (PC-1; PC-2) reflects an intricate web of dramatistic elements, which contrasts significantly with the simpler texts that follow it. This press conference with a corporate speaker was the first text of the post-*Dateline* phase. The press conference was the cornerstone on which GM officials built their strong and effective redemptive strategy for the company and its full-size pickups. The swat team used this genre to begin a more aggressive PR effort to reassign guilt on those attacking GM and its products. The team then enacted other genres reactively and proactively as occasions warranted. The following sections address each of the 11 other genres in the post-*Dateline NBC* phase.

Press Releases

This genre is among the least enacted types in the sample used by GM officials to manage the C/K pickup issue (another being FAQs), but it is among the most potent. Its first use came at a crucial time: Pearce's press conference to debunk *Dateline NBC*'s report on the safety of the pickups' fuel systems. Indeed, press releases were used for press kits distributed at that event and about the class action settlement involving $1,000 coupons for the purchase of a new GM vehicle; otherwise, corporate statements about enacted environments were released to the public. (The press kit and statements are treated separately later.) Nevertheless, the press releases used in conjunction with the press conference served to reiterate and preserve key points that Pearce made during his remarks.

GM officials put out four press releases the day of the press conference. The first one summarizes in 5.5 pages the enacted environments of the company's lawsuit "filed in a state court in Indianapolis against NBC, The Institute for Safety Analysis (TISA) [which helped NBC conduct the test] and its president, Bruce Enz, for defamatory and false statements and grossly misleading and unfair visual representations which were broadcast on the *Dateline NBC* program" (PR-1). The press release says the lawsuit charges that the "*Dateline NBC* program rigged a car–truck crash with incendiary model rocket engines to irresponsibly portray that GM's 1973-1987 full-size pickup trucks are prone to fires in side impact collisions" (PR-1). The press release describes the company's investigation of the crash tests, then outlines "several material aspects" of the *Dateline* report that are "defamatory misrepresentations" made by NBC and TISA. From this information about the enacted environment of the crash tests and *Dateline*'s report, the press release states that the storyline was "preconceived . . . to lead viewers to conclude that the trucks were defective and likely to burn upon side impact" (PR-1). Consistent with its key messages, the press release presents real-world data from third parties (i.e., independent research firms plus state and federal data) of the C/K pickups' safety performance—that the pickups pose no greater risk of injury, death, or post-collision fire than any other comparable full-size pickup and even passenger cars (PR-1).

The other press releases support the company's key messages in other ways. The second press release serves to support the claim that GM faces a "poisoned atmosphere" about the safety performance of the C/K pickups. This release introduces and includes copies of two letters from the Institute for Injury Reduction (IIR) that state the organization would conduct its own test of the C/K pickup fuel tanks for ABC's *PrimeTime Live* news program using "a modified design [to] further enhanc[e] the likelihood of a real-world impact resulting in a fire due to the defect" (PR-2). The third press release (PR-3) presents the chronology of events that led up to GM filing a defamation lawsuit against NBC and holding the press conference, and the fourth press release (PR-4) provides the captions for four photos. Unlike a photo news release where the photo is the subject and the text supportive of it, the form is reversed: The photos support the stories in the captions' texts, which derive from the lawsuit and Pearce's press conference. The captions are long and detailed to make sure that the viewer sees everything that went on at specific points in the staging of *Dateline*'s crashes.

Five months after the press conference about the *Dateline NBC* report, GM and the class of C/K pickup owners reached a settlement in their lawsuit against the company. On July 19, 1993, a prepared statement (PS-11, which is addressed separately later) describes that the settlement requires the automaker to provide certificates for $1,000 toward the purchase of a new GM pickup. Three press releases also were issued that day, each calling attention to specific aspects of the settlement—a tactic that can improve the application of key messages by news organizations as they pay attention to them individually then together, with the statement as an overall organizing device. The first press release about the settlement gives a "brief overview of the current status of GM pickup litigation" as of the date of the settlement (PR-5). The second press release outlines how C/K pickup owners (not necessarily original owners) will be notified of the settlement and how to obtain a certificate (PR-6). And the third press release describes how the settlement works in general, including defining how the certificates could be used, how they work if they are transferred to other people for their use, and what vehicles are eligible for purchase with the certificates (PR-7).

The swat team's choices to enact press releases appear to be functions of the gravity of enacted environments. The press conference, for example, commanded a high level of importance and required an official treatment of the subject matter in the form of press releases. GM's press releases carry the company's logo and are formatted specifically to complement the special letterhead. For example, the use of press releases presented the company's account about the *Dateline* report and the C/K pickups as unique, "breaking" news the company was making. (These texts are unlike prepared statements, which present verbal comments on news that has already been made or is in progress.) The press releases also served to reframe the drama surrounding the issue in a way that journalists and GM communicators could use immediately "as is" or in stories developed with background material provided in other genres.

Video Programming

Over the course of the issue after the press conference, 21 video news programs (approximately 10% of more than 200 programs produced over the ensuing 4 years) for GM employees covered events related to GM's 1973-1987 C/K pickups. Using a format very much like a local television news show, GM officials produced weekly corporate news programs, entitled *GM This Week*, that were videotaped every Wednesday afternoon and broadcast on Thursdays every 30 minutes (between 10:30 a.m. and 3 p.m.) by satellite over a closed circuit to the company's locations around the world.

In every episode, if only because of the nature of the medium, the video news coverage of the C/K pickup issue highlights scenes and related acts and their agents for particular enacted environments in the issue's history. At times, certain people are included as agents of messages important to the story being told. For example, in the very first story about the issue, *GM This Week* describes the outcome of the press conference militaristically, saying "GM has won one battle in its fight to prove its CK pickup trucks are safe" (V-1). Then the segment summarizes the charges in GM's defamation lawsuit against NBC and presents footage of *Dateline NBC* anchor, Stone Phillips, giving an on-air apology to GM and viewers for the "inappropriate [unscientific] demonstration" of exploding fuel tanks on two C/K pickups. The story continues by giving GM employee viewers an idea about the status of the recall campaign started by CAS and the initial judgment against GM in the *Moseley v. GM* trial. An on-screen clip has Harry Pearce stating facts about the pickups' safety: "In terms of side impact fire rates in collisions they are comparable, in terms of overall crash worthiness when we look at a six state data base they are actually the best of the 3 domestic manufacturers" (V-1).

The video news programs stressed the scene for particular events and the acts within them. This approach served an important purpose in keeping employees informed about the issue's status. That is, employees will understand the context within which certain events happened and will be able to recount for other people key messages about those events. The video news programs follow the same formula: present the scene related to particular events, describe the act(s) within them, and present people as agents for the messages that pertain to the enacted environment. For example, in one of the more potent segments about the C/K pickups, *GM This Week* covers the agreement reached between GM and NHTSA that ended the agency's investigation of the pickups.

The segment begins by quoting a story in *The Wall Street Journal*, which called the agreement "a triumph for General Motors" (V-18). The balance of the story includes footage of Peña giving a statement about the terms of the agreement; gives a soundbite of a GM engineering official commenting on the social benefits of the agreement that promotes safety research; and presents very positive reactions to the agreement from one of the leading editors in the auto industry trade press, John McElroy (1994), then editor-in-chief of *Automotive Industries*. McElroy said, "I think that he [Peña] got a call maybe from the President himself . . . that said Frederico are you crazy or what? It's [his decision to recall the pickups, which was against the recommendations of NHTSA researchers] going against what we in the administration want to do which is build bridges with the auto industry" (p. 5). The segment also shows positive reactions from three GM employees (V-18).

Unlike the static, printed material that dominates the PR genres in the case, the video genre demanded that the messages reflect more dynamic, visual, and personal affects. The production of these stories were largely collaborations between the swat team (i.e., Lechtzin and O'Neill) and the video production group of GM. The swat team selected certain enacted environments for video production, then crafted both the verbal and visual components to best depict the drama and drive home the key messages. The result was a strong influence on the thinking of employees about the issue, because those people stood out as the strongest advocates—the ambassadors—of GM and the company's position on the C/K pickup issue. This approach helped establish deep grassroots support for GM, beginning within employees' home communities to induce cooperation between the automaker and its publics.

Newsletters

The internal communications campaign continued in the print medium for GM employees and retirees, who included those of GM's subsidiaries (i.e., Electronic Data Systems, GMAC Financial Services, and Hughes Electronics), and dealers, suppliers, and stockholders—all of whom make up what the automaker calls the "GM family"—a formidable body of ambassadors, even grassroots advocates for the company that numbered an estimated 2.5 million people in North America, based on GM's *1993 Annual Report*. Newsletters published by the corporation and by individual operating units, from each motor division to the subsidiaries, included stories about the C/K pickup issue. Content for these newsletters emanated from a central source: the sensemaking swat team's PR experts (i.e., Lechtzin and O'Neill), who prepared and distributed "communication packages" to internal communications personnel. (This genre is explored in detail in the section on press kits.) This arrangement ensured that all messages were consistent everywhere they appeared for GM family consumption. (The swat team's PR experts also served as the final reviewers of any material that would cover the issue to any public.)

With this kind of central message authority, all internal newsletters (and other texts for any public) would contain the same information that could be laid out differently according to individual newsletter designs. The important point about these newsletters is that they are both permanent and referenceable—employees (and any member of the GM family) could and were encouraged to pass on the information to friends, family, neighbors, and anyone who might want to know more about the issue (N-2, p. 1). These documents present a summary record of enacted environments about the issue, and they variously emphasize pentadic elements in the published stories.

The single most important newsletter published for the GM family, especially for employees, about the C/K issue was a newly minted publication, entitled *GM Focus: Special Report* (N-2). It was released to employees on March 16, 1993, or slightly more than one month after the press conference about *Dateline NBC*. In a letter of transmittal to GM divisional general managers, Bill O'Neill, director of public affairs for GM North American Operations, said the newsletter "was recently developed by our GM Communication and Legal Staff[s]" (N-2, p. 1), which effectively denotes the sensemaking swat team and selected graphics, communications, and production people who prepared the publication for printing. Like *GM This Week*, the newsletter was part of the early foray into a concentrated internal communications effort that sought to make employees "ambassadors for GM" about the C/K pickup issue (N-2, p. 1).

In three of the five stories in the four-page, full-color, tabloid-size newsletter (measuring 14" × 10.75", folded), the publication covers the key points in Pearce's analysis during his press conference, the chronology of events that led up to NBC's apology for its deceptive report, and full-text reprints of NBC's on-air statement on February 9, 1993, apologizing for the report and Pearce's immediate public response that accepted NBC's apology and dropped the defamation lawsuit GM brought against the network. The three stories about the *Dateline* report fill the entire inside, center spread of the newsletter. They emphasize the acts that created the deceptive report and events subsequent to it. In the newsletter's other two stories, scene is emphasized through the actual performance of the vehicles as suggested by empirical and statistical data. In the first set about the *Dateline NBC* report, the language reflects how those involved in the television news report acted in ways with certain agencies (e.g. model rocket engines and remote-control devices) to produce a deceptive program about the trucks.

The two remaining stories of the five in *GM Focus* present the safety record of 1973-87 C/K pickups from state's databases of accident statistics, and the "real-world" performance of the pickups compared to other manufacturers' comparable pickups, citing low fire risk, low injury risk, and few fatal crashes. In this second set of stories, the emphasis is on scene—the real-world performance and safety of the pickups.

Another newsletter, *GM International Newsline* (N-1, N-3, N-4), was produced daily and released internally to GM employees in print and online over an internal computer network (a early kind of intranet but without Web technology). The newsletter routinely featured several selected excerpts of daily news clips, GM stock prices, and communications program reminders about the weekly broadcast of *GM This Week*. This newsletter was prepared by a GM corporate communications staff member, and it often featured complete texts of official statements about issues the company faced. The content of this newsletter emphasizes the action of people and organizations in some scene. The text is typically limited to very short descriptions of what was done, when, by whom, with what, where, for what purpose, and with what results and expected next steps. However, as occasions warranted, full texts of a significant document would be given (e.g., the reprinting of Bill O'Neill's letter to *Dateline* NBC Producer Robert Read [N-1] and a prepared statement about GM filing suit against Peña [N-4]). This newsletter served as an ongoing way to keep employees informed about key internal and external events about which the company placed significant value and wanted employees to know. In this way, *GM International Newsline* was an important channel to get corporate messages in employees' hands each day so they knew what was going on and could talk about matters competently.

Like *GM This Week*, internal newsletters served to solidify the company's key messages and influence the GM family's thinking on the issue. Similar to the video, the swat team orchestrated what enacted environments would be told and how, while working with the corporate and divisional publishing groups. The newsletters have the advantage of relative permanence, as GM family members (primarily employees) could use the texts over and over, including sharing them with others. So cooperation on the C/K pickup issue within the GM family was further strengthened through newsletters and, especially, as people used those texts in their own conversations with others.

Prepared Statements

Of all the genres in this case, GM officials enacted this type of discourse most often, with 25 prepared statements addressing specific enacted environments about the C/K pickup issue. Only *GM This Week* comes close to this level of usage with its 21 programs that covered the issue. Indeed, these two genres represent the primary discourse forms that GM officials used to communicate directly with external and internal publics, respectively. (Numerous articles by third parties were published and are considered indirect communication with publics. This genre is addressed later.) Along with upholding the key messages about the C/K pickup issue, the prepared statements especially and consistently rely on factual or empirical evidence to support claims about the vehicles' design and performance and the company's behavior. The statements also often acknowledge specific claims from opposing groups and advance analyses that debunk those claims and, sometimes, the people or groups asserting them. All statements include a preamble that explains the enacted environment (the context) for a statement, often citing to whom in the company the statement should be attributed. Contact information is also given about whom to call for more information.

Naturally, the statements put the automaker in the best light, and no one would expect anything less. What is important to note is the aggressive attitude reflected in the statements about opposing groups' actions. For example, the beginnings of statements are typically worded plainly and strongly. In response to a letter made public by Executive Director of CAS Clarence Ditlow, GM officials' response begins, "Today's letter from Mr. Ditlow is one more in a continuing pattern of exaggeration and fear-mongering intended to create an atmosphere of hysteria. Obviously, it must be assumed that this is a technique to discourage a rational review of the facts" (PS-5).

In response to Peña's announcement that he would proceed with a public meeting about the safety of the C/K pickups, GM officials' statement said, "The Secretary's action in the 1973-87 C/K pickup matter requires review and resolution by the courts because he is fundamentally wrong in his interpretation of the law" (PS-5). And in a statement responding to "allegations and mischaracterizations" about the pickups, GM officials wrote,

> Every death in a traffic accident is a tragedy. No amount of statistics or other proof of vehicle safety can comfort the loved ones of those affected. General Motors understands that and is fully sympathetic with the grief experienced by the families and friends of crash victims. But the relative safety of any vehicle and its fuel system must be judged on the vehicles' performance in all accidents over time, and not just a few. (PS-17)

After referring directly to a specific scene by asserting the perspective being taken on it, the bodies of the statements often lean heavily on empirical information, usually from third parties or accepted sources that groups opposing GM used. Litigation against GM for alleged defects in the C/K pickups' fuel systems was numerous, suggesting a scene of many angry people taking on a huge corporation. So the news was very "hot" when the class of C/K owners reached a settlement with GM to end its litigation involving the pickups. This settlement ended much pending litigation, quashed the potential for many future lawsuits, and especially spelled waning news media interest since once the settlement was approved by state courts, the story was over. GM officials released two short statements (PS-20, PS-21) that promoted a scene of cooperation between GM and opposing groups and focused on key actions on that settlement. (Accompanying these statements are frequently asked questions for company management and communications professionals' use. See FAQs section.) In these statements, the texts describe the specific enacted environments at the time of each statement, then present the same descriptive paragraph on the general provisions of the settlement.

At the conclusion of the prepared statements, GM officials typically reassert the main idea about the enacted environment (scene) from the opening or take another stab at the actions of opposing parties that threaten the scenic context of the statement. When NHTSA initially announced that a defect may be present, GM officials tendered a statement opposing that action, saying it was "totally unjustified" and that the agency recognized that the trucks "fully met the applicable safety standards for fuel system integrity in collision." That statement concludes by saying, "There is simply no legal or scientific basis on which to seek a recall of these trucks under the Vehicle Safety Act. If necessary, we will defend their safety in court" (PS-16).

Not even 6 months later, GM and NHTSA reached an agreement in which both organizations would "support programs that further motor vehicle safety." The statement about that agreement concludes graciously, "We at General Motors are looking forward to implementing this agreement so that the American public can reap the benefits of this important investment" (PS-18). Nearly 3 years later, GM officials responded to reports that GM "does not care about occupant and product safety," stemming from the McGee case in Ft. Lauderdale, because a memo was discovered that calculated the "value" of each fatality in a vehicle collision (PS-25). The statement said, "Such reckless accusations are typical of conspiracy obsessed contingency fee lawyers and GM critics. GM is a leader in automotive safety and spends million each year on research and product safety improvement" (PS-25). That statement concludes, "General Motors believes that a dollar value cannot be placed on human life. Indeed, the Ivey memo, which GM has produced in litigation for more than a decade, specifically concludes that it is 'impossible to put a value on human life'" (PS-25).

This genre was largely instrumental in structuring how people thought about the C/K pickup issue. Whether long and detailed or concise and focused, each prepared statement highlights the drama in new ways—based on the swat team's enacted environments—and does so in familiar ways, emphasizing the key messages on the issue. The repetition of the key messages and the evidence to back them up were used authoritatively, and new features in the issue's drama gave them new life. The statements, in effect, created new opportunities to advance same messages and supporting evidence in fresh ways to gain public cooperation on the issue with the automaker.

Backgrounders

This genre was especially valuable throughout the issue, because GM officials kept the facts consistent over time, even when detail was added about specific enacted environments to make the fact sheets more relevant to a particular point in the issue's history. The documents could also have been used liberally in virtually every situation to provide people with ample detail about the vehicles in an easy-to-use format. Although they often were named "fact sheets" to ostensibly draw readers' attention, their high level of detail and thoroughness is more befitting of the backgrounder genre. All backgrounders reflect a dominant frame of acceptance about GM's side of the issue and a frame of rejection about the "poisoned environment" promulgated by adversarial groups that suppressed rational discussion of the facts about the pickups' safety performance.

GM officials used a backgrounder in December 1992, a few weeks after the *Dateline NBC* report aired (B-4). That document, entitled *Facts You Should Know about the GM Pickup Truck Controversy*, featured five enumerated facts that were presented on a single page as headings—"FACT 1," "FACT 2," and so on to grab readers' attention—with a statement following each heading. The next backgrounder (B-5), entitled *Facts about GM's 1973-1987 Pickup Trucks* and dated December 18, 1992, created by GM officials, derives from a form letter (WC-4) prepared around the time of the first backgrounder and sent to people who wrote to the automaker about the C/K pickup controversy. (This letter is addressed later as part of the written correspondence genre, but because the text is virtually identical with that of the backgrounder, the textual analysis is given here rather than in both places. The letter version is addressed for special aspects later on.)

This revised text to fit another discourse type is interesting at least because only 2 weeks passed between the preceding backgrounder and this new text based on the letter version (with some revision, mostly in the introduction to set the context more generally rather than anchor it in a person's contacting GM). More important in this recasting of the letter (WC-4) to a backgrounder (B-5) is that the text adopts the letter's narrative approach, unlike the enumeration of key points in the controversy from the first backgrounder. This stylistic change invites the reader to be more involved in the drama behind the facts—just like the swat team—rather than be an interested party to consume the information at face value. In this backgrounder, headings are again used, but they function more to summarize the main idea in the text that follows rather than be a mere signpost to a new fact. This organization gives a reader an idea about what makes up the overall argument that there are no problems or defects with the C/K pickups.

To elucidate on the U.S. Department of Transportation (DOT) and GM's agreement that would end the agency's investigation of the 1973-1987 C/K pickups, GM's public relations swat team assembled a simple and powerful press kit (see section on press kits) that included two key backgrounders that build upon all others before them. The first backgrounder, entitled *Setting the Record Straight on C/K Pickups: The GM/DOT Agreement* (B-8), projects a victorious tone, which was appropriate because it marked the effective end of the debate in GM's favor about the safety of the C/K pickups' fuel systems.

The backgrounder asserts that the agreement "serves public safety far better than the government could possibly have achieved by pursuing a recall of the trucks" (B-8). The backgrounder also asserts familiar messages about the C/K pickup's "superior safety performance," citing the unchallenged statistics about the vehicle's safety based on federal standards and real-world data. Moreover, the text treats the naysayers in more detail than in any other discourse. It cites CAS and the Public Citizen as the two most unhappy groups with the agreement, because they "have a direct financial and political alliance with trial attorneys in ongoing product liability lawsuits against GM. Their position shows more clearly than ever their disdain for public safety when it doesn't advance their agenda" (B-8). Interestingly, throughout the issue, there is little denial of this assertion by these two adversarial groups and plaintiffs' attorneys, which likely contributed to GM's vindication.

The other backgrounder (B-9) in the small but mighty press kit about the GM-DOT agreement gives a point-by-point summary of four key areas in the C/K pickup issue, each with supporting graphs of data comparing GM to comparable Ford and Dodge pickups and to passenger cars—the same graphs used in the press conference. Each point effectively acts as a long caption for each graph, stating the same data and analysis that have marked the public relations discourse from the earliest phase of the C/K pickup issue. The most-detailed backgrounder (B-10) is a lengthy chronological listing of events during the issue's history, from the overall polluted environment to how order was restored. The chronology covers events from February 1972 to December 19, 1994, with descriptions of them and individual contexts.

Backgrounders enacted by the swat team presented selected facts, empirical data, and other key information for certain enacted environments. Yet texts in this genre stand out as some of the more comprehensive yet concise presentations of the critical details in GM's account of the C/K pickup issue and surrounding drama. The result is effective, fairly compact accounts of what was at stake in the drama. By presenting the material as "facts," the texts imply a presumption of authority, credibility, and accuracy that lies with the automaker. Indeed, during the course of the case, many of the facts GM presented went unchallenged (or ineffectively so) and, thereby, became accepted as true. The broad applicability of the backgrounders across publics ensured consistency in their use. When accompanied by other genres (e.g., covering letter, press release, prepared statement), the statements brought the issue into sharper focus for particular enacted environments and affected people's opinions, as suggested in the results of measurements shown in Appendix B.

FAQs

FAQs were rarely used by GM officials, and when they were, they applied to only a couple of complex situations. The FAQs were not necessarily for public distribution, but more for internal use and information by company management and public relations officers. There would presumably have been nothing wrong with the FAQs being released to the public, because they were prepared with the idea that the answers to any questions could be published after talking with journalists or served as additional information to those who wanted it upon contacting the company.

The first instance of FAQs is related to the joint letter to then-President Bill Clinton from the top leaders of GM, Ford, and Chrysler about the dire implications of the decision by U.S. Department of Transportation (DOT) Secretary Frederico Peña to recall the C/K pickups. Peña's action flew in the face of the recommendations of NHTSA researchers. Only four questions and answers (FAQ-1) are embedded in the text of a statement on the letter. (A very short backgrounder [B-7] on what the terms "unprecedented" and "unlawful" refer to within the context of the letter was prepared for GM officials. "Unprecedented" refers to Peña's action as unique because, unlike his predecessors, he ordered a recall of vehicles that met applicable FMVSS standards. "Unlawful" refers to Peña not having the legal power to do what he did to recall the pickups because he can only declare something defective.) Because the chief executives of GM, Ford, and Chrysler were the only ones who signed the letter, the dramatistic context for this FAQ is the act of the letter within the scene surrounding Peña's decision. The questions and answers, then, relate to whether specific people from the United Air Workers (UAW) and other automakers were "approached" to be co-signers. The other questions and answers address what the letter asks the president to do (i.e., "examine if the Secretary is properly interpreting the Safety act . . . [and] compel the Secretary of Transportation to adhere to the law"), and what NHTSA's legal responsibilities are as they relate to the C/K pickups (i.e., the secretary has changed the rules for the C/K pickups to meet a higher standard than what all manufacturers have had to uphold; FAQ-1).

Later on in the case, FAQs supplement prepared statements about particular events in the notification about and the approval process of the class-action settlement by certain state courts. Through this settlement, C/K pickup owners would receive a voucher for $1,000 off the purchase of a new GM vehicle. Interestingly, the same FAQ document was used on three different dates—September 5, 1996 (FAQ-2), about the mailing of notifications to registered owners of C/K pickups; December 26, 1996 (FAQ-3), about the Louisiana State Court's approval of the settlement and an inclusion to cover plaintiffs' attorneys' fees; and March 13, 1997 (FAQ-4), about appeals filed by people who objected to the settlement and their delaying implementation of the settlement—in conjunction with three separate statements about the status of the settlement. Across all three versions of these FAQs, a core set of questions and answers are maintained that address topics like the number of vehicles involved in the settlement compared to the number of C/K pickups on the road, the provisions of the agreement for the various parties to it (i.e., consumers, fleets, and governments), which vehicles are covered under the settlement, any revisions from the original agreement (e.g., allowing certificate holders to purchase any GM vehicle and not just another pickup), the difference between this settlement and the one reached with NHTSA for safety research, how much plaintiffs' attorneys' fees are covered in the settlement, and details about whom to contact for more information.

Given the differences stemming from three enacted environments, there are subtle revisions from one version to the next, especially from the first one to the second, as the contexts differed slightly from one version to the next. For example, the second version more directly answers a question about what an owner of a C/K pickup should do: "There is nothing an owner needs to do at this time. It's important that vehicle owners understand that further court hearings may be held and any appeals from final court approval must be resolved before certificates will be issued" (FAQ-3). The original answer simply gave the details about when notices were mailed to registered owners as of an effective date and time, which is consistent with the revised answer.

In the same second version of the FAQs, the answer to a question about how much plaintiffs' attorneys' fees were part of the negotiations for a settlement is considerably shorter from the original text. The new version says, "We are disappointed that such a large amount of fees was awarded by the court and are in the process of evaluating of we will file an appeal from the fee award [sic]" (FAQ-3). The original text says in two short paragraphs that the notices to registered owners of the pickups would find what fees were covered and "Limits on the amounts of fees that could be requested by law firms that brought the 40 class actions that will be dismissed if the settlement is finally approved were negotiated after the settlement was preliminarily approved by the Court" (FAQ-2). In the third version (FAQ-4), the only change in the FAQs' text is the deletion of the question about plaintiffs' attorneys' fees during settlement negotiations.

Among all the texts enacted by the swat team, the FAQs represent a strong genre to structure people's thinking and induce their cooperation. Whether actual or hypothetical, the questions posed in the FAQs are meant to echo the voice and concerns of the target readers. In this way the FAQs are almost interactive, as the reader assumes the role of questioner and the company gives the answers. The apparent interchange resembles a dialog about information and facts that is very reader-focused. The reader, as questioner, is imbued with power by being the one asking for information, and the company, as answer-giver, is subservient to the reader by giving candid and factual answers to satisfy the reader's needs and establish identification. The interplay of text and reader evoke powerful symbolic action that emphasizes the drama as the swat team enacted it.

Articles and Pitch Calls

Gaining strategically advantageous editorial coverage for an organization requires planning to determine which publication(s) and, often, which writers with special credentials and connections will give the best coverage for the targeted audience(s). It also takes a certain blend of opportunistic thinking and wisdom to know when the time is right for particular articles to see print. Such thinking is very scene-context-oriented. Public speaking events can also bring about a similar advantage, because an expert delivers the message personally at a suitable occasion, and such influence can last beyond the event itself when people talk about what a speaker said and when the speaker's remarks are transcribed for later distribution. Either way, it's no secret that third-party opinions can greatly influence people's thinking about issues. The GM swat team sought public support from third-party experts, even though many articles were written just in response to events pertaining to the C/K pickup issue. Solicited and unsolicited coverage about the issue is voluminous, and it is the former kind and the concomitant calls to engage someone to write a certain article that is the focus here.

The GM swat team proactively sought articles from third-party experts during the course of the issue after the press conference about *Dateline*'s report. Indeed, Lechtzin (personal communication, August 25, 1997) recounted that before the press conference, "No one would listen to us, listen to our side. Well, after *Dateline*, we were able to get media to say, 'There's another side. Maybe they're right, that this is a concerted effort by the plaintiffs' bar to create an issue that doesn't exist.' And after that we were proactive." Making any pitch calls and gaining more supportive editorial coverage became easier in the post-*Dateline* phase because more people (e.g., editors, experts, prominent industry writers, and analysts), who could influence others' thinking, were buying into GM's side of the issue. As Lechtzin (personal communication, August 25, 1997) described it, "It was quite a bit of Bill [O'Neill] and I working the media individually on a regular basis. We were always accessible. We would always talk to five or six key writers. Always sought out the 'friendlies' at the news weeklies and other places and use them."

The swat team worked proactively when Peña decided to recall the C/K pickups against the recommendation of NHTSA researchers and in the face of all other evidence that showed the trucks were safe. As Lechtzin (personal communication, August 25, 1997) recalled:

> That October 17 [1994] until we knocked Peña down—that happened right before Christmas in December—was a very intense period of going out and actively seeking publicity.... I mean, we went out to the point of scheduling Tom Gottschalk [GM general counsel, succeeding Harry Pearce, who was promoted to vice chairman] with the editorial boards of all the key publications in the country. And actually taking him out and getting some very good, strong editorials. It surprised the hell out of Peña.

Articles from independent organizations or experts were, as Lechtzin (personal communication, August 25, 1997) reported, "developed as we were going to manage the issue." Examples of these would include op-ed ("opposite editorial page") articles, like "Clintonites Ram GM" (1993) that ran in *The Wall Street Journal*'s "Review and Outlook" column, and an op-ed piece in *The Detroit News* entitled, "NHTSA: You Call This Science?" (1993). Other articles, Lechtzin (personal communication, August 25, 1997) explained, were "developed and then passed along. We did help a number of third parties prepare material." The basic approach here was to assemble much of the information about the C/K pickup issue, from technical and statistical information about the vehicles' performance to media coverage and dissenting opinions, that resembled a finished piece or was useful background to someone writing a particular article. Some examples of third-party articles developed independently with some help from GM officials include those by Walter K. Olson (1993a, 1993b), senior fellow at the Manhattan Institute, and Philip W. Haseltine (1993, 1994), president of the American Coalition for Traffic Safety.

These genres of articles and pitch calls are geared to "influence the influencers." That is, the swat team's objective was to structure the thinking of journalists, experts, and analysts so they would support and carry GM's key messages about the C/K pickup issue in articles they would publish. In turn, GM's other publics, who consume the influencers' assessments of things, would move closer to identifying with GM. The highly social nature and effects of these genres make them potent forms of symbolic action, especially as each text was tied to hard news being made by the world's largest industrial enterprise.

Pitch Letters

In the course of their public relations organizing about the C/K pickup issue, GM officials never sent out material to journalists without packaging it with supporting documentation. Such pitches to the news media usually came at critical points in the issue's evolution. For example, a 2-page pitch letter (PL-1) to editorial and business editors of every U.S. daily newspaper from William J. O'Neill, GM director of public affairs for North American Operations, summarizes the C/K pickup issue up to May 1993. (The same letter was addressed and sent to GM communicators, inclusive of all corporate communications/public relations professionals across the company, at the same time for their use in keeping members of the GM family informed about the issue's status. See the discussion in the section on press kits.)

The purpose of the letter was to have newspaper editors (and GM's internal communicators) cover the C/K pickup issue fairly and factually, based on the empirical data about the pickups' safety and using attached material in the communication package. The text takes on a scene–agent ratio, as it describes the enacted environments over the course of the issue and what roles specific groups of people (i.e., GM, NHTSA, plaintiffs' attorneys and safety groups, and news media) have taken on, including their subsequent actions. The scene is the debate about the safety of the 1973-1987 C/K pickups, and GM's role is to present the facts and try to maintain a "reasonable, technical discussion" about the pickups.

This role requires GM officials to follow the best interests of the company, from fully cooperating with NHTSA or rejecting specific requests from it, to debunking the claims and reports of critics or commenting on the outcome of litigation. For example, regarding the company's relationship with NHTSA, the letter says:

> On April 30, GM submitted to the National Highway Traffic Safety Administration a 1 1/2-inch thick document that responded to the agency's April 9th request that GM voluntarily recall the vehicles. GM Rejected the request because the design of those vehicles has provided excellent collision protection for both the fuel system and occupants for more than 20 years.... General Motors will continue to cooperate with NHTSA's on-going investigation. (PL-1)

The letter restates key statistics about the sheer quantity of documentation the company provided NHTSA, data from NHTSA's own tests that show the pickups met or exceeded all applicable safety standards, and point-by-point flaws in NHTSA's methodology for its crash-test design, statistical analysis, and review process about the trucks in its investigation.

Regarding the company's role to keep the conversation about the pickups fair and rational amid the slings and arrows of certain critics, the letter asserts:

Yet, it is clear that a small group of plaintiff attorneys, and the so-called advocacy groups they fund, have assumed for themselves the role of advocate, judge and jury relative to the safety of the fuel systems in these trucks. Even as NHTSA began its evaluation of our latest submission, these advocacy groups were promising further public demonstrations. Apparently, they have not been content to allow NHTSA to proceed with a scientific evaluation of the engineering data and statistics that show that in all impacts, the full-size GM pickups are the safest vehicle.
. . .
We will continue to vigorously defend ourselves against the emotional and misleading rhetoric being promulgated by plaintiffs' attorneys and their so-called safety groups. (PL-1)

The letter then binds these scene–agent relationships together in a plea for journalists, if they plan to write about the issue, to do the right thing and treat it fairly, impartially, and factually. As the letter says, "Some members of your profession and some outside independent analysts have viewed the situation and have taken the time to write their opinions. . . . We thought you would want to see some of these and, equally as important, we thought this material would be an important element as you make your editorial decisions and how you decide to cover the issue" (PL-1).

In a package sent to editors at all daily newspapers in the United States (see press kits), a pitch letter (PL-2) dated December 19, 1994, from GM Vice President of Corporate Communications Bruce G. MacDonald seeks the cooperation of those journalists in weighing the facts of the pickups' excellent safety design and performance over the claims advanced by critics with suspect motives and questionable credentials in the area of automotive design, engineering, and safety. The letter leans on the scene of the agreement between the DOT and GM to end the agency's investigation of the pickups and connect actions by GM to "devote over $50 million [and the DOT $27 million] to automotive safety research, anti-drunk driving campaigns, and child safety seat purchases for low-income families and coinvestment" (PL-2). The letter also uses the scene of the DOT–GM agreement to debunk critics of GM and the safety of the C/K pickups. The letter says:

The Center for Auto Safety and Public Citizen, two organizations funded by and closely affiliated with plaintiffs' attorneys in ongoing contingent-fee product liability lawsuits against GM, say they intend to continue their media attacks on the C/K pickups. The critics of these trucks have concocted figures, mischaracterized documents and obscured their motives. As you evaluate the DOT settlement and any future coverage by your publication, we'd like you to know exactly where GM stands. . . .

> In weighing the critics' allegations, I hope you will take the time to review the enclosed fact sheet of information about GM's recent agreement with the Department of Transportation—and about the C/K's undeniably strong safety record in real-world driving. (PL-2)

The two backgrounders that make up the rest of the kit outline the agreement between the agency and the automaker, data about the trucks' performance that was never disputed by any critical group against GM, and the agenda or suspect motives of those critics.

Like pitch calls, the genre of pitch letters works in tandem with other genres to "influence the influencers" on specific news items in the C/K pickup issue. The swat team could zero-in on the salient points of the news and emphasize key messages for readers of news publications. Again, the hard news coming from the world's leading industrial corporation gave the pitch letters and the material they accompanied high degrees of visibility in news organizations. The result was broad coverage of news, GM's take on the surrounding drama, and, ultimately, increasing cooperation between GM and its publics.

Press Kits

This genre was used sparingly but with much impact, because each press kit focused on key enacted environments in the C/K pickup issue and hammered hard on the key messages and used compelling empirical information. The first use of a press kit was for the press conference about the *Dateline NBC* report. Other kits about key events were prepared for and simultaneously sent to both internal communications professionals and external news media professionals. With at least 150 people in attendance at the press conference, all the key people in the news media whom GM officials wanted to have copies of the kit were there—those were the people that would carry GM's message the best. Putting out the press releases over a wire service was supplemental.

The press kit for the press conference (PK-1) served dual purposes: The first, to give attending journalists and other influential people a physical copy of material supporting Pearce's remarks, and the second, to provide internal communications professionals with the same material for their use in informing employees (and retirees, dealers, and suppliers) about this episode in GM's and the issue's history. The press kit includes the press releases described earlier and photographs of significant scenes of the *Dateline* crash tests; three charts that illustrate the comparative statistics for post-collision fires, fatal/major injuries, and projected fatalities among GM, Ford, and Dodge pickups; and a photocopy of the 3-page, November 19,

1992, letter from O'Neill to Read, producer of *Dateline NBC*, citing eight lengthy complaints about the report that aired about the C/K pickups. (This letter is addressed in the section on written correspondence genre.) For internal communications professionals, the same material was provided with a covering memo from a GM director of employee communication, who briefly introduced the kit as that which was given out at the press conference and that an additional item is provided. That item was a memo from O'Neill that presents the names and contact information of people associated with the *Dateline* program so that employees, retirees, dealers, and suppliers, who might be "concerned or outraged" about the report, could send their own opinions to them and a copy to O'Neill.

More than 3 months later, O'Neill sent "GM editors" (i.e., internal communications professionals with specific responsibility for publishing any kind of organization newsletter or program) a package of documents about the C/K pickup case. In a covering memo to those editors, O'Neill said, "we must continue to take aggressive steps in setting the record straight on GM's C/K full-size pickup trucks—both publicly and internally" (PK-2). The same package was sent to "over 2,800 editors and business editors of every U.S. daily newspaper," and GM editors' should plan to publish information from this kit to significantly help members of the GM family be credible spokespeople (PK-2). This package includes six additional items, four of which are articles that were addressed previously, and one that is a fact sheet that was also treated earlier. Next to the kit for the press conference, this package is the most substantial, single collection of information provided for internal and external publicity.

In another communications package (PK-3), the material is substantially less but just as hard-hitting. On November 10, 1994, the chief executives of GM, Ford, and Chrysler (the "Big 3") sent a cosigned letter to Clinton to protest Peña's decision to recall the C/K pickups, because it was both illegal and it set a bad precedent for future vehicles. The auto industry leaders ask Clinton to "address the intolerable state of regulatory uncertainty that will otherwise result from Secretary Peña's decision" (PK-3). (The letter is addressed in more detail in the section on written correspondence.) The package includes a copy of the letter, a covering memo from a GM communications staffer, and notes about key messages related to the letter and definitions for the terms "unprecedented" and "unlawful" regarding Peña's decision.

The covering memo introduces the package and its contents as an important part of the internal communications effort—"to keep employees, dealers and other constituents . . . well-informed on this issue so they can understand it and discuss it" (PK-3). The memo gives recipients a prescription for how to use the contents: use the key messages for anyone from the corporation who would address the issue at any occasion, share the letter itself with employees right away so they know what is going on, and refrain from "develop[ing] material on this issue independent of the attached" but call for advice on how to address the overall issue in more detail (PK-3). The key messages sheet provided in the kit include two specific ideas: (a) "The industry stands together," which means that the Big 3 do not want to have NHTSA enforce safety standards today and have their vehicles held to higher standards at some future date then be subject to a design defect recall, and (b) "Secretary Peña disregarded the advice of his technical advisors," which means that the federal government's own experts said "the vehicles posed *no unreasonable risk to the public*" and there was no reason for a recall, yet Peña decided to recall the trucks, which he could not legally do.

As collections of specific material handily packaged for use by influencers, press kits present selected texts about enacted environments for external and internal targeted publics. This genre allowed the swat team to strategically frame the drama with multiple texts that complemented each other and emphasized key messages in different ways and at the same time. In this way, press kits holistically structure influencers' thinking on many aspects of an enacted environment—and they do so more than could be done with a single text alone. The kits also serve as one-stop resources for various levels of detail and different kinds of information on the issue, making a journalist's job easier to tell the story, for example.

Written Correspondence

Individual letters and memos were written for various purposes, and in some cases, correspondence that started out as person-to-person communication was leveraged to support GM officials' public relations enactments. The correspondence can be put into three groups, according to those publics that the letters and memos address: organization officials, C/K pickup owners, and "GM family."

Written correspondence with any organization's officials addressed specific subjects related to the C/K pickup issue in which those people had a role to play. An early example of such a letter is Bill O'Neill's letter to Robert Read, producer of *Dateline NBC* (WC-1). Immediately after *Dateline NBC* aired its report nationally, O'Neill and the rest of the GM swat team began to thoroughly analyze the report and events leading up to it. One of the results of that analysis was O'Neill's letter to Read that cites many reasons why the report about the C/K pickups was "grossly unfair, misleading and irresponsible" (WC-1). Indeed, this act of unethical reporting is at the center of the letter, but the text reflects a purpose–agent ratio as it asserts that agents responsible for the report acted according to suspect motives.

O'Neill's letter to Read presents eight detailed points that support the contention that the report about the pickups was false and defamatory, and this section reflects an act-scene ratio, where the act of the television report directly caused a scene of increased and ill-founded criticism against GM that tarnished its public reputation. As Lechtzin (1993) summarized, "we asked for NBC to retract what they said because the program did not represent the real-world performance of the trucks, and it had badly hurt the reputation of our company. We also wanted to see the trucks. We wanted to see the cars. We wanted to see the test data" (p. 5). Read's response was that the report was fair and balanced and, in a later letter, that the trucks were junked. On both counts, Read was proven wrong, GM filed a defamation lawsuit against NBC and staged a press conference, and NBC recanted the entire story and apologized to GM on the air to a national audience.

Even President Clinton became involved in the C/K pickup issue. When Peña decided to recall the pickups, against the recommendations of DOT's own experts, GM officials sought to demonstrate the folly of his decision—especially in terms of possible future repercussions on the automotive industry—by obtaining the support from the news media and members of the legislative branch of the federal government. In a very rhetorically significant turn in the C/K pickup case, the chairmen of GM, Ford, and Chrysler, in an act of solidarity, cosigned a letter dated November 10, 1994 (WC-8), that argues Peña's decision will create "needless, unreasonable regulatory confusion." In this way, three of the most powerful leaders of one of the nation's (and the world's) largest industries reflect a strong act–scene ratio by describing how Peña's decision would result in a very equivocal regulatory environment for all automakers. For example, the chairmen said:

> [T]he practical result of the Secretary's decision is that compliance of a vehicle design with a very specific performance requirement of a Federal Motor Vehicle Safety Standard is irrelevant if the Secretary determines years later that the vehicle manufacturer should have selected an equally compliant design used by another manufacturer because it has had better performance in one particular accident mode. . . . This is not rational regulation of the automotive industry, and we are extremely concerned that this decision will establish a precedent which will completely undermine the regulatory process itself as well as the relationship between the industry and agencies that regulate it. (WC-8)

The principle of continuous improvement, then, becomes moot in such an environment, thereby stifling innovation and, ultimately, eroding customer satisfaction. The chairmen asked Clinton to "address the intolerable state of regulatory uncertainty that will result from Secretary Peña's decision" (WC-8). This letter was transmitted by fax to the president at 2:45 p.m. that day, and it was provided to key editors, federal legislators, and internal communications professionals so that they knew what was going on and could act on that news. The results of this high-level communication and supporting publicity were calls for reviews of Peña's actions and the DOT's process, editorials in major publications decrying Peña, and ultimately the GM–DOT agreement to drop the investigation of the C/K pickups and coinvest in safety research and related programs.

With the increasing visibility of the C/K pickup issue in the public after the *Dateline NBC* report, owners of the vehicles understandably became concerned. These people fundamentally wanted to know, as owners of those 1973-1987 models marketed by either Chevrolet or GMC Truck divisions, what the automaker was going to do about the problems with the pickups. A veritable deluge of letters from C/K pickup owners spurred the GM swat team to manage those inquiries in some way, and the chosen discourse was a personalized form letter (WC-3, WC-7) that was signed by a designated representative from GM, Chevrolet, or GMC Truck, depending on where an owner sent the letter. This arrangement ensured that the messages would remain consistent and serve as a simple way to keep track of all the letters that came in and answers that went out. Because the letter's main body text is the same between it and a backgrounder that was issued in December 1992 (as described in the section on backgrounders), the textual analysis is not repeated, but certain similarities and differences among the original version of the letter, a revised version of it, and the backgrounder are worth noting.

The original letter to owners of 1973-1987 C/K pickups was first put into use in early December 1992, almost 3 weeks after the *Dateline NBC* report aired. The fact that the text was essentially unchanged since it was issued is a testament to how well the language structures the issue and is consistent with the company's position on the issue throughout its life. Across the three versions of this text (the original [WC-3], the revision [WC-7], and the backgrounder [B-5]), they concentrate on the scene surrounding the C/K pickups, accent the people who have capitalized on that scene to be opportunistic advocates against the safety of the vehicles, and rely on empirical data from various sources to support claims about the trucks' design and performance. Among all three versions, the only substantive changes occur in the introduction and the closing.

Only 2 weeks after the original version was seeing its first use, its introduction was revised to include a paragraph that briefly describes NHTSA's opening of its own investigation of the pickups. The point of the paragraph was to let people know that the federal government was involved—that "'granting the petition does not indicate that the agency has determined that a safety-related defect exists in these vehicles" (WC-7). The paragraph also asserts confidence that the agency will find that "there is no basis upon which to conclude that these vehicles contain a safety-related defect" (WC-

7). The conclusion was also revised by adding a paragraph that restates the significance of the fact that post-collision fires almost never happen with the C/K pickups. The added text quantifies the rarity of such an event in terms of "a typical 10-mile, 20-minute trip . . . [that] a side collision fatal fire has occurred, on average once in every 115 million trips . . . [and the risk of such fire] is equal to dying while riding a bicycle for 2 minutes, riding a motorcycle for 3.6 seconds or riding in a commercial airliner for 3 minutes and 20 seconds" (WC-7). This marks the first time that explanation is used to define the very low risk of post-collision fires.

The written correspondence provided for the "GM family" targeted employees, retirees, stockholders, and dealers. The covering memos for press kits given to internal communications professionals have already been addressed above, and those documents fit the genre of written correspondence, as they served to introduce the material some received. As another example of covering memo, O'Neill sent one to GM division general managers (WC-6) to introduce the first issue of *GM Focus*, the four-color newsletter on the *Dateline NBC* report and the "real-world safety performance" of the 1973-1987 C/K pickups generally. The memo informs those division leaders how the newsletters will be delivered to their operating units and that all employees should receive a copy. A sample memo of transmittal was attached to give division general managers something to use when they formally gave copies to employees. Other texts were provided in the fashion of e-mail to communications staff to inform them about specific enactments. For example, in the *Moseley v. GM* trial, the automaker was placed under a gag order to not publicly discuss any matter regarding the 1973-87 pickups whatsoever until after the jury delivered its verdict (WC-5). Lechtzin sent an e-mail to GM communications officers that briefly described this scene, asked that all media inquiries be sent to him, and stated "that no person from GM can comment in any way on this subject, not just on the matter before the court BUT ON THE ENTIRE SUBJECT" (WC-5).

In a special letter to GM stockholders (WC-9) dated January 4, 1995, GM Vice President of Corporate Communications Bruce G. MacDonald addressed the settlement reached between the automaker and the DOT that ended the agency's investigation of the 1973-1987 C/K pickups.[12] In this way, the focus of the letter is the scene surrounding the C/K pickup issue at the time, including a description of the general provisions of the agreement. The letter shifts the scene to the general issue about the pickups' safety when it summarizes their performance using the familiar facts about the vehicles meeting and exceeding federal safety requirements, real-world experience, and very low rates of fires, fatalities, or injuries from side impacts. As the letter concludes, it addresses the charges that critics have and would likely make about the agreement with DOT. Here the scene shifts back to the

GM–DOT agreement and emphasizes particular agents who would take certain actions. The letter says:

> Our critics charge that GM knowingly produced and sold a dangerous product and that we 'bought' our way out of responsibility for this products. This is simply false. There is not now, and never was, any legal basis for a recall of the C/K pickup or for a determination of unreasonable safety risk. . . .
>
> The two groups publicly unhappy with the result—the "Center for Auto Safety" (CFAS) and "Public Citizen"—have a direct financial and political alliance with trial attorneys in ongoing product liability lawsuits against GM. Their position shows more clearly than ever their disdain for public safety when it doesn't advance their agenda. (WC-9)

The final statement of the letter resumes the initial scene and places the agents of GM and DOT in focus as taking very prudent action. "From any objective view of the facts and circumstances, General Motors and the Department of Transportation have reached an agreement that benefits everyone" (WC-9).

As the issue wound down, the class of C/K pickup owners settled with GM on a program to provide all registered owners of 1973-1987 C/K pickups with certificates worth $1,000 off the purchase of a new GM vehicle. A group with a vested interest in this agreement was the entire body of GM dealers across the United States. After the settlement was approved by certain state supreme courts and as final appeals were wrapping up—all going toward the automaker's favor—GM officials sent a message to all franchised dealers on June 10, 1997. The text (WC-10) was sent over GM's Dealer Communication System (DCS), which was an e-mail system among dealers, GM, and GM's car/truck divisions. The text begins by describing the situation with the settlement as it courses through the appeals process and what the outcome would be once the settlement is affirmed. The purpose of the letter then focuses on what a dealer's role is in answering customers' questions and basic rules for transferring certificates from original holders to other parties. The key point that inspired the DCS message was that GM officials were "informed that some dealers have been solicited to purchase coupons. Aside from the fact that no coupons have been issued and that coupons will not be issued until after all appeals are successfully concluded, there are provisions that apply to dealers" (WC-10). The letter concludes by assuring the dealers that they will receive detailed information about handling the certificates when the appeals process is complete and the settlement is affirmed.

Being one of the case's most personal genres, written correspondence afforded the swat team the advantage of direct, one-to-one contact with organizational leaders outside GM, customers, employees, stockholders, and dealers. From the president to GM assembly line workers, letters helped make the drama more immediate to the addressee by establishing his or her stake in it. The result is a record of focused symbolic action to individuals in GM's key publics, who gradually increased their levels of cooperation with the automaker on the issue and helped bolster its corporate reputation.

THOUGHTS ON TEXTS AND PROCESS

Across all the genres and their individual texts that GM officials enacted, it is clear that scene is the single most important element, being the one that draws in agents and their actions, purposes, and agencies. In only a few instances, like written correspondence, did scene take a back seat to other pentadic elements; however, those texts still reflected scenes because so much was understood about the issue by the participants in those communication acts. The fact that scene is so pivotal in all of GM's public relations discourse makes sense, given the swat team's organizing process. Indeed, the use of the many different genres of public relations discourse grew out from the swat team's organizing processes and served to structure people's thinking about the C/K pickup issue, doing so dramatistically. The relationship among dramatistic features means that the GM swat team relied heavily on context—the enacted environments—to enact dramas about the issue through particular public relations texts that more closely resembled the enacted dramas of the automaker's publics. This is the essence of consubstantiality, or the inducement of cooperation, between the company and its publics.

GM's sensemaking swat team clearly developed public relations genres in ways that emphasized both process and product (see Smudde, 1991). Driven by the contexts of enacted environments, the team established key messages that would be emphasized to selected publics, then designed a strategic plan to communicate those messages in the best ways to establish consubstantiality with the automaker's publics. Consequently, the team's enacting certain PR discourse genres was purposeful and authoritative as they fulfilled the plan's objectives. The team's continued monitoring of the environment, measuring public opinion and awareness about the issue (like that shown in Appendix B), and tracking press coverage gave them the right information about how well things were going. So just like other writers, the swat team "used a genre's exigence to fulfill organizational purposes, for example, to proclaim the company's success. So [these] writers achieve[d] organizational purposes in fulfilling broader generic functions" (Cross, 1993, p. 142).[13]

The GM swat team had a formidable task in its public relations organizing about the C/K pickup issue over the 6 years covered in this case study. The bottom line to the swat team's organizing was "not to create too much stir that would cause people to react against us" (Lechtzin, personal communication, August 25, 1997). This point was especially important during the time between *Dateline NBC*'s report and Peña's decision, when the team sought to not "put too much heat out there that would cause the NHTSA administrators to have to do something" (Lechtzin, personal communication, August 25, 1997). The task now for this project is to evaluate the case addressed in this and the preceding chapter for lessons it teaches us. The method is also evaluated for how well it works. All this research and analysis is used to formulate a program for the dramatistic organizing of public relations.

6

LESSONS FROM THE METHOD AND CASE

This volume was designed to discover the rhetorical and organizational nature of public relations by advancing a unique analytical method, testing it on the case of the GM 1973-1987 C/K pickup truck controversy, and deriving a practical program for public relations. The method synthesizes theories of rhetoric and organizations and applies discourse analysis to discern patterns of symbolic action in the organizing processes of PR officials. The analysis of the case demonstrated how public relations is an organizing activity that functions dramatistically and features symbolic action to induce cooperation between an organization and its publics. This final chapter brings everything together to answer this project's three research questions: (a) How successful was GM's public relations in managing the issue? (b) What does the case study teach us about the practice of public relations? (c) How effective is the Burke–Weick combination as a way to translate the case into its rhetorical and organizational aspects? This chapter closes by suggesting future research areas.

EVALUATING THE SUCCESS OF THE CASE

The first research question for this volume is, "Based on the application of the analytical method, how successful was GM's public relations in managing the issue?" Taken together or separately, the analyses of the case in Chapters 3 to 5 reveal that GM's sensemaking swat team was very successful when managing the issue among many publics over a long period of time. Early on in the case, the NHTSA did appear to have a case, and GM's own statistics made public in a published statement could have spelled a different turn in the case. The skillful use of additional third-party evidence and support, plus the political hullabaloo about and loud dissent against Peña for his suspect motives, squelched any debate of statistical significance in the C/K pickups' safety record. Indeed, the swat team's overall success is all the more impressive given that certain parties on both sides of the issue were enacting their own kinds of corporate advocacy (see Schuetz, 1997) in a complex, very equivocal environment that lasted over a prolonged period.

The team's public relations efforts successfully achieved the vindication of GM's 1973-1987 C/K pickup trucks among the company's publics, especially as the majority of people believed the company was "going in the right direction" on the issue (see Appendix B). From a traditional PR standpoint, keys to that redemption were at least three things:

1. Consistent and aggressive adherence to and evidential support for a core set of messages about the trucks' safety, GM's conduct, and opponents' suspect motives against the company and its vehicles.
2. A high level of support from prominent, influential people (i.e., safety experts, industry analysts, publication editors, independent auto industry writers, other auto industry leaders, and key federal legislators) who actively and publicly voiced their support for GM.
3. The marked reduction in the importance the news media placed on the issue, including falling public awareness of it (see Appendix B), after the agreement between GM and NHTSA and the settlement of class-action suits brought against the company.

Separate legal actions were brought against the company to oppose the class-action settlement and to sue the company for the pickups' fuel-system design by individual plaintiffs. However, these actions were largely unsuccessful and garnered limited, short-lived media coverage that had no affect on GM's redemption. A study by the PRSA (2000) offers a reason why GM was successful as it leveraged the credibility of outside sources in support of its key messages. The study shows that the public's most-trusted sources of information about a company come from respected third parties, including "experts" and "print news sources" (p. 12).

On a deeper level, this project's analytical method reveals more compelling reasons why GM was successful. From a logological perspective, we see the bigger picture of the dramatic action of the C/K pickup issue over time. We also learn about the public relations organizing of GM officials. Much of the issue was intertwined with legal matters, from litigation against the company for alleged defects in the pickups to disputes about federal laws

Lessons From the Method and Case 125

pertaining to vehicle safety and agency jurisdiction.[14] There were multiple representatives on the two opposing sides, each beset with their own agendas. There were many events that folded into one another, like episodes in a drama, where organizational representatives acted in certain ways that conformed to their agendas. Many of the actions were various acts of communication, especially from GM, advancing selected ideas for specific situations to influence other people's thinking. As a result, we get a good sense of the equivocal, ever-changing environment faced by the GM swat team, and we also see something of the opposing groups' enacted environments. Most importantly, we see how the swat team's organizing and the issue itself evolved through symbolic action to reach redemption for GM and vindication of the 1973-1987 C/K pickups.

From the vantage point of the public relations texts that grew out of organizing behavior, we discover finer detail about how the swat team used language to structure people's thinking about the issue and particular aspects of it. Each text functions as an individual symbolic act that is tied to a particular scene or context in the issue's history. Even when separate texts—like a backgrounder, press release, and pitch letter—are used for the same episode in the issue's drama, they are simultaneously separate in their specific generic qualities and united in their appeal for people to identify with the drama enacted by those texts. Thus, the effectiveness for all PR discourse on the issue derives from both the discourse form and the language about the scenes, actions, agents, agencies, and purposes.

The case history shows that GM's internal and external publics slowly but increasingly identified with the company's position, and they especially did so at particular points in the issue when significant events favored GM. When certain publics, primarily those in the "GM family," were invited to participate and information about the issue resonated more on their terms, identification appears to have become stronger. The general public came to identify with GM's position on the C/K pickup issue as third parties supported GM, news organizations and the federal government agreed with GM's empirical data about the pickups' safety, groups opposing GM lost credibility and favor with the news media, and GM family members enacted the issue's drama with friends, neighbors, and others on a personal level.

Across both the logological and dramatistic dimensions, the context for the C/K pickup issue expanded and contracted based on individual episodes in its history. At times, the issue was portrayed as one that affected the personal safety of individuals, other times it stood as a dangerous social problem, sometimes it was cast as a political wrangling, and still other times it fell somewhere else. Such expansion and contraction of the issue's context is understandable, as GM's sensemakers selected enacted environments and sought to structure people's thinking about them. In this way, identification was doubtless contextual and achieved over time among GM's publics as the messages about the issue often reflected their perspectives.

Taken together, these rhetorical and organizing dimensions demonstrate why GM's public relations organizing was successful. The result is that the swat team's enacted dramas about the issue more closely resembled those of the automaker's publics' enacted dramas, thereby inducing cooperation between them. When this view is joined with how the issue played out, we better understand why the GM team's public relations organizing was successful and the company was redeemed. The next step is to turn those reasons into lessons for engaging in future public relations work and formulating a corporate public relations program.

WHAT THE CASE TEACHES US

This second research question is, "What does the case study of GM's C/K pickup trucks teach us about the practice of public relations?" As was made apparent in the case study, plus the related research and analysis, the work of public relations practitioners is systematic, reflecting both rhetorical and organizational aspects. More specifically, public relations emphasizes a dramatistic orientation during practitioners' organizing processes to communicate something important within an organization and selected publics. We saw from the analysis of the case how the rhetorical and organizational aspects flow through public relations activity. Specifically, a logological perspective spurs retrospective (i.e., past-focused) and prospective (i.e., future-focused) analysis of an issue during PR organizing. Organizing entails the ongoing processes for making sense of equivocal environments for internal and external publics, where PR professionals work with people from other functional areas or affiliated groups. Identification provides the rhetorical focus on people's attitudes and their social interactions, from organizing to PR texts themselves. The pentad focuses analysis on the structure of the issue's drama and discourse about it. Whether there is a lot of time or very little time for public relations organizing and symbolic action, these dimensions generally account for how practitioners craft their texts for specific publics.

These insights from the case reveal a systems view of public relations that can be modeled as shown in Fig. 6.1. Unlike other models (e.g., Cutlip et al., 1994; Gonzales-Herrero & Pratt, 1996), this model of the dramatistic organizing of public relations presents a recursive process that consists of five phases, with feedback/feedforward links (i.e., the arrows between phases) among them, and entry and exit points. Models proposed by Cutlip et al. (which is a circular diagram of PR process features) and Gonzales-Herrero and Pratt (which is a complex curve of multiple PR-related tasks) show how one stage passes to the next rather linearly and provide no linkages or cycling back and forth within and among phases to accommodate the real, creative, problem-solving work of PR practitioners on either an *ad hoc* (i.e., project) or ongoing (i.e., organizational function) basis.

The process, as teased out from the case study and illustrated in Fig. 6.1, is recursive, because from the time an issue commands an organization's attention and action, public relations practitioners cycle within and through the phases any number of times. PR officials may even return back or link to previous phases to revisit something and briefly go forward or link to upcoming phases to tend to something in their problem-solving efforts that would, ultimately, resolve the issue. In such a recursive process, "There is constant creation, re-creation, evaluation, and re-evaluation of what's been thought of, written, understood, tested, thrown out, edited, etc. . . . [A practitioner] refers back to previous ideas, interpersonal transactions, and elements of the project in order to move [it] ahead" (Smudde, 1991, p. 319). The following analysis describes the process and model shown in Fig. 6.1.

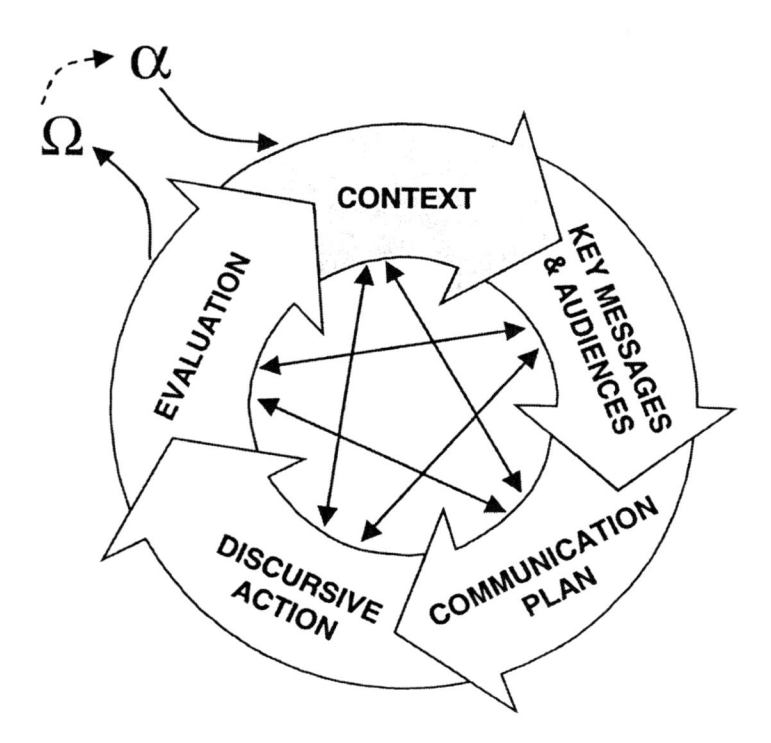

FIGURE 6.1. Model for the dramatistic organizing of public relations.

Entry and Exit Points

Conspicuous features of the model are the points labeled "α" and "Ω." These features are significant because, very frequently, such models typically depict a process already in motion without formally accounting for how the process begins and ends and begins again in tune with the flow of events from the environment that must be addressed, primarily on a project level. Such features are consistent with what has been described in the case study and supported by research. Of course, the process would be continuous as it involves the ongoing work of practitioners in the public relations function.

These points in the model mark where practitioners begin and end the process for their dramatistic organizing of public relations. In the case study about GM's C/K pickup issue, there was a definable beginning (i.e., the public announcement that the CAS and Public Citizen were going to file with NHTSA a recall petition about the trucks) and ending (i.e., the GM–NHTSA agreement that stopped all investigation on the pickups and, soon after, the class-action settlement between GM and owners of 1973-1987 C/K pickups). These points are important because the process cannot begin at any phase, but it proceeds in an evolutionary way from the moment someone or some group places importance on an issue that the organization must address through to its resolution. That person or group may be either internal or external to the organization, and issues may run the gambit from a new product launch to a community catastrophe.

Whatever the source, the entry point "α" denotes that the order of things for the organization is in some way polluted or in need of attention of some sort, and a team of PR professionals and experts in other organizational areas could be assembled to address the issue throughout its life cycle. The exit point "Ω" denotes that an issue has "come full circle" and is resolved, achieving redemption in some way and restoring order to the organization. Upon the exit of the process, practitioners should conduct a final analysis of the issue and their organizing of it. Sometimes the exit from the process is only temporary, as suggested by the dotted arrow from "Ω" to "α." If the C/K pickup issue becomes prominent again, the process would reengage. In this case, "α" denotes the reentry point to the process, if the issue again becomes important at a later time to someone or some group.

Context

Intuitively, to properly understand an issue, action, event, or the like requires us to know about the things going on around it that are (or are not) related to it. With symbolic action as the basis for the dramatistic organizing of public relations, this firmament of properties from social situations are "systematically (that is, not incidentally) relevant for discourse" (van Dijk, 1997, p. 11) and make up context. Minimally, participants, their acts, their agencies, their purposes, the scene, and other discourses all make up something's context. Like the case study analysis, the rhetorical (i.e., logological and dramatistic) and the organizational natures of a situation must be enacted and documented.

In terms of organizing, it is from an equivocal environment that people select certain features and make sense of them intersubjectively for social situations. For public relations organizing, the uncertainty within an environment poses rhetorical opportunities. The case study showed that while reducing this uncertainty about what is going on, PR officials also identify areas for possible symbolic action. In this way, practitioners define context by reducing rhetorical equivocality. In a very real way, as PR officials reduce the rhetorical equivocality to define context, they enact Weick's (1979b) recipe, "How can I know what I think until I see what I say" (p. 133). Practitioners' enactments for rhetorical opportunities comprise samples from the flow of experience, first, taken by each person individually for closer inspection and, next, selected in a group process of sorting out which enactments (including previously retained ones) make the most sense to share publicly in ways that would induce cooperation between a company and its publics.

Such enactments are part and parcel to practitioners' investigation of the motives behind a situation and planning for specific symbolic action by naming the act (the corporate message), the scene (the environment or context to which the message refers), the agent (the person[s] who will act as the corporate representative), the agency (the chosen public relations discourse genre), and the purpose (to inform, persuade, inspire, inform, debunk, etc.). This sensemaking activity reduces rhetorical equivocality and results in an enacted environment—"an orderly, material, social construction that is subject to multiple interpretations" (Weick, 1988, p. 307)—on which practitioners act symbolically. That environment, or context, may be enacted as an order of things that is already polluted or one that is in danger of being polluted, and some person or group is guilty and must seek purification through either mortification or victimage to reach redemption.

In rhetorical terms, as the 3-chapter analysis of the case showed, context frames a social drama enacted in discourse. Context subsumes the logological progression of social moments that creates what Duncan (1989) called a "social bond" that is attained "through identification which occurs in the enactment of guilt redeemed through victimage" (p. 436). These social moments can be thought of as texts—the symbolic action of individuals either individually or collectively. Within the scope of public relations, the context concerns the logological progression of things, beginning with a stable order just before something upsets it. From there, context addresses who or what may have caused the problem, their level of responsibility for it, and how order can be restored for the organization and its publics. In this way, context is as much retrospective as it is prospective about the drama of a particular event, issue, situation, or other enacted environments.

Key Messages and Audiences

Having made sense of the environment that the organization faces, the trick now is to figure out how to make it resonate with other people—to craft key messages about it with which target publics will identify. Based on the selected and retained enacted environments, key messages reflect different but related aspects of its larger drama. Like those developed by GM officials in the case study, key messages comprise the most important points of an issue that corporate officials believe they must emphasize with target publics. They must also reflect areas of common ground, striking a favorable balance between the organization's point of view and the audiences' concerns and needs. Defining key messages for particular publics, then, follows the recipe, "How can I know what others should think until I see what I want them to say?" Key messages serve as a kind of outline or list of the dominant features in the issue's drama that are enacted textually, based on the context and in any combination of PR genres.

To be useful during the planning and discursive action phases, key messages are documented simply, shared, and retained with corporate leaders and PR officials managing the issue. The main reason for this approach is to maintain message consistency and mutual understanding among corporate people involved in the issue. To capture the key messages that organizational officials want publics to understand, buy into, and act on is to help ensure consistency. And having a central team that orchestrates and is the authority for communication to all audiences also keeps consistency intact.

In general terms, as an extension of the lessons from the case, a PR official must also do his or her homework on the organization's principal audiences, which ones must be targeted, and what their demographics are. Research into audiences can be both quantitative and qualitative, using methods like surveys, focus groups, and secondary research from other sources (e.g., other department analyses, periodicals and published articles, and government reports) about target audiences. A customer relationship management (CRM) system also can be an especially powerful tool for audience analysis because it is a veritable Fort Knox of data of and about present, past, and prospective customers (i.e., primary publics/stakeholders) and whom they rely on, especially the kinds of communication/news media they prefer, product/service history, and many other dimensions that can and should be tracked that can give needed insights for public relations work.[15] Stakeholder analysis, too, can be a valuable approach, as it "demands the ability to determine where parties agree and disagree in terms of what they believe to be facts regarding an issue and the evaluation of it" (Heath, 1997, p. 29). How to go about such research is not addressed here because it is outside the scope of this volume and is covered well in other sources, such as Bivins (1999), Sinickas (1997), Stacks (2002), and Watson and Noble (2005). The important point is that the target publics are the focus of the key messages, which guide practitioners in their discursive action—to make sure the most important points are emphasized with publics effectively, ethically, and strategically.

Communication Plan

After making sense of things and deciding what to say and to whom, the next step is to define a way to systematically enact the drama about an issue. Developing a communications plan is a function of the PR team's organizing process, which GM officials did in the early history of the C/K pickup issue. The research about an organization's context, messages, and audiences forms the foundation on which to build a reliable plan. A communications plan documents all the relevant dimensions to advance an organization's view on something over time, like an issue, crisis, organizational change, milestone achievement, market positioning, and so on. The plan, then, is critical to the work of those in the public relations function. Those people use the communications plan as a recipe to obtain particular results by conveying consistent messages in a common voice that balance the needs of the company and its publics by using the appropriate genres to share information, obtain feedback, and cause specific actions and consequences. To meet this need, three principles guide corporate communications activities:

1. *Focus on business needs*: From strategic goals to new customers, focusing on an organization's needs means the appropriate communication solutions come naturally. In this way, public relations focuses on helping target audiences to identify with the company's key messages and act on them supportively.
2. *Be the company's eyes and ears*: Public relations is a boundary-spanning function that collects and shares information about what is going on within an organization's internal and external environments, including what people are thinking and saying about the company, its market, and the industry. From this information, recommendations for next steps to take may be tendered.
3. *Direct communication on behaviors*: Communication focuses on action by helping people understand, buy into, and apply corporate messages. For example, a company would want journalists and industry analysts to know key messages, embrace the ideas

and insights that are presented, favorably cover the company, and use its views to guide their thinking. For employees, they should understand what is going on in particular situations, buy into them, and apply information about the situation to move the company forward.

A complete template and rationale for a communications plan for the dramatistic organizing of public relations is presented and discussed in Chapter 7. It derives from the case, my professional experience, and research. Having a good plan is essential, because "The act of strategic planning requires us to work through issues and helps guarantee that you will keep your head while everyone else is losing theirs" (Bailey, 2000, p. 51).

Discursive Action

At this point it is time to turn all the sensemaking and planning into action. Enacting the communication plan through discursive action is the high point to public relations. It is the time to get the word out, obtain results that are in line with business needs, and meet PR objectives. This phase is also the true test of practitioners' preparation and the communication plan.

In tune with the plan, public relations officials enact an issue's drama in specific kinds of PR texts that best present publics with key messages about that drama. This point is central to the strategies toward redemption enacted by GM officials in the case study. The choice and timing of each text was defined in the previous phases and specified in the plan. Although the overall context has been defined and key messages have been developed, the actual discourse that weaves the two together must be prepared, focusing on specific episodes or scenes in the entire drama. As Chapter 5 showed, the subsequent discourse about an issue enacts the context PR officials defined. As Eggins and Martin (1997) said, "an interactant setting out to achieve a particular cultural goal is most likely to initiate a text of a particular genre, and that text is most likely to unfold in a particular way—but the potential for alternatives is inherent in the dialogic relationship between language and context" (p. 236).

During the preparation of individual PR texts, an audience-centered approach may result in some refinement of key messages, as PR officials pragmatically apply their knowledge of the context and effective, ethical communication to the task at hand. Furthermore, a text can only be effective if the writing works well for the audience in the right genre. Whatever the purpose of PR discourse may be (e.g., to persuade, inform, debunk, or motivate), that purpose guides practitioners in how they use language in selected genres to structure people's thinking about an issue.

To meet someone's needs on their terms increases the probability that the message will be accepted and understood, then subsequently embraced and acted upon. This challenge was met by GM officials who enacted the C/K pickup issue's drama in any text they created based on the communication plan. At a textual level, certain attributes of messages are instrumental in inducing cooperation with an audience: "proximity or immediacy, concreteness, the vital, suspense, repetition, familiarity, simplicity, novelty, conflict, activity, repetition, visual and vivid, content, elite personalities, messages with affective content, and humor" (Ferguson, 1999, p. 149). These attributes reflect various ways people may come to identify with messages. At a basic level, the more a message affects people personally and projects a sense of urgency, the more likely they are to pay attention to it and, potentially, act on it.

Practitioners can strategically and ethically emphasize one or more key messages over others, especially through the individual dramatistic features of act, scene, agent, agency, and purpose to craft texts for target audiences. Chapter 4 showed how pentadic elements were selectively emphasized in a representative text from the C/K pickup issue, and Chapter 5 revealed how pentadic elements were employed within and across many PR discourse genres. Elements of the pentad can be used to order one's perception of reality, where people select one of the five elements to emphasize over the others. This approach reflects how one's worldview orders the rhetorical aspects of a text. This approach also calls attention to ethical principles, as people can view the same situation differently and possibly mask truth in a situation to serve one's own ends.

For example, by focusing on the scene, someone subordinates the agent, act, agency, and purpose as functions of the scene; or by emphasizing the agent, the other elements are subordinated to that agent. Ling (1970) shows, regarding Sen. Edward Kennedy's (D-MA) televised statement about the death of Mary Jo Kopechne on Chapaquidick Island, Massachusetts, in 1969, that the pentad can be applied for unethical purposes. Kennedy's focus on the scene of the incident subordinated him as a victim of it, and the scene was one over which he had no control, thereby absolving him of the responsibility for Ms. Kopechne's death. Conversely, PR professionals can—and must—use the pentad in ethical ways, which Burke would expect from these writers of "secular prayers" (Burke, 1984a, p. 323). As the case study showed, by emphasizing a pentadic element from which all others would radiate, a PR professional can truthfully, accurately, and appropriately frame an issue and enact its drama in texts to establish identification with target publics.

As issues evolve, like the C/K pickup issue did over a 6-year period, changing contexts may require practitioners to enact more or fewer key messages for publics than those in the original plan. Such adaptability is necessary to make sure the issue is managed as effectively as possible. The main point here is an intertextual one: Practitioners must make sure that, across all texts that will be used, certain messages will be given in particular ways that are best-suited for chosen discourse forms, meet audiences' needs, and ethically advance communication objectives. This intertextual dimension means "the line separating internal and external communications becomes more suspect and corporate messages become more interrelated," from newsletters to television (Cheney & Dionsopolous, 1989, p. 145). This interrelationship among texts does not mean every person gets each message identically in any genre; it means that members of each audience receive the same message in the appropriate language and form that suits them collectively. The result, generally speaking, is that audiences are more apt to identify with the messages and cooperate with an organization's cause.

An effective way for PR officials to raise a message's level of importance for an audience is to find advocates or "thought leaders" (a kind of "elite personality") who have a high level of credibility with an audience and will advance an organization's messages effectively with it. Thought leaders were a critical part of GM officials' plan to manage the C/K pickup issue. Advocates outside an organization "persuade public audiences about public issues," and advocates within an organization "shape internal company culture by offering personal, social, and economic incentives for productivity" (Schuetz, 1997, p. 239).

Of the two types of thought leaders, those within an organization (and even all its members) can act as ambassadors of it and its messages to the organization and its external community. These insiders, as demonstrated by GM officials' use of PR texts that targeted the "GM family," represent a key link to family, friends, and neighbors about "what's really going on," and possess a unique grassroots level of credibility than can shape the public's thinking on an issue. Internal and external thought leaders do not necessarily have to be used together, depending on the issue and the strategic communications plan. However, as the case study showed, the combination of internal and external advocates working on the same cause can spell powerful influence within constituent groups. Enacting PR discourse requires flexibility to adapt to the varied needs of separate audiences, master the many forms of texts, and write messages with which audiences can identify.

Evaluation

Feedback is essential about whether the PR discourse is having the effects that are specified in the communications plan. That feedback is rarely volunteered from target publics and must be obtained systematically. In the case study, GM officials constantly monitored the environment and how their texts and key messages were being received and used by the automaker's various publics. (See Appendix B for example measurements.) Evaluation programs provide practitioners with a way to monitor the environment for contextual changes, publics' attitudes about an issue, and their receptivity to key messages. From this information, practitioners can adjust their messages, the plan, and discursive action to better induce cooperation between the organization and its publics. With this new information, the cycle may continue indefinitely until the issue is finally resolved.

The focus of an evaluation of public relations organizing is the communications plan's objectives—that they are measured according to certain criteria that help define success. Those criteria are the goals, which measure success in meeting the objectives at the end of a project, and the leading indicators, which measure progress toward meeting the goals at predetermined points along the way. Furthermore, the critical success factors anticipate areas that may have a positive or negative affect on things, and those factors can help in the explanation of success or failure as well as suggest opportunities and barriers that could be or could have been accentuated or avoided. Appendix D addresses how goals, leading indicators, and critical success factors work, and it summarizes central evaluation issues for a communications plan. In addition to these approaches, public relations practitioners could employ this project's analytical method to examine their own cases (and even those of other organizations) of PR organizing.

Designing a traditional evaluation program for public relations organizing is beyond the scope of this project, and useful discussions of this area can be found in sources like Stacks (2002), Watson and Noble (2005), and Sinickas (1997). One useful perspective is that of Lindenmann's (2006), in which he argued that public relations evaluation must encompass outputs (i.e., immediate production of discourse and reception by audience), outtakes (i.e., audience's participation in the communications), outcomes (i.e., the degree of change in the audience's opinions, attitudes and/or behavior patterns as a result of having been exposed to and become aware of messages directed at them), and outgrowths (i.e., longest term, cumulative effect of the entire communication program and products on the minds of the audience). The key point of evaluation is that practitioners must measure regular (ongoing), milestone (periodic or ad hoc), and overall (end times) efforts and effects of public relations organizing, analyze the results, then apply those findings to make improvements anywhere they are necessary.

Linkages

Like the entry and exit points, the feedback/feedforward links in the model shown in Fig. 6.1 are unique when compared with other conceptions of the public relations process. Like the linkages in Weickian cause maps and borne of the notion of recursiveness, these links help account for the dimensions of PR practitioners' problem solving. It would be unreasonable to assume that people do only the work expected in a given phase without also considering things they learned in the past, are addressing in the present, and anticipate for future phases.

As people work in any given phase, they attend to the principal matters that concern them then, but they also consider the many other dimensions of the PR problem they are trying to solve. The GM swat team on the C/K pickup issue clearly demonstrated this point in its organizing. People call on, or link to, aspects germane in other phases, past experiences, anticipated situations, or the experiences of others for information, adjustment, enhancement, feedback, lessons learned, and so on. In this way, practitioners engage in recursive cognitive activities during which they "regenerate or recreate their own goals in light of what they learn" (Flower & Hayes, 1982, p. 381). The recursive nature of public relations organizing means the process is highly flexible and can quickly accommodate new situations or actions as they are needed.

HOW WELL THE METHOD WORKS

The third and final research question for this project is, "How effective is the combination of Burke's rhetorical theory and Weick's theory of organizing as a critical method for translating the case into its rhetorical and organizational aspects?" The analytical method is a way to analyze the simultaneously rhetorical and organizational dimensions of public relations (or any kind of communication for that matter), which gives a critic a flexible approach to analyze organizational discourse. The method is a flexible one, because it allows a critic to strike an appropriate balance between the rhetorical and the organizational, as Table 2.1 indicated, and do so by isolating texts based on discourse genres. By tempering Burke's dramatistic method with Weick's theory of organizing, a critic can directly and simultaneously address the rhetorical aspects of organizational discourse and account for the enactment of specific kinds of corporate discourse, as modeled in Fig. 6.1. In this way, Burke's and Weick's ideas are much less divergent than they are tangent when it comes to understanding organizational discourse, generally, and public relations, specifically.

An application of the method to public relations discourse reveals something about people's rhetorical choices and how they make sense of the equivocality of enacted environments and their symbolisms. The ensuing symbolic action reflects a drama and serves as the means for establishing identification among members of many audiences. On an organizational level, we can make sense of the rhetorical dimension of human action in organizations. That is, the sensemaking process is made up of the symbolic action among people to induce cooperation and establish identification among them across loosely coupled systems. That symbolicity comes from human action during the process of organizing, which is largely evolutionary. Ecological change can be understood not just in terms of enactment, selection, and retention, but also rhetorically in terms of order, pollution, guilt, purification, and redemption and integrated with the pentadic elements of scene, act, agent, agency, and purpose that reveal human motives that lie behind enactments that contribute to organizational evolution.

If we view public relations as a staff function of management, much like that described by Heath and Nelson (1986), it helps organizations adopt a stance to their environment for the purpose of achieving their goals (Long & Hazelton, 1987). Reactive, adaptive, dynamic, or catalytic stances (Crable & Vibbert, 1985) to enacted environments means that public relations practitioners are "boundary spanners" (Aldrich & Herker, 1977; Cheney & Vibbert, 1987) as they gather information about environments to reduce rhetorical equivocality about a given issue or crisis.

In a Weickian sense, boundary spanning by public relations practitioners involves "loose coupling" between that group of people and cycles from the organization's environment (Weick, 1969, 1979b, 1988). By itself, public relations involves "interlocked" communication behaviors among practitioners whose responsibility it is to span boundaries; enact events from within and without an organization for issues, developments, crises, opportunities, and so on; make sense of environments by reducing uncertainty and rhetorical equivocality; select those that are appropriate for any public reports about enacted environments; and retain other enacted environments for future sensemaking activities.

Public relations subsystems can manage issues, crises, events, and so on through cycles of obtaining input from the environment and organizational policymakers, transforming those inputs into communication goals, objectives and campaigns, and producing output in the form of discourse for specific publics within the internal and external environment (Long & Hazelton, 1987). In this way, the boundary spanning of public relations officials can help maintain an organization's image and legitimacy by providing important information about an issue or crisis to appropriate internal and external publics (Aldrich & Herker, 1977).

Perhaps the most significant point to uniting Burke's dramatistic critical method and Weick's theory of organizing is the common ground between them. That is, the ideas that Burke presents can be explained further by ideas advanced by Weick, and vice versa, as Tompkins (1987) pointed out (also see Smudde, 2008.) For example, from Burke's perspective, the role of a "public relations counsel with a heart" can be to cultivate a "charitable attitude toward people that is required for purposes of persuasion and co-operation, but at the same time maintain our shrewdness concerning the simplicities of 'cashing in'" (Burke, 1984a, p. 166). This humanistic role requires this counsel to "give attention to superstructural adjustments" (Burke, 1984a, p. 184) in the symbolisms of a society (i.e., enact events from the flow of experience and make sense of enacted environments through consensual validation).

Put in another way, public relations practitioners make sense of the enacted symbolisms or symbolic action of present, past, and anticipated enacted environments, which reflect an order of things, to induce cooperation through identification. The analytical method capitalizes on the consubstantiality of the core theories and the pragmatic usefulness of discourse genres, all of which make it well suited to the critic's task of making sense of corporate communication and the practitioner's task of communicating an organization's view of the order of things with its publics.

IMPLICATIONS

This volume can serve as the springboard for additional research and application. That future work should not be limited to just traditionally academic pursuits. Indeed, both the professional and the scholarly communities have a fair share of opportunities to build knowledge about the rhetorical and organizational nature of public relations.

Practical Issues for PR Professionals

What are the implications of this project for public relations professionals? In specific terms, we find that the model and the analytical method can be tools to help practitioners make sense of public relations organizing and its symbolic action about enacted environments to induce cooperation between an organization and its publics. By applying them to particular cases of PR organizing, the model and the method also help establish how PR works and can be done effectively. Separately, each tool focuses on the rhetorical and organizing dynamics of public relations in different and complementary ways. The analytical method provides a calculus to develop a holistic view of a communications effort, from the broad context of an issue as it evolves to individual texts enacting episodes in the issue's drama. The model serves as a practical heuristic for public relations organizing—strategic planning—from a project level to a broad department management level. Both are complementary as the method provides the necessary calculus to undergird the model, and the model illustrates the systematic application of the method in the organizing process.

In general, we reconfirm the importance of communications professionals, who "are in the business of producing symbols. They, much more than others in the organization, tell various publics 'what the organization is.' They share identity, manage issues, and powerfully 'locate' the organization in the world of public discourse" (Cheney & Dionsopolous, 1989, p. 139). Because organizations function within a larger context of social, political, economic, technological, and cultural environments, they communicate symbolically with internal and external publics in many ways. Yet, "despite all other measures of what a company is or should be, what really counts is the meaning internal and external people enact on behalf of or in response to it" (Heath, 1994, p. 118). It is indeed the case that PR professionals "attempt—admittedly with varying degrees of success—to control the ways internal and external environments discuss such key concepts as values, issues, images, and identities" (Cheney & Vibbert, 1987, p. 173). The ways to "control" environments are addressed in the process of strategic planning, which is the substance of the final chapter of this volume.

As an organization makes certain choices about controlling what and how to communicate with its publics, ethics becomes bound together with public relations. At the heart of an ethical stance about PR are issues related to the equivocality of responsibilities, values, and rights of an organization's internal and external publics that may be at odds with the organization's own values and goals (Seeger, 1997a). The objective, then, is to reduce the ethical equivocality as much as possible during the process of organizing so that practitioners can make both the right decision and do what is right and just. Accordingly, communications with internal and external publics should conform to and uphold ethical principles, where the ideal ethic is that of dialogic, or two-way communication (see Johannesen, 1990). It is, therefore, important to consider that "[i]f an organization fosters two-way communication," as Heath and Bryant (1992) asserted, "it is likely to increase trust that it is acting in the interests of others and thereby foster their willingness to act in the interest of the organization" (p. 263). In this regard, trust is a function of a fundamentally moral position from which an organization operates, enacts communication, invites participation from its publics, and ensures its ethical principles are known, understood, and upheld.

Scholarly Issues for Researchers

Like that for practitioners, what are the implications of this project for scholars? This study, which sets up a unique analytical method and demonstrates its workability as a critical orientation, is the first step for other projects. This study's critical orientation does not limit a critic to examining only public relations discourse. The theoretical underpinnings derive from theories that are open to any kind of symbolic action and organizing behaviors among people in any social collective. The opportunities to apply dramatistic organizing to texts are truly universal.

One next step would be to measure employees' reactions to public relations discourse directed at them and external audiences. Such measurement could focus on, for example, a discourse's dramatistic elements derived from an enacted environment about a specific issue. The approach could include a content analysis of publications produced within a company for its employees and retirees, interviews with employees and retirees about their impressions of some corporate discourse, surveys of employees' opinions about examples of corporate discourse, or any combination of these methods. These diverse measurements would augment the approach employed in this project.

In another approach, an ethnographic study of public relations could trace organizing cycles as they happen and assess the dramatistic dimensions of strategic planning, discourse development, and results obtained over an issue's curve of history. Such an investigation could reveal new insights about the process of a PR swat team to determine how well the team did in its PR organizing. Studies of reader reception of the texts would reveal the degrees to which publics were induced to cooperate with the organization.

Taking into account the role of the Internet in corporate communications, research could be conducted on the affect of online PR on an organization and its publics. This kind of project would test the model for the dramatistic organizing of public relations to determine how much such pervasive and technological change affects the PR process. In a broader view, organizations tend to influence other organizations' processes for organizing, and this observation is at the heart of institutional theory. The theory behind the process model of the dramatistic organizing of public relations in Fig. 6.1 might be further developed by integrating institutional theory to account for the enactment process, sensemaking, and ecological change, taken dramatistically through the rhetoric of rebirth.

With a strong research base, theoretical framework, and analytical method applied to a case example, we have seen deeper into the organizing and symbolic action of public relations professionals, whose work focuses on trying to establish identification between an organization and its publics. The result is that we discover very useful insights about why rhetorical and organizing aspects are so interrelated and codetermine the success or failure of public relations action. We also derive practical lessons from case examples that show how best to formulate and conduct public relations programs. And we find that the critical approach developed in this project is universally useful by practitioners and scholars alike. So, accounting for the simultaneously rhetorical and organizational nature of public relations shows it to be a profoundly dynamic phenomenon with broad implications for both study and practice.

7

CONCLUSION: STRATEGIC PLANNING FOR AND VALUE OF PUBLIC RELATIONS

Public relations is the measured and ethical use of language and symbols to inspire cooperation between an organization and its publics. A key phrase is "measured and ethical," which directly implies metaphorically a strategic bias to the practice of public relations, not merely or only tactics. It also implies literally the application of methods of measuring performance and success. Strategy and the process of strategic thinking can be viewed as a systematic, forward-looking approach for a situation that, given certain parameters (e.g., knowledge, experience, research, timing, budget, resources, enacted environment), defines what must be achieved, how achievements will be made, and why the approach can be determined successful or not.

The case of GMs' C/K pickups and other cases addressed in the literature all share at least one vital characteristic: Strategic planning was involved somehow. Granted that one cannot know precisely what an emergency situation may be or become, one must not be caught without at least some idea—a contingency plan—for managing some problem, organizational crisis, disaster, or issue. Practitioners fulfill two principal roles: tactician/specialist or manager/generalist (see Dozier, L. Grunig, & J. Grunig, 1994). In the rush of daily work, PR professionals must guard against the temptation to engage primarily tactically in these and any situations. To focus on tactics instead of strategy risks diluting the effectiveness of their efforts and the value of their contribution in the long term. Public relations professionals must take a step backward at the outset to enact and share a vision with management and clients that blends the best strategic thinking with the cleanest tactical execution.

This final chapter focuses on what is perhaps the pivotal part of public relations work—strategic planning—that specifies how certain resources must combine into a focused approach for the successful dramatistic organizing of public relations that adds value to the organization. The chapter begins with a summary about why public relations professionals are immediately at a disadvantage with organizational management but can turn that disadvantage around. Next, the chapter argues for formal yet pragmatic theory-practice bridge building between rhetoric and public relations. From here, the chapter presents a prescription for enacting the dramatistic organizing approach for public relations through formal strategic planning that is in tune with organizational expectations and practice-area needs. The chapter wraps up and this book concludes with a final analysis about public relations' value contribution to organizations that brings ideas full circle.

THE IMPACTS OF HISTORY, TACTICAL BIAS, AND SEMANTIC BAGGAGE

First, the good news. Executive management has high expectations for public relations and wants it to succeed. Now, the bad news. Executive management typically does not value public relations as strategic but, instead, as tactical. Why is this? The answer is profoundly simple and hinges on at least three things: public relations' history, bias for tactics, and weak identification with management perspectives of business.

History

We know much about the historical evolution of the practice of public relations over the past century and even beyond (see Cheney & Vibbert, 1987; Cutlip, 1994, 1995, 1997; Cutlip et al., 1994; Ewen, 1996). The formal practice of "public relations" does not emerge until 1889, as Westinghouse competed with Edison General Electric over the establishment of alternating electrical current over direct current, and Westinghouse created the first, formal public relations position (Cutlip, 1995; Cutlip et al., 1994). Until this point, the responsibilities that eventually came to be associated with public relations were referred to under terms like "publicity," "promotional activity," and "press agent," all of which were closely associated with coverage of corporate activity in the press. The term and function of "public relations" then was still fairly new but not without a heavy load of semantic baggage, as it "became institutionalized in the large public agencies that arose to meet several environmental challenges [of social order (labor unions), political order (Roosevelt's New Deal), economic order (the Great Depression), and technological order (radio and 'mass culture')]" (Cheney & Vibbert, 1987, p. 169).

Public relations and those who have practiced it are seen through a negative terministic screen. That screen seems based on negative first impressions. As J. Grunig and Hunt (1984) said, "in its early development, public relations was equated with persuasion and/or propaganda [i.e., a secular approach to 'propagating the faith' about an organization]. Most people still have that concept of public relations today, explaining the common suspicion, mistrust, and even fear of it" (p. 21). For example, growing out of the labor movements in the early 1900s, primarily in the steel, oil, meat-packing, and railroad industries, and fertilized by muckraking journalistic practices about what was going on, both business and government alike adopted aggressive practices of public communication and defense (Cutlip, 1997). So in the eyes of business and government leaders, public relations was seen as an essential means to combat hostility and court public favor, but in the eyes of the public it was seen as a way to manipulate people's thinking about issues. Even more recently, as Cutlip (1995) said, contemporary social critics claim that the ideal of "free and robust debate" that is at the heart of our culture is in grave danger of being "seriously imbalanced by the large, money-stuffed war chests and armies of skilled communicators that the powerful special interests can put into the field of debate" (pp. 280-281).

From William Henry Vanderbilt's 1882 statement, "'the public be damned'" (Cutlip, 1995, p. 188), to today's sense and reference from terms like *spin* and *spinmeisters*, negative terministic screens have long guided people's thinking about public relations and public relations professionals. In this light, public relations might be seen as heartless, as Burke (1984a) seems to have thought when he referred to his book, *Attitudes Toward History*, as "Manual of Terms for a Public Relations Counsel with a Heart" (p. i). At worst, public relations suffers from a poor image—an unscrupulous endeavor of wordsmithing or shameless image-mongering. Cases like the staged Federal Emergency Management Agency news conferences about its response to California wildfires in 2007 support such a negative terministic screen, or frame of rejection. But cases like Johnson & Johnson's management of the Tylenol poisonings show that a more positive terministic screen, or frame of acceptance, can apply. It is the latter that Burke may have wanted to establish, as considered in Chapter 1, if only because he saw that a comic corrective about public relations practitioners of his time was needed to help them be more heartful in their work.

Bias for Tactics

The key to understanding the force of history on people's views of public relations is tactics. After all, the public experiences what PR professionals do, not the thinking and the process behind it. Yet public relations as a field has done a poor job of promoting itself. As Budd (2003) found, "Public relations is too short-sighted, too fragmented . . . to mount any true industry offensive. World-class PR demands world class political skills, attributes in short supply" (p. 380). Remember, too, Budd continued, that public opinion has been long on mistrust toward business, but it can best be overcome by deeds, not words alone. The field, then, still faces a difficult task to better inform the public, inspire a cooperative attitude, and result in supportive actions toward the profession. According to the PRSA's ethics code, practitioners are called to "enhance the profession," which means to do so for anyone—especially those outside the field.

The tactical bias that runs through public relations is especially evident in what it teaches. Numerous textbooks and trade books are available about how to write specific forms of public relations discourse. In comparison, far less work has been published about strategy and strategic planning specifically for public relations, but examples like Botan (2006), Ferguson (1999), Moffitt (1999), Oliver (2007), Potter (2006), and Steyn (2003, 2006) are available, even though they cover the topic in isolation from the larger organizational picture. Courses in public relations writing are important to any curriculum for the field, but they must not be the only courses in the curriculum. Furthermore, PR writing courses must be framed properly as the realm of discourse enactment within the larger context of strategic public relations and its value contribution to an organization. Many seminars are offered annually by stalwart organizations (e.g., PRSA, IABC, Regan Communications, Melcrum Publishing, the Word of Mouth Marketing Association, and et al.) that frequently feature "how-to" sessions about communication channels and opportunities. For example, during one 2-week period in March 2008, I received nearly 50 e-mail invitations to such events, approximately two-thirds of which were focused on tactics, while the rest leaned more toward management-related matters. In a related vein, conferences for professionals and scholars alike accomplish similar ends by showcasing examples of public relations successes and failures—more the former than the latter, especially at PRSA and IABC events. Finally, we also see in our journals (both scholarly and practice-based) much emphasis on what was done—the literal discourse—of public relations efforts through case examples or lived experiences.

There is immediate satisfaction from tactics—a rush from seeing work come to life. That is why tactics are so attractive and easy to focus on. It also explains why, on one hand, there is much celebration of especially successful work and, on the other hand, much confusion about why public relations should be involved as a strategic function. A tactics bias, then, must be meticulously shifted to a strategic bias. If we think of attention as an economic commodity (Davenport & Beck, 2002) like iron ore, silicon, and so on, the means *and* the ends for getting and maintaining attention are both integral. Tactics are the ends of public relations, but the means that makes them possible and successful is the intense strategic planning that must be done in advance and enacted effectively.

Weak Identification with Business Perspectives

Public relations' history and a bias toward tactics will not result in public relations being included at the table with the rest of management. All too often, public relations students and many practitioners shy away from or avoid mathematical parts of the job. Public relations is largely a language-based business, but so is statistics. How else do we draw inferences or conclusions about quantitative results and make our cases about them? Management needs and wants quantitative data, but management will also accept qualitative data. The whole point is a basic one of argumentation—if you make a claim or recommendation, you must have the evidence and reasoning to back it up. But as Budd (2003) observed, "practitioners tend to behalf [sic] historically rather than scientifically . . . they do what they have always done and, often, can't explain to a top manager's query why they do it that way and what effect it has" (p. 377). The reason for this may be that "There appears to be pervasive fear in our profession about having PR efforts measured by anything less than their effect on a business metric" (Oates, 2006, p. 12). This inability to identify with management and its perspectives of the business translates into a potential loss of trust, especially with the chief executive officer, who needs sound advice from competent and strategically oriented advisors, including PR professionals (see D'Aprix, 1997, 2001; Garten 2001; Hipple, 2007; Lukaszewski, 2001a, 2001b, 2001c, 2008; Oates, 2006). In a speech at the 2007 Melcrum Summit in Chicago in Fall 2007, D'Aprix provided further analysis:

> You see we have this fatal flaw. We fall in love with communication tools that promise simple solutions to complex problems. We also love craft. Our senior leaders, on the other hand, love outcomes. If you deliver craft and they want outcomes, don't wonder why they don't value what you do for the organization.
> As well respected British consultant Bill Quirke recently reminded a group of communication professionals like us, leaders care about arriving at the destination. They play by what he called "big boy and big girl rules." Communication professionals, on the other hand, love the journey. It's a dangerous difference for us. (cited in Murray, 2007, ¶ 37-38)

Even more to the point about public relations' weak sensitivity to business perspectives is the matter of semantics. In their organizing behaviors, public relations professionals and management tend to think differently and do not speak the same language. Between the two, as D'Aprix alluded, management uses the language of objectivity, process, data, logical and novel alternatives, and so on, to secure competitive advantage. At the same time, management tends to avoid the language of subjectivity, holism, intuition, magical solutions, and the like, which public relations people tend to favor. This semantic difference was brought into sharp relief by Lukaszewski in 2003 during a special PRSA chapter professional-development event in Milwaukee and is at the heart of his book, *Why Should the Boss Listen to You?* (2008). During his 2003 session, he gave a simple and insightful analysis of the term, *integration*. For public relations people, the term refers to synthesis, the bringing together of disparate but complementary organizational functions for a single cause that would result in success. For management, the term refers to systematic/scientific improvement in resource allocations and the processes in which they are applied, even to the extent that certain resources (human, physical, financial) may be reduced or eliminated. Just imagine what "integrated communications" means to either group and how significant the differences in sense and reference are. It is no wonder that public relations professionals cannot "get a seat at the table"—or as L. Grunig, J. Grunig, and Dozier (2002) called it, be included in the "dominant coalition" (p. 141)—or are not viewed as valuable and valued strategic advisors. Public relations people and management often are not consubstantial—they do not speak the same language and share enough common ground. The most effective leaders, however, use both quantitative/objective and qualitative/subjective information, thinking, and acting (Mintzberg, 1994).

What is the solution? It is not just creating a strategic plan itself. Newsom and Haynes (2008) addressed the development of strategic plans, but ironically, their treatment of the subject makes strategy more of a *tactical* matter of professional survival (i.e., creating a specific form of discourse that management demands) rather than a matter of proving PR's real strategic value to an organization. Most importantly, this myopic approach to strategic plans prevails in public relations instruction, where students are given essentially a recipe of things to address in a document so they can show *what* they will do, *when* and *how*. It still misses the mark about *why* within the organization's big picture. Students graduate and begin their careers thinking they know how public relations helps organizations, but they only know the strictly PR side of it. Hipple (2007) got closer as he called for more specific perceptual and actual links between public relations and business strategy by (paraphrasing Edward Bernays) "putting yourself on equal ground with executives and their advisors" (p. 17). This does not mean everyone in public relations must earn MBAs. But it does mean, as a recent report from the Arthur W. Page Society (2007) also argued, public relations people must understand, embrace, and apply business/management concepts and methods more effectively, systematically, and most of all, strategically. As Quirke (2008) said, "Communication must be based squarely upon business strategy or it will unknowingly work against it. It is not enough to tell employees what the strategy is, you have to equip them to deliver ion it. Existing communication practices are usually based on the old, implicit, strategy and will work against the new one if not realigned [with the business strategy]" (p. 31).

The solution is the dramatistic organizing of public relations *with management* within a single system for what Anthony (1988) called the processes of strategic planning, management control, and task control. They are processes that are owned by management and involve all levels. Within this system, strategic planning takes key management initiatives and supports top–down and bottom–up planning processes. This area involves deciding on an organization's goals and the strategies to attain them through goal setting, budgeting, and rolling forecasts. Management control supports planning by providing organizational insight, communication, and focus. It involves managers influencing other organizational members to enact the strategies by monitoring plan performance, supporting the analysis of alternatives, and taking corrective action. Task control involves making sure specific tasks are carried out efficiently and effectively. It is tactics- or transaction-focused and is the province of the literal results sought in the strategic planning process and measured according to the management control process.

This system leverages organizational knowledge and insight by blending these processes into a single, synchronous, and ongoing system to better implement strategies, strengthen decision making, and make management at all levels more effective. The system's process is typically engaged annually, and any *ad hoc*, project, or contingency planning would follow a similar path, being in synch with the organization's overall strategic plan and the PR function's strategic operating plan. Indeed, when time is especially of the essence, public relations leaders' strategic thinking is internalized and supported by extensive experience and knowledge of what works and what may not. Such strategic thinking in these situations involves a compressed process covering most or all elements of a strategic plan, resulting in efficient and effective management decision making that is in tune with the organization's bigger strategic picture (see Bazerman, 1998).

It is interesting that the starting point for the strategic planning process is really the end point—management thinks about what it wants the organization ultimately to be, then figures out how it will get there. And everyone has a role in this, starting with management and including employees. As Fig. 7.1 shows, developing the strategic plan (i.e., "planning efforts") is a top–down process that begins with management as it sets the course for the company about the level of strategies, and operating activity (including budgeting) is a bottom–up process that begins at the tactical level with employees who have the expertise and experience with the day-to-day demands that propel the company forward on its course to success. During the bottom–up process operational units examine management's strategies, decide what is doable and what is not, and allocate resources to ensure success. Key assumptions about the organization's current and anticipated future environments also are noted and understood by all parties. Both processes *together* result in a complete view of the business from all perspectives and focused on one vision for the company (also see Drucker, 1994; Robert, 1998, 2006). It may take some time to consistently demonstrate public relations' value before others embrace the value contribution of PR. The planning, budgeting, forecasting, consolidating performance data, analyzing performance data, reporting on results can, must work in public relations' favor.

This whole top–down and bottom–up process can take some time to complete, and it is contingent on an organization's culture and systems. In the end, the result is (a) a single strategic plan for the entire organization and (b) individual strategic operating plans for each organizational function. Operational plans, budgets, and forecasts must all "roll up" to organizational plan, budget, and forecast. Such an approach ensures that everyone is working toward the same ends and they all understand how everyone else will help get there. All parts of the plans are the same, but the content differs because each operational area has its own plan to fulfill the expectations specified in the organization's plan.

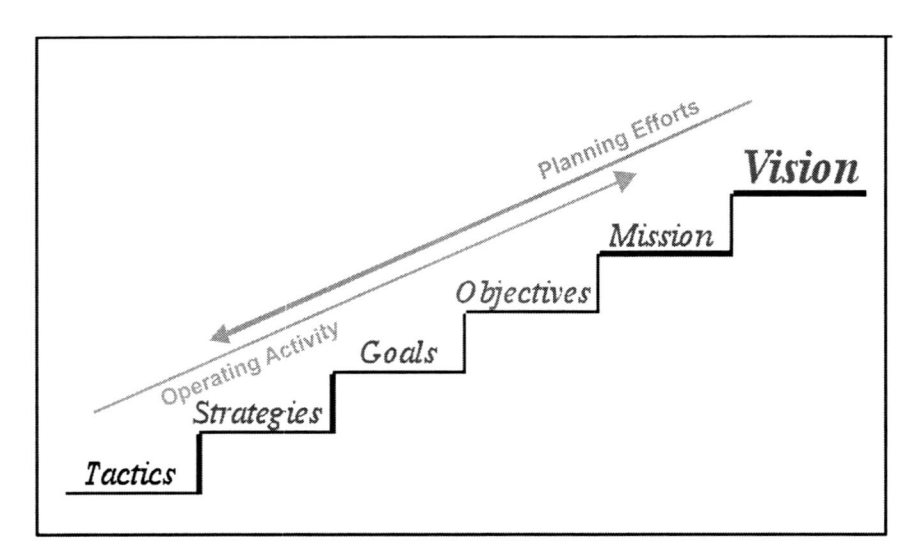

FIGURE 7.1. Strategic planning process model.

The key parts of an organizational plan are the company's vision, mission, objectives, goals, strategies, and tactics. Other aspects may be required (e.g., situation analysis, critical success factors, leading indicators, budget, timeline, evaluation scheme, etc.), which will be addressed later on and especially so for public relations. Here is how the key parts of a strategic plan interrelate. *Objectives* are the high-level things a company wants to achieve over a defined period of time (e.g., 1 year or more), and *goals* are specific measurable aspects that combine with and affirm that the objectives have been achieved. *Strategies* define the steps toward achieving objectives, and *tactics* are the specific efforts that must be done to enact a particular strategy. All of these must fall within the scope of the company's *mission*, which is a statement about what business the company is in, and gets the company closer to realizing its *vision*, which is the ultimate thing a company wants to be and needs to apply resources as effectively as possible over time to get there. Figure 7.1 shows how these features of strategic planning build one upon the other.

There is one caveat: Strategic plans go out of date essentially as soon as they are finalized and approved (see Drucker, 1994). The reason is that the process to develop a plan rests on information about an organization's enacted environment, which is really a snapshot in time. Certain assumptions also were made about the future. So because things change quickly inside and outside an organization, aspects of a strategic plan (at the corporate or operating levels or both) must be flexible enough to accommodate change and still achieve success. Public relations' inherent boundary spanning capabilities become more potent this way. Here, too, rests the potency of rhetorical theory for the management and practice of public relations.

USING RHETORICAL THEORY IN PRACTICE

Do people in industry knowingly use a theory of rhetoric to help them do what they do? I don't know, but I strongly suspect the vast majority of them do not overtly use any theory of rhetoric in their work. They may, however, covertly do so, if they have been introduced to one, it somehow "stuck" with them, and they use it in their communication with others.[16] But this issue is less the matter on which I have chosen to dwell here. Rhetoric is the very substance of organizing and the strategic planning, management control, and task-control processes. My focus, instead, is more predictive: Will and can theories of rhetoric ever be formal tools of the trade for public relations practitioners? I believe the answer is yes and no. The synthesis of theories of rhetoric and organizing will not solve completely the weak business acumen that tends to prevail among PR professionals, but it does offer a systematic means to better account for and thrive in the simultaneously rhetorical and organizational nature of public relations that concerns practitioners at any level.

I address two basic dimensions to my position on the topic. First, pragmatism prevails in our nation and across industry, and it is appropriate but limiting. For rhetorical scholars and practitioners in public relations, the issue is whether *and* how to cross the chasm between theory and practice. Second, the matter of bridging that chasm is possible so that practitioners have a good idea about how rhetorical theory can help them add value to their organizations. That bridge building is possible through active application of practice with theory.

A Pragmatic Attitude Prevails

Take a step back in history. For our nation, as Boorstin (1958) said, a high level of pragmatism[17] has always been at the heart of our forebears' work to colonize a foreign land, build a nation, and establish a democracy. Early American colleges, "concerned more with the diffusion than with the advancement or perpetuation of learning [unlike their ancient European counterparts]" (Boorstin, 1958, p. 178), were founded "not to increase the continental stock of cultivated men, but rather to supply its particular region with knowledgeable ministers, lawyers, doctors, merchants, and political leaders" (p. 181). Looking back on it all, from Harvard's founding in 1636 as the first higher-education institution in the colonies, to Emerson's philosophy of self-reliance, to Jack Welch's turnaround of General Electric and his subsequent place as a business icon, pragmatism has been often privileged in America's thinking and acting—and that is okay. But there is more.

Fast forward to today's industrial milieu and public relations practitioners. Like the vast majority of professionals, public relations people work hard and are proud of their work. Their bosses (and *their* bosses) expect public relations action to add value to the organization. That value is something beyond the planning, execution, and measurement of public relations campaigns and tactics. Adding value is the primary concern of all business functions. To do so means, on one hand, that a functional area's contributions have simultaneously bolstered the organization's mission and moved the business closer to realizing its vision. On the other hand, adding value means pragmatically that a functional area has helped enhance (or at least not hurt) a company's financial position through its allocation of resources and budget versus actual expenditures. Not that every organizational function has to be cash-positive, because even a function that tends to heavily depend on expenses (like public relations does) can spur income-making opportunities that drive things like sales, donations, and so on. Public relations has the added benefit of sparking crucial attitude-changing opportunities that enhance image, reputation, perception, brand equity, and so on, that also affect the financial picture. The link between the two—public relations actions and corporate income/gross receipts—is a tenuous thing to measure directly at best, and is outside the scope of this book, but the point is relevant to the pragmatism of public relations practice. Here, too, we must recall the semantic disparity that often prevails in the organizing behaviors between management and public relations professionals. We also start to sense a clash between the proponents of quantitative and qualitative perspectives.

Sadly, I believe the prevailing pragmatic attitude is overprivileged. A tendency in industry to seek recipes (privilege tactics) for effective corporate communications dominates, as professionals are increasingly asked to "do more with less," "work smarter," and adhere to other slogans meant to inspire excellence in work, but as Deming (1986) said, they "generate frustration and resentment" (p. 67). Public relations discourse is the sum of many people's enactments shared, selected, and retained according to organizing recipes during the process through which they make sense of what is going on and what must be done. As Weick (1979b) said, recipes are "the means to generate structures that have the characteristics you want. . . . Adapted to organizing, the question becomes: given our need for a sensible enacted environment, how do we produce it?" (pp. 46-47). This quest for recipes eschews the direct application of theory. Witness the great variety of "how-to" seminars and luncheon meetings at PRSA chapters in everything professional communicators might need to enhance their tactical skills.

Indeed, I have heard a few professionals (and sometimes students—the horror!) say something like, "Ah, forget this theory crap." But consider that it is not enough to "just do it," because someone would act out of instinct without taking the time to ensure success by systematically applying principles of effective, ethical, and strategic communications. Likewise, I have heard others say something like, "We can't act until we've identified all possible angles," but consider that it would be wasteful to "plan to the nth degree," because we could run out of time, squander resources, and settle for completing only some of everything we would like to have done. All this is in line with Aristotle's distinction between "right opinion" and "knowledge"; whereas, the former means someone possesses a basic competence about public relations, but lacking the latter, that person does not understand truly why public relations adds value to an organization and society. In a Burkean frame, it is also akin to the motion-action dichotomy: The former involves someone merely "going through the motions" of or following recipes for public relations assignments/tactics, whereas the latter involves someone organizing more purposefully and strategically within the big picture and the little pictures of their public relations work for the larger organization.

The fundamental difference between these two perspectives is a way of thinking—should public relations practitioners think more pragmatically or more conceptually? I believe the answer is, "Yes!"—and rhetorical theory can have a place in it. Theory informs practice, and practice informs theory. They are harmonious.

Theory-Practice Bridge Building

We know that many public relations professionals tend to be a methodical lot, preferring to plan a route to success, identify the various avenues and detours that may come along the way, embark confidently on the trek they have plotted, then measure results and outcomes. There are elements of analysis, planning, executing, evaluating, and celebrating. Through it all, practitioners have to know *how* to do the work and *why* the approach they take is sound. In this sense, there are advantages to being both "book smart" and "street wise." That is, theory and practice have a place in everything a public relations professional does, even as a citizen in the community.

As a professional communicator, it is important to pay attention to current thinking and approaches—the why as well as the how—to effective public relations. A grounding in both theory and practice, then, will help practitioners do better in their work. The result: They secure the results they want, sharpen their abilities, stay on top of current ideas, and add to the body of knowledge about public relations.

There are many examples of scholarly work that applies rhetorical theory specifically to public relations, and just a few include individual works by Boyd (2004), Cheney (1983b, 1991), Cheney and Dionisopoulos (1989), Courtright and Slaughter (2007), Crable and Vibbert (1995), J. Grunig (1993a), Hearit (1996), Heath (1992b, 1993, 2001, 2006), Ihlen (2002a, 2002b, 2004), Miller (1989), Terry (2001), Vasquez (1993), and book-length treatments by Cheney (1991), Cragan and Shields (1995), Elwood (1995a) and Toth and Heath (1992). Although works such as these are part of the body of knowledge about public relations, they are still very much untapped by industry. The fact of the matter is academic work tends to stay in academia and is scarcely tantalizing to the vast majority of professionals we would like to think are salivating for it. Even though implications *to* industry may be given, they are meant as focal points primarily for scholars and students, not industry practitioners—those who have already "been there and done that."

Because of my experience in industry and the cross-pollination from academe along the way, I believe theories of rhetoric can and do work as formal tools in the professional practice of public relations. I have done it and seen it. But here is the big issue: I believe theories of rhetoric will not be applied in the near term as formal tools of the trade for public relations prac-

Strategic Planning and Value 153

titioners like "six sigma"[18] has been for General Electric (see Pande, Neuman, & Cavanagh, 2002) or the ROPE (research, objectives, programming, and evaluation) model (Hendrix & Hayes, 2007) for communications professionals. Theories of rhetoric have not been made pragmatic enough for business use, even though echoes of them may be discovered in textbooks but none foreground them like six sigma. Our expectations should be more modest, focusing on the long-term, because attitude change will rest on the successful proof of concept for this theory-practice bridge that we build. This is the point of this book.

Pragmatic applications of rhetorical theory to public relations practice must be designed so that they blend the best of both worlds, even to harmonize qualitative and quantitative analyses of a business. In addition to this volume (including Smudde, 2004b, 2008), I have designed a way to apply Michel Foucault's rhetorical system (Smudde, 2007) to work more like theory-practice recipes that professionals can use. Another prescribes how image repair theory should be made more palatable to practitioners (Smudde & Courtright, 2008).[19] Such approaches would help practitioners see that (a) rhetorically based approaches to public relations truly can be *usable* and *useful* for adding value to organizations and (b) such theory-based approaches can be truly *used* successfully to plan, execute, and measure public relations action. To enable such usability, public relations rhetoricians must address the field in a pragmatic way for practitioners so it can further strengthen their cases about public relations' value in addition to quantitative performance analyses like six sigma. My prescription is that these smart people in academe and industry must prepare and present theory-driven and case-based analyses that explain the following:

1. What rhetorical theory is and what its value-added benefits to public relations can be.
2. Which rhetorical theory applies and why (i.e., choose theory effectively).
3. How it works systematically—in general and in specific (i.e., at both the macro- and micro-levels) regarding case examples, especially from varied organizations and industries.
4. How to make a rhetorical theory work *prospectively* for one's own communications opportunities and in synch with strategic planning, execution, and measurement (qualitative and quantitative).

Let me review this prescription from the bottom up. The prescription's last point about using rhetorical theory prospectively is important. Although critique and rhetorical criticism are traditionally anchored in retrospective analysis (i.e., looking at an artifact to investigate it for what it was and is), there is no reason why critical methods cannot be used prospectively to the benefit of future discursive action. In this way, we move from traditional critique (which looks back on extant discourse) to prediction (which looks forward to planned discourse). Criticism and rhetorical theory, then, become something more strategically potent—a tool for planning and enacting more effective discourse rather than an exercise attaining 20/20 hindsight. This prospective view is especially relevant to business because spending too much time looking in the rearview mirror means the advantage from looking down and preparing for the road ahead has been lost and the opportunities that go with it.

The third point of my prescription is the idea that rhetorical theory must be usable through systematic application. To a certain degree, rhetorical theory should be presented heuristically so application of it mimics other effective management decision-making tools. The idea is for rhetorical theory to be sufficiently easy for practitioners to understand and apply in nonacademic settings. The result would enable practitioners to move forward in their work and add value to their organizations. For example, practitioners should feel confident that they can devise an effective communications plan that encompasses not only the traditional aspects of public relations, but also gives them ways to account pragmatically for critical dimensions at the macro and micro levels beyond the traditional, like motives, argument structure, dialectic, intertextuality, and power.

To get to this point, practitioners must be able to choose a relevant rhetorical perspective effectively, which is my prescription's second point. There are a lot of perspectives to choose from, and practitioners will need criteria about how to select one or more rhetorical theories to apply in some situation. Any theory-driven, case-based explanation of rhetorical theory must provide practitioners (plus scholars and students) with sufficient guidance about how to choose a rhetorical perspective that fits not only a communication opportunity and all its dimensions, but it must also fit a practitioner's perspective of public relations, management's view of the business, corporate policies and procedures, and other relevant environmental factors inside and outside an organization. Some amount of taxonomic explanation may be required here, leaning on best practices of symbolic/rhetorical action from various situations, organizations, industries, and so on.

All these aspects of my prescription have as their foundation my prescription's first point: a firm understanding of what rhetorical theory is and how it can add value to a public relations function and the organization overall. We should not assume that practitioners understand and would use rhetorical theory in ways intellectuals do. Walking a mile in practitioners' shoes with theory and practice can make the relevance to corporate viability and professional vitality all the more potent for them. (It may even help improve rhetoric's image and inspire some useful and ethical collaboration between professionals and academics.)

Rhetorical Theory as a Strategic Framework

The process model given in Chapter 6 summarized the major steps involved in a public relations effort, large or small, simple or complex. It recognizes the Weickian notion that public relations professionals make sense of what is going on through communication and, in particular, discover what they think after seeing what they want to say in key messages about the enacted environment (context). Although a communications plan springs from a particular context (and even anticipates future ones), it must reflect back on and support an organization's overall strategic plan. Any public relations work, however, must be understood for what it is and not treat everything like a crisis. Doing so could be overreactive, squander resources, and risk stakeholder trust (see Smudde & Courtright, in press) in management's ability to know the difference among mere problems, organizational crises, disasters, and issues to manage (Smudde, 2001). Public relations practitioners must have a thorough understanding of a company, its business, future direction, products and technology, market, and regulatory matters along with strong competence in communication (see D'Aprix, 1997, 2001; Lukaszewski, 2001a, 2001b, 2001c; 2008; Hipple, 2007; Holstein, 2008).

This requirement is clearly met by the GM officials who handled the C/K pickup issue. As an organizational function, public relations has a stake in helping a company achieve its objectives. That stake is defined by the company's high-level strategies to meet its objectives. In this way, what are strategies to the company are objectives to the functional departments. For example, if one of a company's objectives is to attain market leadership, one corporate-level strategy could be to establish a market niche in which the company can legitimately lead. That corporate strategy is one that public relations can support, which makes it a PR objective. (There would be other corporate strategies PR could not support, like improving product functionality, which would fall under a product engineering function.)

As the measured and ethical use of language and symbols to inspire cooperation between an organization and its publics, public relations professionals do more than retell any organizational story. In the dramatistic organizing of public relations, practitioners create discourse ethically that emphasizes its dramatic dimensions and invites the involvement of the publics with the organization in communication about it. In this way the unifying, consubstantial elements of both Burke's and Weick's theories (see Table 2.1) come into real play. What practitioners know about the how *and* the why of public relations is more important than whether the how outweighs the why, or vice versa. (This latter orientation often needlessly and unfortunately divides industry and academe.)

Building a useable bridge between rhetorical theory and public relations practice is an essential and needed approach for planning, understanding, and evaluating public relations action. In this way theories of rhetoric can be strategic tools of the trade for public relations practitioners, *if and only if* they can be bridged with the pragmatic need of adding value to the public relations function and the organization. Again, the best of both worlds must be blended in this quest. That will begin to be possible through prospective, case-based analyses that cross the theory-practice chasm.

PROSPECTIVE, STRATEGIC, AND RHETORICAL PUBLIC RELATIONS

How can a system of rhetoric and criticism help a public relations practitioner achieve specific results strategically? The answer to this question stems from the method used in the C/K pickup case study and relies on Burke's tools for critical analysis—terms for order, identification, and the dramatistic pentad—individually and, especially, as a system within the context of Weick's ideas about organizing. Separately and together these tools reveal important dimensions at both the micro- and the macro-levels about the symbolic action of public relations. After all, too, prospective, strategic planning is something that, in tune with Burke's view, befits the nature of humans as perfection seekers.

In a nutshell, a practical methodology for the dramatistic organizing of public relations would be a dramatistic one (Smudde, 2004b). For example, an issue's evolution can work for an organization in a proactive way to establish a new order that is at least as close as possible to what it wants. Issues that matter to an organization and its publics are literal dramas that have scenes, acts, agents, agencies, and purposes. The dramatistic quest for an organization is to inspire cooperation between itself and its publics by enacting an issue's drama that is one with which audiences will identify. The public relations discourse that is used enacts that drama and an issue's dramatic dimensions, which also invites the involvement of publics with the organization. Let's look at how public relations professionals can apply Burke's tools proactively and strategically to their organizing at the micro- and macro-levels.

Applying Terms for Order to Public Relations

Burke's (1970) cycle of terms for order is his tool for tracing out history terministically, and it can help us understand the context, even the drama, of the symbolic action of public relations. A logological approach can help us understand the dynamics of such symbolic action through order, pollution, guilt, purification through either mortification or victimage, and redemption (Burke, 1970; Brock, 1995, 1999). Describing issues logologically chronicles the rhetorical context and the evolution of an issue to restore order for an organization. Fig. 7.2 shows and briefly describes the general logological progression of matters across four phases, all of which echo Burke's terms for order.

Intuitively, to properly understand an issue, action, event, or the like requires us to know about the things going on around it that are (and maybe are not) related to it. With symbolic action as the basis for public relations, this firmament of properties from social situations are "systematically (i.e., not incidentally) *relevant* for discourse" (van Dijk, 1997, p. 11) and make up context. Minimally, participants, their acts, their agencies, their purposes, the scene, and other discourses all make up something's context. The rhetorical (i.e., logological and dramatistic) and the organizational natures of a situation must be enacted and documented, especially in the form of a strategic public relations plan that supports an overall business plan and has specific measurable objectives that link to the business plan's objectives.

In terms of the organizing process for public relations, it is from an equivocal environment that people select certain features and make sense of them intersubjectively for social situations. For public relations organizing, the uncertainty within an environment poses rhetorical opportunities. While reducing this uncertainty about what is going on, public relations officials also identify areas for possible symbolic action. In this way, practitioners define context together (perhaps with others in an organization, like management, attorneys, engineers, etc.) by reducing rhetorical equivocality. In a very real way, as public relations officials reduce the rhetorical equivocality to define context, they enact Weick's (1979b) recipe, "How can I know what I think until I see what I say" (p. 133). Practitioners' enactments for rhetorical opportunities comprise samples from the flow of experience, first, taken by each person individually for closer inspection and, next, selected in a group process of "sensemaking" (Weick, 1979b, 1995) sorting out which enactments (including previously retained ones) make the most sense to share publicly in ways that would inspire cooperation between a company and its publics.

In rhetorical terms, that environment, or context, frames a social drama enacted in public relations discourse. Context subsumes the logological progression of social moments that creates what Duncan (1989) called a "social bond" that is attained "through identification which occurs in the enactment of guilt redeemed through victimage" (p. 436). These social moments can be thought of as texts—the symbolic action of individuals either individually or collectively. Within the scope of public relations (as depicted in Fig. 7.2), the context concerns the logological progression of things, beginning with a stable order just before something changes it. From there, context addresses

PHASE 1: Order	PHASE 2: Pollution & Assignment of Guilt	PHASE 3: Purification	PHASE 4: Redemption
The state of things about and for an organization, what it stands for, and what it offers is stable.	Something from within, without, or both upsets or significantly changes the stability of things, and blame or responsibility must be assigned for it on the public stage.	Efforts to make things right gradually secure the public's approval, where the success of one side over the other becomes increasingly apparent, especially as an organization accepts responsibility of it own accord or is saddled with responsibility by others.	• For an organization that secures the public's favor, final vindication of it is given and a new order is created, which would bolster its image and credibility. • For an organization that does not secure the public's favor, it must cope with the new order, which (adversely) affects the organization's reputation and credibility.

FIGURE 7.2. Four-phase logological progression of public relations matters.

who or what may have caused the problem (whether internal, external, or a combination of both), their level of responsibility for it, and how order can be restored for the organization and its publics. In this way, context is as much retrospective as it is prospective about the drama of a particular event, issue, situation, or other enacted environments. That is, public relations officials can not only make sense of how the order of things changed, but they can also plan to ethically "pollute" the order of things to achieve certain objectives, like those related to the launch of a unique product into a market or the introduction of a new public policy to remedy a social situation.

Achieving Identification in Public Relations

Symbol systems place humans in the realm of action—symbolic action—and beyond mere biological motion. For Burke (1969b), rhetoric is a function of language "as a symbolic means of inducing cooperation in beings that by nature respond to symbols" (p. 43). This definition expands the traditional notion of rhetoric as persuasion—that rhetoric is an element of symbolic action, which includes persuasion and identification. Identification entails simultaneous unity and division—it is rooted in the inherent division among people because of their physical separateness, and language helps them bridge that condition to become "consubstantial," to find common ground or "substance" (Burke, 1969b). Indeed, identification is perhaps the most-often used concept of Burke's when applied to the study of organizational communication and, specifically, public relations.

Public relations officials work hard to make sense of the environment that an organization faces to find common ground, or inspire cooperation between an organization and its publics. A big part of achieving this goal is to figure out how to make selected events in an environment resonate with other people inside and outside the company, while they craft key messages about it with which target publics will identify and develop a strategic plan to guide the application of those messages and other aspects of public relations efforts. Based on what is understood about an organization's internal and external environments, key messages reflect different but related aspects of any event's or issue's drama. Key messages are not the final public relations texts; they make up the most important points of an issue that corporate officials want to emphasize with target publics in the texts (e.g., press releases, speeches, backgrounders, press conferences, etc.) they do prepare. The key messages must also reflect areas of common ground, striking a favorable balance between the organization's point of view and the audiences' concerns and needs. Key messages serve as a kind of outline or list of the dominant features in the issue's drama that are enacted textually, based on the context and in any combination of public relations discourse genres.

To be useful during the planning and execution of public relations symbolic action, key messages are documented simply, shared, and retained with corporate leaders and public relations officials managing an issue. The main reason for this approach is to maintain message consistency and mutual understanding among corporate people involved in the issue. To capture the key messages that organizational officials want publics to understand, buy into, and act on is to help ensure consistency. And having a central team that orchestrates and is the authority for communication to all audiences also keeps consistency intact.

In general terms, a public relations official must also do his or her homework on the organization's principal audiences, which ones must be targeted, and what their demographics are. The key is to enact dramas about something (e.g., issues, product, service, event) that are consistent with or complementary to target publics' dramas about those things. Research into audiences can be both quantitative and qualitative, using methods like surveys, focus groups, and secondary research from other sources (e.g., other department analyses, periodicals and published articles, and government reports) about target audiences. Stakeholder analysis, too, can be a valuable approach, as it "demands the ability to determine where parties agree and disagree in terms of what they believe to be facts regarding an issue and the evaluation of it" (Heath, 1997, p. 29). The important point is that the target publics are the focus of the key messages, which guide practitioners in their symbolic action—to make sure the salient points about the enacted drama are emphasized with publics effectively, ethically, and strategically. Public relations professionals can measure and nurture identification with publics through audience analyses, ensuring that the right messages are in the right discourse at the right time.

Public relations officials enact an issue's drama in specific kinds of public relations texts that present that drama in the best ways for publics and emphasize key messages about it. The genre set for public relations includes 30-some kinds of discourse listed in Table 2.2 in Chapter 2. Although the logological context has been defined and key messages have been developed, the actual discourse that weaves the two together to enact the drama must be prepared, focusing on appropriate pendatic aspects in the entire drama. The subsequent discourse about an issue enacts the drama public relations officials defined logologically. As Eggins and Martin (1997) said, "an interactant setting out to achieve a particular cultural goal is most likely to initiate a text of a particular genre, and that text is most likely to unfold in a particular way—but the potential for alternatives is inherent in the dialogic relationship between language and context" (p. 236).

During the preparation of individual public relations texts, an audience-centered approach may result in some refinement of key messages, as public relations officials pragmatically apply their knowledge of the context and effective, ethical communication to the task at hand. Furthermore, a text can only be effective if the writing works well for the audience in the right genre. Whatever the purpose of public relations discourse may be (e.g., to persuade, inform, debunk, or motivate), that purpose guides practitioners in how they use language in selected genres to help structure people's thinking about an issue.

To meet someone's needs on their terms—to achieve consubstantiality—increases the probability that the message will be accepted and understood, then subsequently embraced and acted upon. At a textual level, certain attributes of messages are instrumental in inducing cooperation with an audience: "proximity or immediacy, concreteness, the vital, suspense, repetition, familiarity, simplicity, novelty, conflict, activity, repetition, visual and vivid, content, elite personalities, messages with affective content, and humor" (Ferguson, 1999, p. 149). These attributes reflect various ways people may come to identify with messages. At a basic level, the more a message affects people personally and projects a sense of urgency, the more likely they are to pay attention to it and, potentially, act on it.

As issues evolve logologically (see Fig. 7.2), changing contexts may require practitioners to enact more or fewer key messages for publics than those in the original plan. Such adaptability is necessary to make sure the issue is managed as effectively as possible and any changes can be accommodated in the strategic plan (or vice versa). The main point here is an intertextual one: Practitioners must make sure that, across all texts that will be used, certain messages will be given in particular ways that are best-suited for chosen discourse forms, meet audiences' needs, and ethically advance communication objectives. This intertextual dimension means "the line separating internal and external communications becomes more suspect and corporate messages become more interrelated," from newsletters to television (Cheney & Dionsopolous, 1989, p. 145). This interrelationship among texts does not mean every person gets each message identically in any genre; it means that members of each audience receive the same message in the appropriate language and form that suits them collectively. The goal is to establish common ground between an organization and its publics. The result, generally speaking, is that audiences are more apt to identify with the messages and cooperate with an organization's cause.

Applying the Dramatistic Pentad to Public Relations

To Burke (1973), because language is "the dancing of an attitude" and shapes our views of reality, guides our behavior, and generates our motives for our actions, human action could be understood through drama. He developed dramatism as a method to derive a literal statement about human motivation (Burke, 1968b, p. 448; see Brock, Burke, Burgess & Simmons, 1985). Dramatistic analysis proceeds through the pentad (Burke, 1969a), a cluster analysis of the terms that name the act (what was done), scene (where it was done), agent (who did it), agency (how that person did it) and purpose (for what reason the person did it). Ratios of these five terms show relationships between them and in which term the greatest attention is placed to discover motivation for the act.

Public relations texts grow out of organizing behavior among public relations practitioners and the people with whom they work. The logological context practitioners define is part and parcel to their investigation of the motives behind a situation and planning for specific symbolic action by naming the act (the corporate message), the scene (the environment or context to which the message refers), the agent (the person[s] who will act as the corporate representative to which the message will be ascribed), the agency (the chosen public relations discourse genre), and the purpose (to inform, persuade, inspire, inform, debunk, etc.). This sensemaking activity reduces rhetorical equivocality and results in an enacted environment—"an orderly, material, social construction that is subject to multiple interpretations" (Weick, 1988, p. 307)—on which practitioners act symbolically.

Using pentadic analysis, we discover finer detail about how language is used to structure people's thinking about an issue and particular aspects of it. Each text functions as an individual symbolic act that is tied to a particular event in an issue's history, as suggested in Fig 7.2. Even when separate texts—like a backgrounder, press release, and pitch letter—are used for the same episode in an issue's drama, they are simultaneously separate in their specific generic qualities and united in their appeal for people to identify with the drama enacted by those texts. Thus, the effectiveness for all public relations discourse on the issue derives from both the discourse form and the language about the scenes, actions, agents, agencies, and purposes. Two simple examples are shown in Table 7.1. (Note that in the case of an organiza-

TABLE 7.1. The Pentad and Public Relations Discourse Examples

	PRESS RELEASE	PRESS CONFERENCE
Screen	Specific situation	Actual place of event
Act	What was done or needs doing	Addressing news media and public
Agent	Quoted official(s)	Corporate official(s) & selected dignitaries
Agency	Press release	Oral comments & supplemental texts
Purpose	Announce news	Personally address issue

tion being the agent, the agency may be a spokesperson or the particular kind of public relations discourse that is enacted.)

Inherent in the practice of public relations is the effective management of information for multiple audiences simultaneously. This managing of multiple or diverse audiences means the role of the pentad can be especially powerful, because it give practitioners a way to systematically break down and analyze the dynamics among the constituent dramatistic parts of an organizational situation (e.g., issue, crisis, disaster, opportunity, or other matter). In effect, public relations practitioners are working with various publics' ideas—multiple dramas—about what is going on. In this way, having multiple publics means there will be multiple dramas about any given issue, crisis, or other matter. So the symbolic action that public relations practitioners enact dramatistically about something should help target audiences to identify with the drama that is articulated in public relations discourse. In practice, public relations practitioners can employ diverse strategies to target any given audience or set of target audiences. Practitioners, then, can be working with multiple genres of public relations discourse in systematic efforts to enact a particular drama in symbolic terms. Furthermore, depending on the complexity of an organization's environment, a public relations practitioner can coordinate multiple dramas and concomitant symbolic actions about different matters simultaneously, and each probably would have its own release date. In the end, this dramatistic approach should lead, ideally, to establishing identification between diverse publics and an organization as the drama an organization enacts about some matter in its discourse is closely aligned with the dramas that its publics enact about the same matter.

Examining public relations texts dramatistically reveals public relations officials' use of language to structure publics' thinking about issues and inspire cooperation. Practitioners can strategically and ethically emphasize one or more key messages over others, especially through the individual dramatistic features of act, scene, agent, agency, and purpose (and attitude, if using Burke's hexad) to craft texts for target audiences. Elements of the pentad can be used to order one's perception of reality, where people select one of the five elements to emphasize over the others. This approach reflects how one's worldview orders the rhetorical aspects of a text.

This approach also calls attention to ethical principles, because people can view the same situation differently and possibly mask truth in a situation to serve one's own ends. As we saw in chapter 6, one element of the pentad may be used to emphasize part of a drama and, consequently, subordinate other pentadic elements. Again, Ling's (1970) analysis of Senator Edward Kennedy's 1969 televised statement about Mary Jo Kopechne's death is a useful example. In his statement, Kennedy's focus on the scene subordinated all other pentadic elements of agent, act, agency, and purpose, thereby making them functions of the scene in which the two people were a part and, most important, victims at its mercy. This example presents important lessons about ethical decision making for public relations professionals. Not only must public relations officials accurately and honestly assess situations, but also they must use the pentad to guide them in their discourse development. The result would be what Burke (1984a) might refer to as "secular prayers" that truthfully, accurately, and appropriately frame an issue and enact its drama so that target publics identify with it.

A STRATEGY FOR THE DRAMATISTIC ORGANIZING OF PUBLIC RELATIONS

A strategic plan for the dramatistic organizing of public relations based on the ideas in this volume is presented here. It features concise explanations for each dimension a practitioner must address. The template is designed to be flexible so that it can be used for situations of varied levels of complexity, from new product launches to crisis management. Such flexibility is also important as contexts shift and the plan needs to be revised in ways that accommodate those shifts but still uphold its objectives.

The first half of the plan—from the situation analysis through objectives—sets forth the philosophy behind what should be communicated, why, and for what results. This framework is vital, because it gives practitioners the foundation for their symbolic action. The other half of the plan—from strategies through evaluation—presents a methodology for what must be done to successfully and ethically inspire cooperation among target publics. This method is the focal point when implementing the plan for discursive action.

Situation and Its Context

The context of a public relations situation includes the specific matter that needs attention and the surrounding environment that an organization faces. The statement defines the public relations situation logologically and in sufficient detail, especially differentiating it as a problem or opportunity, an organizational crisis (e.g., product tampering, facility explosion), a disaster (e.g., hurricane, terrorism effects), or an issue (e.g., public safety, fair trade practices). The situation itself may affect the organization in either a positive way or a negative way. The statement about it should also define anyone involved in the plan and draw attention to any special considerations (e.g., resources, bureaucracy, or politics) for the team's organizing processes. The statement may require a separate document if the description is lengthy. The opportunity may reflect one of several rhetorical angles. For example:

- To overcome or correct a negative perception of the organization, its products, or its services
- To manage an issue that someone or some group says is important and must be addressed by your organization
- To conduct a specific one-time project or achieve a well-defined one-time objective
- To develop or expand a continuing program or to maintain and improve an existing positive situation
- To address a particular public policy issue that affects or is affected by the organization

By applying sufficient research about the situation and its effects on the organization and its environment, you can define the logological context by answering certain questions in as much detail as possible. Remember that the situation can be as much one you purposefully and *proactively* create to achieve a competitive advantage for your organization as it could be one in which you purposefully and *reactively* defend your organization. The key questions are:

- What was the cause of the situation that adversely changed the way things were internal and/or external for your organization?
- Whom or what may be solely or partially responsible for the situation and to what extent?
- How can a solution be implemented and benefits enjoyed by the organization and those affected that effectively restores order by either your company asserting mea culpa, accepting all or some responsibility for the opportunity, then proposing a solution; or another party taking sole or shared blame for the situation and advancing a solution?
- How will you know that the public is satisfied with and acts on the solution, thereby restoring order for them and your organization?

Key Audiences

Because many PR situations facing organizations are rarely of interest to the general public, you must identify the key groups of people inside and outside your organization who must receive the messages and determine what they want to know. Consider the following:

- What do your audiences want to know, and how can the messages be tailored to address their self-interests?
- What are the characteristics of your target audience, and how can demographic information be used to craft messages that demonstrate common ground between them and your organization?
- How can any audience help the organization achieve its objectives and be inspired to cooperate?

You may have different levels of audiences (i.e., primary, secondary, and tertiary) that suggest degrees of importance that any audience may play in the communication plan. If so, the second point can especially guide you in addressing each audience level appropriately.

Key Message Platform

The analysis of the situation and audiences yields the basis for a key message platform. It is a concise outline of specific ideas about the public relations opportunity's rhetorical context that you want target audiences to understand, embrace, and act upon. The messages should be tailored for each audience to help inspire their cooperation with the organization. A key message platform consists of two parts: (a) a thesis, theme, or slogan that states the big-picture idea; and (b) a series of specific message points that backup the thesis. The idea is that such a platform helps corporate officials "stay on message" and helps audiences remember the key "take aways" even if they forget everything else.

- How can the messages best be crafted to establish identification between target audiences and the organization?
- Will the messages work to achieve the plan's objectives?
- Are the messages designed to inform or change attitudes and behaviors?
- Are the organization's expectations realistic?

The key messages should ethically and sufficiently enact the drama about the scene, act, actors involved, means for doing the acts, and reasons for doing them within its logological context. The key message platform should also identify any particular ratios of pentadic elements that should be emphasized to establish identification. A successful key message platform is one that inspires publics to cooperate with the organization because they identify with the drama the organization enacts in its discourse.

Objectives

Objectives for communications plans are statements about the high-level communication results a company wants to achieve over a defined period of time. Specific objectives are more meaningful than general ones that merely try to "increase awareness" about something, for example. Each objective addresses four dimensions which correspond to the acronym EGAD: (a) the *effect* sought (knowledge/ awareness, attitudes, behaviors, discourse outputs), (b) the *goal* or measurable amount of the effect sought, (c) the target *audience*, and (d) the *deadline* or date for achieving results (also see Hendrix & Hayes, 2007). Here are a few examples:

- Increase awareness by 30% among state lawmakers about the adverse impact of proposed corporate tax legislation before the end of the legislative session.
- Improve consumers' attitudes to 65% approval for the organization's handling the effects of the chemical spill by December 31, 2009.
- Achieve a 15% lift in sales among all customer segments by the end of the campaign.
- Pitch two new-business stories to trade publications each month during the year.

Note that the objective requires a *benchmark* so you know the context of the degree of improvement for any effect sought. To achieve your objectives, the target audiences must receive, understand, believe, and act upon the messages. A statement about the benchmark for an objective can and should be given immediately with the corresponding objective.

Strategy Statements

Strategy statements, or "strategies," outline conceptually how the plan's objectives will be achieved through certain categories of activities. Strategies may be broad or narrow in scope, and they must be associated with one or more objective. The most efficient strategies are those that help you achieve more than one objective. Strategy statements indicate what you will do generally and give you room to articulate what you will do specifically and tactically for each strategy statement. For example, in tune with the above objectives:

- Provide audiences with salient information about the affects of the proposed corporate tax legislation.

- Use credible sources to demonstrate sound decision making about the chemical spill.
- Allow for audience participation in the launching of the new product line.
- Use verbal cues with journalists about new-business cases.

Tactics

Tactics are the specific means you will use to fulfill each of your strategies. Planned and developed according to pendatic analysis, tactics may be written, spoken, or visual means to facilitate communication between an organization and its audiences. Tactics are part of the task-control process and include myriad possibilities for literal public relations action, applying people (e.g., corporate officials, reporters), discourse types (e.g., news releases, face-to-face meetings), or technology (e.g., Internet, wire services). For example, in tune with the above strategies:

- Write and distribute press releases and fact sheets about the organization's position on the proposed corporate tax legislation. Marshall industry support in a joint letter to the people of the state and the governor. Hold a news conference about a solution. Post all relevant written, video, and audio content on the Internet in selected places.
- Write an op-ed piece with the CEO about the situation and publish it in major newspapers. Invite third-party experts to comment on the organization's process and hold a news conference on the findings. Have small-group, face-to-face meetings between senior managers and supervisors as part of any organizational change program.
- Hold a product launch event in downtown New York, Chicago, and San Diego to allow people to experience the new product. Invite news organizations to cover it.
- Hold meetings with editorial boards of key publications (trade and general business) about customer success stories.

Given the situation's logological context and grounds for inspiring cooperation, a hierarchy of communication channels can be devised to select the most appropriate discourse genres for the situation and your audiences; whereas, the more personal the communication is the better. A useful hierarchy of channels begins with one-to-one, personal communication and builds to broad-based, mass communication channels.

Critical Success Factors

To make sure you have considered as many ways your strategic communication will be successful, you must show what things could affect it (positively and negatively) when trying to meet your goals. Those factors can come from several directions. For example:

- Opportunities: Occasions when an organization can capitalize on the situation to garner support and build its image
- Barriers: Include but are not limited to ideological, attitudinal, or social opposition to or legal, regulatory, or institutional restrictions on an organization doing what it believes it should to solve the problem in the way it wants
- Environment (internal and external; based on the situation analysis): Business issues fuel communications, like low profitability undermines the company's and its leaders' credibility; product problems and failures damage the company's reputation; third parties are reluctant to endorse the company; a merger or acquisition diverts attention to organizational changes
- Resources: Staff required to fulfill communications objectives is sufficient and supplemented by knowledgeable and experienced outside help to take on intensive special projects when required

Leading Indicators

Along the way, you must regularly make sure your plan is on track. You do this by measuring how well things are going in your quest to meet your goals and achieve your objectives. Your leading indicators must be (a) measurable and specific ways you can regularly monitor your progress against your objectives and (b) consistent with your evaluation methodology addressed here. You should check your leading indicators at predetermined intervals (e.g., weekly, monthly, quarterly) so you can make any adjustments. Here are some quick examples:

- Meet monthly with 10 to 15 randomly selected employees and the CEO to discuss company performance and the market, obtain feedback on internal issues, and determine effectiveness of communications
- Make 60 calls per month with key editors about company news and editorial opportunities
- Have 15 or more conversations each quarter with analysts on company progress, key messages, and direction

- Gain two or more commitments each month for significant editorial coverage
- Secure one to three speaking opportunities each month
- Submit three or more entries to strategically important award competitions each quarter

Timetable

A timetable, either outlined in text or presented in a chart, must show the start and finish of all events within the context of the communications plan. This approach helps to ensure that all events, leading indicators, and milestones are met when planned. Key questions to answer in creating a timetable are:

- Can the program be done in the time allotted?
- Can the results be achieved in the time allotted?
- What contingencies can be made if any time is lost?

Budget and Resources

This is an outline and explanation of what will be needed for each aspect of the plan and how much each aspect will cost during the sequence of events. It also summarizes total costs and, if appropriate, makes any comparisons to similar or related programs. Include items like postage, mileage, labor, overhead, and 10% for unforeseen expenses. Identify major supporters and financial resources. Bottom line: The benefits of the plan justify the costs for doing the work.

Evaluation

Now you must measure how effective the plan was toward inducing cooperation with target publics. This step should employ quantitative research methods, like written or phone surveys and content analyses of media coverage, and/or qualitative research methods, like focus groups and one-on-one interviews. The methods used here must be consistent with those used in the leading indicators, and measuring outputs, outtakes, outcomes, and outgrowths are integral. Some key questions to answer when designing your measurement scheme are as follow:

- How will I measure the success of reaching the plan's objectives?

- How have the critical success factors affected the plan's success?
- What have my leading indicators told me?
- Can I create a means for continuous feedback from my target audiences?
- Did the target audiences receive the messages?
- What was the extent of any print and broadcast media coverage?
- How was the organization portrayed in media reports?
- What do people think about the organization now as compared to their opinions before the plan was implemented?
- Did the plan fall within budget and were the resources sufficient?
- What unforeseen circumstances affected the plan's success?

Compile the data, analyze the results, and report on the findings. Also state your conclusions and propose ways to act. Use this report to help you create future evaluations and communication plans. Finally, you should take the opportunity to note ways to improve things along the way and at the end of the project. Your postmortem should address how to do things next time, including alternative methods, discourse, channels, and so on.

Basic Plan Workability

In a strategic PR plan, how the team would make its objectives a reality is possible through unique public relations strategies. For example, to meet the objective for establishing a market niche that a company can lead, possible PR strategies could include obtaining key media coverage and industry analyst support of the company and its market niche leadership, sharing information on the market positioning and future direction with the company's "family" of employees and affiliated organizations, and recruiting customers and "influencers" to speak on behalf of or write articles about the company based on their successes with its products.

Embedded in the PR plan's objectives are specific, measurable goals, and PR strategies are supported by tactical activities to get certain results specified in the plan. All of these and other elements are covered in the plan template, which also incorporates the rhetorical and organizational dimensions of the Burke–Weick synthesis—the dramatistic organizing of public relations. So, the fundamental mission for any communications plan—even the public relations function—is to inspire cooperation between an organization and its publics by structuring people's thinking about something in ways that use language effectively and ethically in appropriate PR genres.[20]

PUBLIC RELATIONS' VALUE CONTRIBUTION

A strategic approach for the dramatistic organizing of public relations, on a broader level, should not be developed in isolation from other functional areas, especially if its focus is an annual plan for corporate publicity or a concentrated promotional effort, like a product launch. Public relations works among other operating areas of an organization. Marketing, finance, legal, human resources, research and development, sales, and operations could all be affected by and benefit from public relations. These functions may deserve to be included in the PR plan in some ways, depending on the business needs and the company's overall strategic plan. For example, marketing's promotional advertising could be timed with editorial placements in publications. Financial performance should be echoed in relevant press releases, company backgrounders, and conversations with influential people in the media or among industry analysts. Legal staff should review PR discourse before it is released and may require management of legal issues. Human resources may require certain employee communications about new benefits plans or other internal programs or issues. Research and development may have created a break through technology that works more simply, cheaply and effectively than anything available. Sales would need published articles and success stories about the company and its customers. And operations would look to PR to publicize major product or service achievements that affect the company, its customers, and the competition.

These kinds of organizational needs show how deeply public relations can penetrate an organization. Even going a step further, public relations can help corporate leaders reach out to their publics by communicating what they and the organization stand for in the market and society. So an overall strategic communications program would integrate PR with executives and other corporate functions to build stronger relationships with an organization's internal and external publics that "create and protect [its] brand and reputation" (Caywood, 1997, p. xi). Through such planned integration, public relations practitioners can anticipate corporate or policy issues that may gain importance and account for them in the formal communication plan.

Key to public relations' success is delivering value. That concept can mean many things and has been the focus of numerous books and articles in the trade press. Very basically, value means something has been made better than before or enables something to become better than it was. It is not necessarily tied to strictly financial measures of price, cost, asset worth, and so on. Nonfinancial measures can and should be linked to it (see Epstein & Birchard, 2000). For public relations, value is added constantly, but the traditional measurements for it have been problematic (e.g., advertising equivalences, clip counts, etc.), but they are at least useful as initial data point to indicate where to further measure campaign initiatives against business objectives (Oates, 2006, p. 12). In terms of any organization's "business," public relations is part of the *value chain* that brings a finished product, service or other output to a market or target public or customer.

Any organizational function exists within a defined value chain of other functions, and each function contributes to the organization's success or failure. In this way public relations is as important as research and development, finance and accounting, manufacturing, customer service, human resources, and so on. The value that each function contributes is just different, but it must be significant. As long as each organizational function is utilized, each one is expected to add value in specific ways, financial and nonfinancial. Functions that contribute significant value are retained and, perhaps, augmented. Those functions that add little, no, or take away value could well see their resources reallocated or eliminated. Indeed, concerted efforts have been made to determine more appropriate and accurate ways to account for public relations' value (e. g., Horton, 2006; Paine, Draper, & Jeffrey, 2008; Swedish Public Relations Association, 1996). Although it is not within the scope of this project to present any particular approach for calculating PR's value, it is vital to know that it must be done, ample sources are available, and appropriate methods must be used to do the job.

Value is demonstrated through measurements of performance, which are orchestrated through the single system of strategic planning, management control, and task-control processes covered earlier. A strategic plan includes performance measures in obvious places: goals, leading indicators, budget/resource allocations, and evaluation scheme. To determine value contributions, management controls are key, and performance measurements are the ways of tracking how well an organization and its operating units are getting the results needed to achieve objectives and realize the vision. Such measurements are based on data that are collected daily and reported on each day, week, month, and quarter—whichever periods are needed. These reports give management the information it needs to run the business, and the reports show employees how their work is paying off (or not). In general, accounting for value must minimally include regular and formal reporting (e.g., expenses, meetings, memos, progress reports, etc.) about the management of the public relations function and its constituent pursuits.

This work is part of a *corporate-wide* system for management control called a "performance measurement" or "performance management" system; the latter term refers to software solutions that undertake the measuring of organizational performance (see Geishecker & Zrimsek, 2002). For public relations, this system would naturally help to fulfill the principle of "enhancing the profession" by being a tool for making the business case for public relations, the role it and its people play, and the value it contributes in dynamic times within and outside an organization. A performance-measurement system, as defined by the American Institute of Certified Public Accountants (AICPA) and Lawrence Maisel in their 2001 report, *Performance Measurement Practices Survey Results*, is one that "enables an enterprise to plan, measure, and control its performance and helps ensure that sales and marketing initiatives, operating practices, information technology resources, business decisions, and people's activities are aligned with business strategies to achieve desired business results and create shareholder value." Simply put, a business measures what it must to make sure it achieves its objectives and goals.[21]

Performance measures focus on *both* financial and nonfinancial aspects of the business (see DeWaal, 2002; Epstein & Birchard, 2000; Schiemann & Lingle, 1999). The measures are often taken through quantitative methods, but qualitative methods can and should be used as well for the most complete picture. Financial measures alone only show you where the company has been and only in terms of its revenue, cash and equivalents, debt, and obligations. Financial measures are inherently lagging indicators about what happened in the past, not leading indicators for the future. Sales could be linked to public relations, for example, by using a CRM system to track customers influenced by specific PR tactics. Add to this approach online data-analytics systems, like that offered by BusinessWire, that can track and trace people's use of public relations discourse from an initial click on a press release to the final sale (Laura Sturaitis, personal communication, October 27, 2008). These links to sales would necessarily tie public relations to other financial measures instead of just output-related costs. Nonfinancial measures take into account things beyond finances that add value to the company and cause one to look to the future. Nonfinancial measures, like brand recognition, community efforts, customer satisfaction, education, and so on, show key factors driving the business and indicate where a company is headed. Nonfinancial measures in public relations typically cover outtakes, outcomes, and outgrowths, and if conditions permit, these can be linked back to financial measures. In the C/K pickup case, the "Voice of the Public" surveys demonstrated nonfinancial performance measurements nicely. Indeed, the attitudinal ferment toward the company in the face of the situation did not hurt its financial performance and, in some ways, it may have helped while the news media, advertising, and public relations showed the company's and its products' strengths. Moreover, along with the case study, the surveys show how a quantitative *and* a qualitative approach can complement and provide greater support for each other's findings. Financial and nonfinancial measures together, then, make up a complete view of how well the business is doing in realizing its vision and fulfilling its strategic plan.

The trick in measuring performance effectively is to select only the things that are critical drivers of performance under the strategic plan. Public relations would have financial and, especially, nonfinancial measures to address. So the availability of key information is essential in measuring performance and achieving success. And that key information comes from both internal and external sources that keep tabs on all aspects of the business important to management, employees, suppliers, investors, partners, and the like. Most importantly, cause-and-effect relationships among the financial, customer-focused, business-process, and innovation/learning domains of a business (see Kaplan & Norton, 1996) help to determine which things are strategically important to measure and report on.

According to the American Productivity and Quality Center (2002), "performance measures allow employees to gain a greater sense of accountability, personal ownership, problem solving, and priorities based on stakeholder [e.g., employees, investors, suppliers, customers] needs. Organizations are likely to experience improvements in performance, fairness, objectivity, consistency, response time, and decision making. Performance measures also allow organizations to implement a common language and to be alerted to issues on the horizon." (Think of the benefits at least to public relations' image with management.) Organizations apply a performance management system based directly on the company's strategic plan. Effective performance measures should focus on key/strategic business factors; be a mix of past, present and future; balance the needs of all stakeholders; start at the top and flow down to the bottom; and have targets that are based on research and reality rather than being arbitrary (Coveney, Ganster, Hartlen, & King, 2003).

Any performance management system that tracks a company's results effectively against a corporate strategic plan will reflect the following characteristics, as described in Coveney et al. (2003):

- Align top-level strategic objectives and bottom-level initiatives.
- Identify opportunities and problems in a timely fashion.
- Determine priorities and allocate resources based on those priorities.
- Change measurements when the underlying processes and strategies change.
- Delineate responsibilities, understand actual performance relative to responsibilities, and reward and recognize accomplishments.
- Take action to improve processes and procedures when the data warrant it.
- Plan and forecast in a more reliable and timely fashion.

Again, the measurements can be taken in either or both quantitative and qualitative ways. It is important for everyone in an organization to know that performance expectations are defined on an annual basis and applied periodically. This means that management begins a year with certain expectations, and each department works toward meeting or exceeding those expectations. The assumption is that performance expectations for the year will be met or exceeded as defined in the corporate strategic plan. Only a major circumstance, like a severely faltering economy, a new and aggressive competitor, a devastating natural disaster, or unexpected heightened demand for a company's offerings, would significantly affect its ability to achieve its objectives and probably require changes to the strategic plan and each department's work.

Major corporations, including GM and others, already recognize public relations' value by including it as a stand-alone, executive-management function. But the vast majority of organizations do not. Public relations professionals must understand their organizations' basic business issues, management theory, performance measurement, and the work of their peers in other organizational functions. The bottom line: Public relations' value can only be known and appreciated when it can be clearly demonstrated as directly linked to an organization's business strategy and performance. The dramatistic organizing approach to public relations subsumes the salient features of successful public relations and, most important, connects the dots between the operating function and a larger organization's business. Furthermore, the dramatistic organizing approach to public relations applies a qualitative, critical-analytical method that can balance quantitative, scientific management methods. As the case study showed, the strengths of the former can make up for weaknesses in the latter, and vice versa.

APPENDIX A
Sample Public Relations Discourse About the C/K Pickup Issue

PREPARED STATEMENT

The following is a statement from General Motors on the December 8 announcement by the National Highway Traffic Safety Administration that it plans to investigate fuel tank safety of 1973-1987 GM full-size pickup trucks:

...

We welcome the agency's decision because it will move the fact-finding process away from the sensationalized, wildly exaggerated charges of the last few weeks. Recent experience has demonstrated that the media is not the appropriate venue in which to investigate and resolve such a complex technical matter. Given that, the initiation of a formal NHTSA investigation, based upon fact and sound engineering, statistical and related science, and the directly relevant federal safety standard, is desirable.

After a full investigation, we trust and believe the agency will conclude -- as any fair reviewer would -- that there is no basis upon which to conclude that these vehicles contain a safety-related defect.

The commencement of the agency's investigation is a continuation of the inquiry recently begun by the NHTSA. This in no way suggests that the vehicles are unsafe or that they should be recalled.

Some people may feel that, given the facts, it is regrettable to undertake such a costly and time-consuming process at this critical time for the agency, the industry, the economy and our company. However, we at General Motors fully understand the agency's need for more time to review the available data and we welcome the seriousness with which it is conducting its inquiry.

Contact: Bill O'Neill and Ed Lechtzin at GM Public Relations/Washington
202-775-5008

# # #

Reprinted with permission.

PRESS RELEASE

GENERAL MOTORS CORPORATION
General Motors Building, Detroit, Michigan 48202

NEWS

For Release Immediately, Monday, February 8, 1993   Contact: Bill O'Neill or
Ed Lechtzin
(313) 556-2027

DETROIT -- General Motors contends the **Dateline NBC** segment that showed rigged car-truck crashes to unfairly characterize that GM's 1973-1987 full-size pickup trucks are prone to side impact post-collision fires is part of an orchestrated campaign by plaintiff lawyers and others to create a "poisoned atmosphere" designed to prevent a correct, scientifically based evaluation of the trucks.

At a press conference to announce the filing of a suit against the National Broadcasting Company and The Institute for Safety Analysis, Harry Pearce, a GM executive vice president and general counsel, also produced a January 25, 1993, letter from the Institute For Injury Reduction (IIR) that he said reinforced GM's claim. (A copy of the letter is attached.)

In the letter to IIR supporters, Ben Kelley, head of the organization founded and funded by trial lawyers, solicited funds to stage a "GM Pickup Truck Fire Test" by the "contractor used by **Dateline NBC** at our suggestion, with a modified design further enhancing the likelihood of a real-world impact resulting in a fire..."

"It is clear that these people will go to any lengths to forward their viewpoint," said Mr. Pearce. "They are not satisfied with misrepresenting GM's own experimental tests, but have admitted that they would 'modify' a vehicle to get a fire to occur. This is blatant deception."

Mr. Pearce also showed a second letter -- from Cindy Raffles of the IIR to IIR Founders and Sustainers -- asking for help in locating "a GM insider -- past or present, identified or not -- to be interviewed about the company's attitudes, practices and misperformance."

According to her letter, IIR is "working with CBS **Prime Time Live** again, this time on an analysis of GM's current mammoth difficulties -- most of them self-made -- including making a safe product." **Prime Time Live** is actually an ABC program. (A copy of her letter is attached).

\# \# \#

2/8/93

Reprinted with permission.

BACKGROUNDER

FACTS ABOUT GM'S 1973-1987 PICKUP TRUCKS

The National Highway Traffic Safety Administration (NHTSA) in December opened an investigation into the safety of GM full-size pickup trucks built between the 1973 and 1987 model years. However, the agency itself has emphasized that "granting the petition does not indicate that the agency has determined that a safety-related defect exists in these vehicles." We welcome the agency's decision because it moves the fact-finding process away from the sensationalized, wildly exaggerated charges of the last few months. After a full investigation, GM trusts and believes the agency will conclude -- as any fair reviewer would -- that there is no basis upon which to conclude that these vehicles contain a safety-related defect.

General Motors is committed to building safe products. For more than half a century now, GM has been a pioneer in automotive safety research, design and manufacturing. The issue is not as simple as some of our critics would suggest. The following explanation provides facts that our critics have known -- but have chosen to ignore.

The 1973 Through 1987 C/K Pickup Trucks' Safety Record
The best available field data clearly show that, specifically in side collisions, the risk of fatal injury to full-size 1973-1987 model year pickup truck occupants has been essentially the same for occupants of GM, Ford and Dodge pickups.

State accident surveys show that these GM trucks have experienced an extremely low rate of post-collision fires, around the same as that of full-size pickups sold during the same years by the other two major manufacturers. Why is this important? Because the fuel tanks in those other manufacturers' trucks were located right where the critics seem to want them: between the frame rails. Those other trucks aren't defective, and ours aren't either.

The Critics Are Wrong
Certain lawyers -- and advocacy groups they fund -- have been saying recently that the side-mounted fuel system on these trucks is unsafe. The U.S. government has a tough safety standard for this very issue of side-impact, post-collision fuel system integrity. This standard first became effective for pickup trucks in the 1977 model year. Since the 1978 model year, the standard has required that the trucks' fuel systems be able to withstand a 4,000 lb. side-impact barrier collision at 20 mph.

- **Fact:** In most cases, these trucks substantially <u>exceed</u> the requirements of the federal fuel safety standard.

- **Fact:** In 1972, five model years before the 20 mph standard was required, GM tested its C/K model pickups against its own **30 mph** side moving barrier performance objective, using a standard Society of Automotive Engineers (SAE) 4,000 lb. barrier. The trucks met this internal GM objective.

- **Fact:** Over the years, GM has continued to test and improve the fuel system on these trucks. In 1981, GM even considered applying an internal 50 mph vehicle-to-vehicle side-impact objective to these trucks -- an energy level well beyond the energy level of the government standard. Between 1981 and 1984, we tested 22 car-to-truck crash tests at 50 mph in a development program. As a result of what we learned, improvements were made and implemented with the 1984 models.

<u>We do not apologize for improvements we make. That's what safety leaders do. They make improvements over time.</u>

The Side-Mounted Fuel System Design Is Not Defective

These lawyers' groups and their self-proclaimed safety experts would have you believe that GM knew of a defect but proceeded with its design anyway. That charge is absolutely untrue. GM engineers never knew of any "defect" because there isn't one.

As they do with all products, GM engineers examined design alternatives very carefully including the design suggested by our critics. They concluded that our side-mounted design offered excellent safety performance. And contrary to what the critics have been saying, this design was **rigorously tested**.

- In one side-impact test done in 1972, a 4,500 lb. station wagon was propelled at 35 mph directly at the filler neck of a new 1973 pickup truck. What little fuel seepage there was -- less than a teacup -- came from the weld seam which was promptly redesigned before this truck went into production.

These Critics Are Misleading The Public

One typical, favorite tactic of these groups is to mischaracterize a manufacturer's efforts to go beyond required safety standards.

- You may have seen some videos on the news or other TV shows, in which a truck's fuel tank leaks in a collision. These people would have you believe that these videos show production vehicles -- like the one you may own -- undergoing routine tests at levels comparable to the government standard. But that's not what the videos show.

- In fact, these videos show the <u>developmental</u> tests of <u>experimental</u> fuel systems being struck **at 50 mph**, part of a process intended to improve fuel system performance.

These groups also contend that our totally new and redesigned 1988 model year trucks are proof that all our previous designs (and especially those we sold from 1973-1987) are faulty. That too, is a **gross distortion and blatant manipulation of the facts.** The truth is that the all new 1988 model design was improved in many ways over the previous models. But that's what we hope to do with every new model car and truck -- stretch ourselves to implement new technology, make progress, provide constant safety improvements over time.

Post-Collision Fires Are Extremely Rare Events

You may have gotten the impression from media reports that post-collision fires are common events. For example, the head of one of these groups recently made the wildly irresponsible charge on national television that post-collision fires in these GM trucks might be happening "daily." They definitely are not.

GM is not saying that these post-collision fires <u>never</u> happen. They do unfortunately occur and they can and do occur in every model car and truck on the road. But the critics haven't told you how rare these events are. For example, in the 1973-1987 C/K pickup truck population alone, a crash fatality where there was also a post-collision fire has occurred once in every 1,172,000,000 (1.17 billion) miles driven. Put in terms of a typical 10-mile, 20 minute trip in one of these trucks -- another way to understand the nature of this risk -- a side collision fatal fire has occurred, on average, once in every 115 million trips.

# # #

Reprinted with permission.

WRITTEN CORRESPONDENCE

November 10, 1994

The President of the United States
The White House
Washington, D.C. 20500

Dear Mr. President:

Secretary Federico Peña's decision that a safety defect exists in certain General Motors C/K pickup trucks, if allowed to stand, threatens the entire automotive industry by creating needless, unreasonable regulatory confusion.

In essence, the practical result of the Secretary's decision is that compliance of a vehicle design with a very specific performance requirement of a Federal Motor Vehicle Safety Standard is irrelevant if the Secretary determines years later that the vehicle manufacturer should have selected an equally compliant design used by another manufacturer because it has had better performance in one particular accident mode.

Basically, the Secretary's approach to motor vehicle safety means the industry cannot rely on federal safety standards to design its cars and trucks. Inevitably, after years of production, some designs will always exhibit better performance than other designs in some specific accident subcategory, and in some constructed test, not based on a performance standard. The Secretary's approach means that the vehicles performing less well could be subject to recall and increased product liability exposure, even though they met or exceeded a directly relevant performance requirement of a federal standard.

This is not rational regulation of the automotive industry, and we are extremely concerned that this decision will establish a precedent which will completely undermine the regulatory process itself as well as the relationship between the industry and agencies that regulate it. We hope that, as President, you will address the intolerable state of regulatory uncertainty that will otherwise result from Secretary Peña's decision.

Sincerely,

Robert J. Eaton
Chairman and CEO
Chrysler Corporation

Alex Trotman
Chairman and CEO
Ford Motor Company

John F. Smith, Jr.
President and CEO
General Motors Corporation

Reprinted with permission.

PITCH LETTER

General Motors Corporation

December 19, 1994

Dear Colleague:

As you know, General Motors recently reached agreement with the U.S. Department of Transportation concerning our 1973-87 full-size C/K pickups. The government has agreed to end its investigation of the C/K side-mounted fuel tanks. The Transportation Secretary's initial decision will be voided and the investigation will be closed. That is consistent with the recommendation of National Highway Traffic Safety Administration experts -- and reportedly the legal advice of the Department of Justice. For good reasons, the safety performance of these trucks will no longer be under review by the government.

The Center for Auto Safety and Public Citizen, two organizations funded by and closely affiliated with plaintiffs' attorneys in ongoing contingent-fee product liability lawsuits against GM, say they intend to continue their media attacks on the C/K pickups. The critics of these trucks have concocted figures, mischaracterized documents and obscured their motives. As you evaluate the DOT settlement and any future coverage by your publication, we'd like you to know exactly where GM stands.

First, GM's commitment to safety continues strong and unwavering. Rather than expend resources litigating against the government, even from a position of strength, GM has agreed to devote over $50 million to automotive safety research, anti-drunk driving campaigns, and child safety seat purchases for low-income families -- programs in which DOT will join and coinvest approximately $27 million. These programs will advance automotive safety in concrete ways that will make travel safer and better protect the American public against accidents and injuries.

Second, GM's faith in its engineers, designers, dealers, and employees is steadfast. GM is determined to defend the quality and integrity of their work.

Our critics charge that GM knowingly produced and sold a dangerous product, and that we "bought" our way out of responsibility for this product. That is simply false. There is not now, and never was, any legal basis for a recall of the C/K pickup, or for a determination of unreasonable safety risk. The C/K pickups protect their occupants as well as or better than most vehicles on the road today, in side impact collisions as well as in collisions generally.

In weighing the critics' allegations, I hope you will take the time to review the enclosed fact sheet of information about GM's recent agreement with the Department of Transportation -- and about the C/K's undeniably strong safety record in real-world driving.

Please feel free to contact me if I can be of any further assistance.

Sincerely,

Bruce G. MacDonald
Vice President
Corporate Communications

Reprinted with permission.

WRITTEN CORRESPONDENCE

General Motors Corporation

January 4, 1995

Dear GM Stockholder:

As you know, General Motors recently reached agreement with the U.S. Department of Transportation concerning our 1973-87 full-size C/K pickups. The government has agreed to end its investigation of the C/K side-mounted fuel tanks, the Transportation Secretary's initial decision will be voided, and the investigation will be closed. For good reasons, the safety performance of these trucks will no longer be under review by the government.

This outcome is consistent with the recommendation of National Highway Traffic Safety Administration experts that the investigation should be closed because C/K pickups do not pose an unreasonable risk to safety.

There will be continued media coverage of this crucial issue, much of a negative nature generated by our critics. The public interest in motor vehicle safety is well served by the DOT/GM agreement, and we would like you to know exactly where GM stands.

First, GM's commitment to safety continues strong and unwavering. Rather than expend resources litigating against the government, even from a position of strength, GM has agreed to devote over $50 million to automotive safety research, anti-drunk driving campaigns, and child safety seat purchases for low-income families -- programs in which DOT will join and coinvest approximately $27 million. These programs will advance automotive safety in concrete ways that will make travel safer and better protect the American public against accidents and injuries.

Second, GM's faith in its engineers, designers, dealers, and employees is steadfast. GM is determined to defend the quality and integrity of their work. GM's case was strong and clear throughout the government's investigation, one of the most comprehensive ever conducted:

- The C/K pickup meets or exceeds all federal safety requirements, including particularly the government standard for fuel system performance in side collisions.

- The real-world experience of C/K pickups demonstrates that they protect occupants well against injury in collisions. GM's 1973-87 C/K pickups have a significantly lower rate of fatal injury in side collisions than the vast majority of other models in use -- less than half the rate of passenger cars generally, in fact, and a lower rate than 95 percent of all the cars on the road.

General Motors Building 3044 West Grand Boulevard Detroit, Michigan 48202

January 4, 1995
Page 2

- In side impacts by another motor vehicle, C/K pickups have a significantly lower rate of fatal or major injury than pickups made by GM's two leading competitors.

- In side impacts, the risk of a fire occurring in a C/K pickup is remote and no different than the risk in full-size pickups made by GM's competitors.

- At least 50 passenger car models on the road today have a fire rate in fatal side impacts that is higher than, or statistically indistinguishable from, that of GM's C/K pickups.

Our critics charge that GM knowingly produced and sold a dangerous product and that we "bought" our way out of responsibility for this product. That is simply false. There is not now, and never was, any legal basis for a recall of the C/K pickup or for a determination of unreasonable safety risk. The C/K pickups protect their occupants as well as or better than most vehicles on the road today, in side impact collisions as well as in collisions generally.

The two groups publicly unhappy with the result -- the "Center for Auto Safety" (CFAS) and "Public Citizen" -- have a direct financial and political alliance with trial attorneys in ongoing product liability lawsuits against GM. Their position shows more clearly than ever their disdain for public safety when it doesn't advance their agenda.

From any objective view of the facts and circumstances, General Motors and the Department of Transportation have reached an agreement that benefits everyone.

Sincerely,

Bruce G. MacDonald
Vice President
Corporate Communications

Reprinted with permission.

APPENDIX B
Public Awareness and Opinion About the C/K Pickups

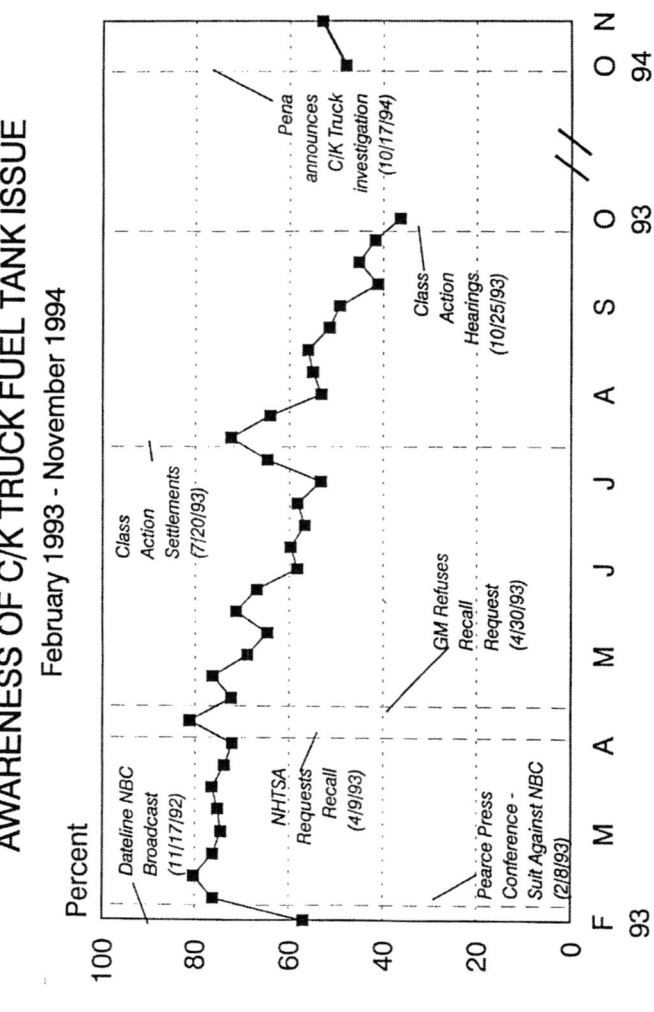

AWARENESS OF C/K TRUCK FUEL TANK ISSUE
February 1993 - November 1994

Dateline NBC Broadcast (11/17/92)
Pearce Press Conference - Suit Against NBC (2/8/93)
NHTSA Requests Recall (4/9/93)
GM Refuses Recall Request (4/30/93)
Class Action Settlements (7/20/93)
Class Action Hearings (10/25/93)
Pena announces C/K Truck investigation (10/17/94)

Source: Voice of the Public – Daily Tracking
Audience: General Public; Adults 18+
Sample Size: 267
Margin of Error +/- 5.9

Have you seen or heard anything recently about pickup truck fuel tanks?

*NOTE: Question added End of February 1993

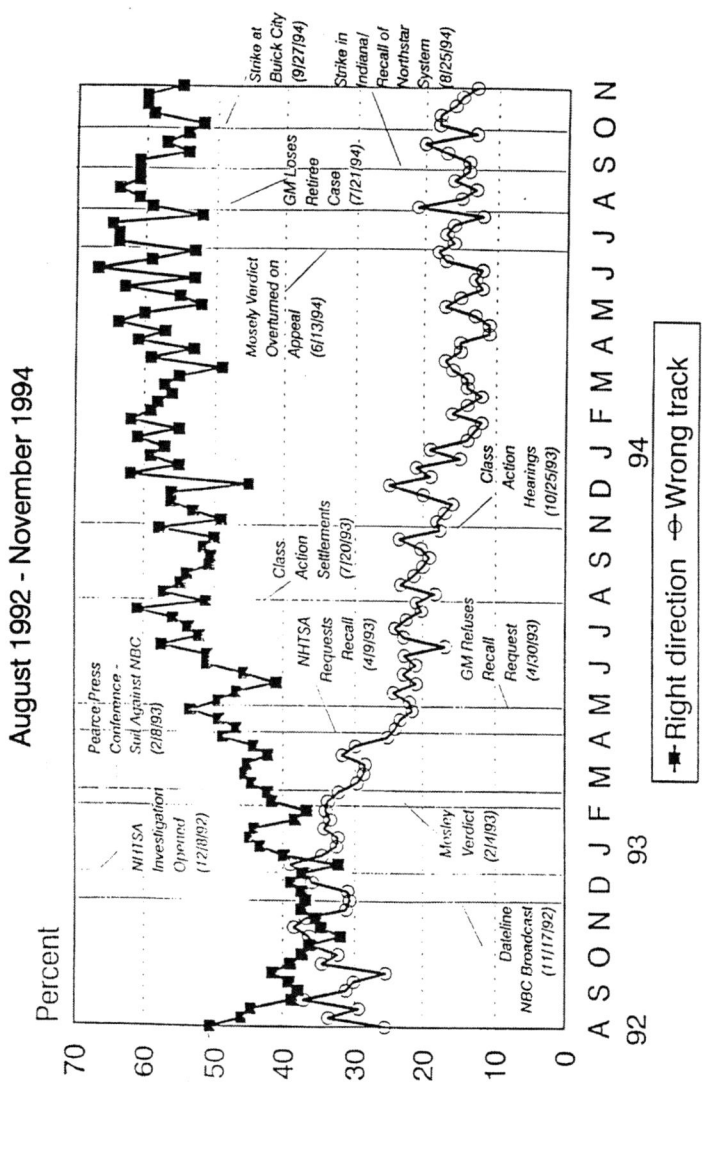

GM RIGHT DIRECTION vs WRONG TRACK: CK TRUCK EVENTS
August 1992 - November 1994

Events annotated on chart:
- Dateline NBC Broadcast (11/17/92)
- NHTSA Investigation Opened (12/8/92)
- Pearce Press Conference - Suit Against NBC (2/8/93)
- Mosley Verdict (2/4/93)
- NHTSA Requests Recall (4/9/93)
- GM Refuses Recall Request (4/30/93)
- Class Action Settlements (7/20/93)
- Class Action Hearings (10/25/93)
- Mosely Verdict Overturned on Appeal (6/13/94)
- GM Loses Retiree Case (7/21/94)
- Strike at Buick City (9/27/94)
- Strike in Indiana/ Recall of Northstar System (8/25/94)

■ Right direction   ○ Wrong track

Generally speaking, would you say that General Motors is going in the Right Direction or has it pretty seriously gotten off on the Wrong Track?

Source: Voice of the Public -- Daily Tracking
Audience: General Public; Adults 18+
Sample Size: 300 per week/1,200 per month

APPENDIX C
General Motors Public Relations Texts Used*

---

*Permission has been granted to the author for the use and quotation of excerpts from the texts outlined here.

BACKGROUNDERS (B)

TEXT NO.	DATE	TITLE/TOPIC
B-1	11/16/92	1973-1987 General Motors C/K pickups: Compliance and beyond [released with a statement and two other backgrounders of same date; deals with allegations that the pickups are unsafe]
B-2	11/16/92	Post-collision fires are extremely rare events [released with a statement and two other backgrounders of same date; deals with allegations that the pickups are unsafe]
B-3	11/16/92	General Motors a leader in automotive safety [released with a statement and two other backgrounders of same date; deals with allegations that the pickups are unsafe]
B-4	12/8/92	Facts you should know about the GM pickup truck controversy
B-5	12/18/92	Facts about GM's 1973-1987 pickup trucks
B-6	5/7/93	General Motors response to NHTSA: Summary
B-7	11/10/94	Thoughts on "unprecedented" and "unlawful" [part of package sent about the letter to President Clinton from the CEOs of the Big 3]
B-8	12/19/94	Setting the record straight on C/K pickups: The GM–DOT agreement [printed on press release letterhead]
B-9	12/19/94	GM 1973-1987 C/K pickup truck [captions for a series of graphs showing statistical relationships between the pickups and other vehicles; uses press release letterhead]
B-10	1/23/95	An abbreviated chronology of key events that have occurred regarding GM's 1973-1987 full-size C/K pickups
B-11	4/18/95	C/K class action cases—background [summarizes key points on lawsuits filed against the company regarding the C/K pickups; this text accompanied a prepared statement of the same date]

FREQUENTLY ASKED QUESTIONS (FAQ)

TEXT NO.	DATE	TITLE/TOPIC
FAQ-1	11/10/94	FAQs embedded as part of statement about the letter sent to President Clinton by the CEOs of the Big 3
FAQ-2	9/5/96	Questions & answers regarding the 9/3/96 mailing of court-approved notices in the C/K class-action settlement agreement

General Motors Public Relations Texts Used 193

| FAQ-3 | 12/26/96 | Questions & answers regarding the status of the C/K class-action settlement agreement—as of December 26, 1996 |
| FAQ-4 | 3/13/97 | Questions & answers regarding the status of the C/K class-action settlement agreement—as of March 13, 1997 |

NEWSLETTERS (N)

TEXT NO.	DATE	TITLE/TOPIC
N-1	11/19/92	*GM International Newsline* [reprints full text of W. J. O'Neill's letter to R. Read, *Dateline NBC* producer]
N-2	3/16/93	*GM Focus: Special Report* [full-color, four-page, tabloid size; dedicated to the press conference and the issue in general]
N-3	4/13/93	*GM International Newsline* [covers NHTSA information request and GM's response]
N-4	11/18/94	*GM International Newsline* [reprints full text of statement PS-16; includes items on other topics]

PITCH LETTERS (PL)

TEXT NO.	DATE	TITLE/TOPIC
PL-1	5/20/93	Dear GM Communicators [pitch letter signed by W. J. O'Neill; introduces background information on C/K safety and attorney groups' motives]
PL-2	12/19/94	Dear Colleague [pitch letter signed by B. G. MacDonald; sent to editors to affirm key messages and introduce backgrounders on NHTSA agreement]

PRESS CONFERENCE (PC)

TEXT NO.	DATE	TITLE/TOPIC
PC-1	2/8/93	Harry Pearce press conference: February 1993 [video]

| PC-2 | 2/8/93 | In the matter of: General Motors Media Briefing: Harry Pearce – 2/8/93 [transcript] |

PRESS KITS (PK)

TEXT NO.	DATE	TITLE/TOPIC
PK-1	2/8/93	Press conference [prepared for event with Harry Pearce regarding *Dateline NBC*]
PK-2	5/20/93	Dear GM Editor [selected documents about the issue in general]
PK-3	11/10/94	C/K pickup truck update [concerns letter from Big 3 CEOs]
PK-4	12/21/94	C/K pickup informational package [collection of material sent to editors, writers, and dealers]

PRESS RELEASES (PR)

TEXT NO.	DATE	TITLE/TOPIC
PR-1	2/8/93	General Motors today filed suit against the National Broadcasting Company (NBC)... [released with the H. Pearce press conference]
PR-2	2/8/93	General Motors contends that the *Dateline NBC* segment that showed rigged car–truck crashes... [released with the H. Pearce press conference]
PR-3	2/8/93	The following chronology describes the contact between General Motors and *Dateline NBC*... [released with the H. Pearce press conference]
PR-4	2/8/93	The following are captions for the attached photographs... [released with the H. Pearce press conference]
PR-5	7/19/93	The following is a brief overview of the current status of GM pickup truck litigation...
PR-6	7/19/93	The following describes the procedure under which registered owners of GM's eligible full-size pickup trucks will be notified of the class-action settlements...
PR-7	7/19/93	Under terms of the settlement in the class actions involving 1973 to 1987 model C/K full-size pickup trucks, registered owners will have the opportunity to receive certificates for $1,000...

PREPARED STATEMENTS (PS)

TEXT NO.	DATE	TITLE/TOPIC
PS-1	11/16/92	The following statement deals with a news report on the release of documents by General Motors regarding its 1973 through 1987 model light-duty pickup trucks.
PS-2	12/2/92	General Motors statement on data submitted to NHTSA.
PS-3	12/3/92	General Motors spokesperson's statement regarding reports that NHTSA administrator is recommending an investigation of GM's 1973-1987 C/K light-duty pickup trucks.
PS-4	12/8/92	The following is a statement from General Motors on the December 8 announcement by the NHTSA that it plans to investigate fuel tank safety of 1973-1987 GM full-size pickups.
PS-5	12/8/92	The following is General Motors' response to a letter from Clarence Ditlow [executive director of the Center for Auto Safety] to General Motors on December 8, 1992.
PS-6	12/16/92	Spokesperson's statement to be used to respond to media inquiries regarding NHTSA's 12/16/92 information request in its GM pickup truck investigation.
PS-7	12/18/92	Spokesperson's statement to be used to respond to media inquiries regarding NHTSA's 12/16/92 information request in its GM pickup truck investigation—updated 12/18/92.
PS-8	2/9/93	GM response to NBC retraction [for *Dateline NBC* report on the C/K pickups]
PS-9	3/11/93	GM files two separate motions in Moseley case.
PS-10	4/9/93	Statement by William J. O'Neill, director of public affairs for General Motors' North American Operations, on the letter issued 4/9/93 by the NHTSA on GM's 1973-1987 full-size pickup trucks.
PS-11	7/19/93	General Motors today issued the following statement regarding the announcement that a settlement has been reached in class-action suits involving GM's 1973-1987 full-size pickups.
PS-12	10/17/94	General Motors statement regarding the announcement by the DOT of an initial defect determination relating to GM's 1973-1987 full-size C/K pickups.
PS-13	11/3/94	General Motors statement on Congressman Carr's call for an inspector general investigation of DOT secretary Peña's 10/17/94 action regarding GM C/K pickups.

PS-14	11/10/94	Statement concerning the letter sent to President Clinton by the CEOs of GM, Chrysler and Ford [embeds FAQs as part of the text]
PS-15	11/15/94	General Motors statement in response to transportation secretary Peña's 11/15/94 announcement that he will proceed with a public meeting in the C/K pickup truck issue.
PS-16	11/17/94	Statement attributable to Thomas A. Gottschalk, general counsel of General Motors Corporation, on the filing of a complaint by General Motors in the U.S. District Court for the Eastern District of Michigan (Detroit) naming Transportation Secretary Frederico Peña, the U.S. Department of Transportation and the NHTSA, and seeking a declaratory judgement and injunctive relief with regard to the Vehicle Safety Act and to GM's 1973-1987 full-size pickup trucks.
PS-17	12/6/94	The following statement has been issued by General Motors in response to the allegations and mischaracterizations regarding GM's 1973-1987 C/K full-size pickup trucks.
PS-18	3/7/95	General Motors statement regarding the agreement signed by the DOT and GM on March 7, 1995, ending the government's investigation of GM's 1970-1990 full-size pickups.
PS-19	4/18/95	GM spokesperson's statement regarding action taken by the U.S. Court of Appeals in Philadelphia in the GM C/K pickup class-action suits.
PS-20	9/11/95	General Motors statement regarding media reports on the settlement of a C/K pickup product liability lawsuit in Oklahoma and media reports of sanctions against GM in the case.
PS-21	9/11/95	General Motors statement in reply to the 9/11/95 press conference by plaintiffs' counsel announcing settlement of four C/K pickup cases.
PS-22	9/5/96	General Motors statement in response to the mailing of notifications to owners of C/K pickups involved in class-action lawsuits.
PS-23	12/26/96	General Motors statement on status of the settlement of class-action litigation involving C/K pickups.
PS-24	3/13/97	General Motors statement on status of the settlement of class-action litigation involving C/K pickups.
PS-25	2/16/98	General Motors statement regarding *McGee vs. General Motors*.

VIDEO PROGRAMMING (V)

TEXT NO.	DATE	TITLE/TOPIC
V-1	2/11/93	*GM This Week*: "Truck fire lawsuit" [GM drops defamation suit against NBC]
V-2	2/25/93	*GM This Week*: "Fuel tank reax [reaction]" [interviews with employees, dealers, and customers about press conference]
V-3	3/25/93	*GM This Week*: "NBC probe" [results of NBC probe into the *Dateline NBC* report on the pickups]
V-4	4/8/93	*GM This Week*: "Truck" [C. Ditlow accuses GM of withholding information]
V-5	4/15/93	*GM This Week*: "Trucks" [W. J. O'Neill statement on NHTSA request for voluntary recall]
V-6	4/22/93	*GM This Week*: "GM Truck Trial" [GM requests new trial in *Moseley v. GM* case]
V-7	5/6/93	*GM This Week*: "GM Truck/NHTSA" [GM rejects call for voluntary recall]
V-8	5/14/93	*GM This Week*: "GM truck papers" [data show pickups' safety]
V-9	12/23/93	*GM This Week*: "Truck settlement" [Philadelphia judge approved class-action settlement]
V-10	3/17/94	*GM This Week*: "C/K pickup lawsuit" [plaintiffs' attorneys filed lawsuit against GM for conspiracy to suppress information]
V-11	4/21/94	*GM This Week* : "Martinez/C/K pickups" [NHTSA head disqualifies self from ruling on pickups]
V-12	6/2/94	*GM This Week* : "CK update" [*Detroit News* says DOJ cannot fully prove a case against pickups]
V-13	6/16/94	*GM This Week* : "CK Georgia appeal" [GM wins in appeal in *Mosley v. GM* case]
V-14	10/20/94	*GM This Week* : "CK pickup/Pena" [NHTSA initial ruling that the pickups have a defect]
V-15	11/3/94	*GM This Week* : "C/K truck reax" [GM asks DOJ to settle the C/K issue in court]
V-16	11/17/94	*GM This Week* : "C/K truck update" [Peña decides against litigation and schedules a public hearing]
V-17	12/1/94	*GM This Week* : "C/K update" [covers reaction to erroneous report by C. Ditlow about an accident in Chicago over Thanksgiving]
V-18	12/8/94	*GM This Week* : "CK agreement" [GM and NHTSA reach agreement to settle issue and end C/K investigation]

V-19	3/16/95	*GM This Week*: "C/K settlement" [GM and NHTSA sign settlement agreement]
V-20	4/20/95	*GM This Week*: "GM truck coupons" [U.S. Court of Appeals in Philadelphia overturns proposed class-action settlement]
V-21	9/14/95	*GM This Week*: "CK truck update" [four lawsuits settled out of court]

WRITTEN CORRESPONDENCE (WC)

TEXT NO.	DATE	TITLE/TOPIC
WC-1	11/19/92	Mr. Robert Read [letter to *Dateline NBC* producer from W. J. O'Neill about the report on C/K pickups]
WC-2	12/2/92	Customers letters [from E. Lechtzin; informs GM communicators about form letters to respond to C/K pickup owners who write the automaker and all correspondence to the company should be directed to designated PR officials who will handle the responses]
WC-3	12/2/92	Dear GM (or Division) Truck Owner [form letter to owners of 1973-1987 C/K pickups who write to GM or one of its divisions]
WC-4	12/14/92	Updated customer letter on 1973-1987 pickup trucks [from E. Lechtzin; informs communicators that the form letter to customers has been revised and all correspondence to the company should be directed to designated PR officials who will handle the responses]
WC-5	1/4/93	GM pickup truck product liability trial—Atlanta [interoffice memorandum from E. Lechtzin informing GM communicators about the gag order given by the judge in the *Moseley v. GM* trial]
WC-6	3/16/93	C/K pickup truck special report [covering memo to GM division general managers about *GM Focus*, N-1]
WC-7	12/16/92	Dear GM Truck Owner [revised version of form letter to C/K pickup owners who write to GM]
WC-8	11/10/94	The President of the United States [signed by CEOs of the Big 3]
WC-9	1/4/95	Dear GM Stockholder [signed by B. G. MacDonald; summarizes the C/K pickup issue]
WC-10	6/10/97	DCS Message: General Motors Dealers [covers aspects about the class-action settlement certificates]

NOTES

1. I was an employee of General Motors from 1989 to 1997, and was working in GM's Service Technology Group at the company's Technical Center in Warren, Michigan, when GM began managing the issue of the safety of its 1973–1987 C/K pickup trucks and, subsequently, the controversial story about the trucks that aired on *Dateline NBC*. I watched the program that evening in November 1992 when it was broadcast. In February of the following year, I listened intently with a few of my fellow employees to a live radio broadcast of GM's response to *Dateline*'s story. As I listened to the coverage of the dramatic press conference, I could imagine the scene, the spokesperson from GM, and the material evidence he used to buttress his statements about the story's content. I remember being impressed by the well-crafted, detailed arguments that the speaker presented and being struck by the profound implications this event and the entire issue had—and would have—on GM, NBC, and other organizations, as well as on the practice of public relations. This study had its impetus in that personal experience.
2. Grunig (2005) presented a similar typology but used different terms that are congruent with Pavlik's: "1) research actually used *in* the practice of public relations; 2) critical, evaluative research *on* the practice of public relations; and 3) research *for* the practice of public relations—theoretical research that develops and tests strategies and methods that can be used in practice." I find Pavlik's more usable and useful because it is better defined. The prepositions Grunig emphasized in each of these three areas leaves much ambiguity to what each could refer.
3. Burke viewed his rhetorical theory both as epistemological under the term *logology* and as ontological under the term *dramatism* (Burke, 1978, 1985). My references to Burke's rhetorical system focus both on rhetoric as a way of knowing through symbolic action and on humans as symbol users (see Brock, 1985, 1995; Brock et al., 1985; Chesebro, 1992). My synthetic application of Burke's dramatistic critical method with Weick's theory of organizing functions both as a way

to explain how people are symbol users in the process of organizing and how people engage in symbolic action to make sense of enacted environments.
4. Another party—news media—plays a supporting role, but the opinions of journalists can be classified to fit into either of the two principal parties' roles or in neither role if coverage merely recounts events as they occurred. The general public and various other constituencies play additional roles in this case, but are in the background as benefactors of the symbolic action of the two main parties. Such benefactors include those who chose to enter litigation (individual or class actions) against GM, which means they subscribed to and participated in the non-GM groups' view of order.
5. The verdict in the *Moseley v. GM* trial was later overturned on an appeal. This reversal contributes to GM's purification and is addressed accordingly.
6. Although GM officials managed the C/K pickup issue publicly to achieve consubstantiality with the company's stakeholders, other GM staffs may well have played a part in quelling the issue. For example, GM officials engaged in the usual product and corporate advertising, which would bolster the image of the truck's current models and the corporation. And like many companies, GM has lobbyists working at the U.S. capitol and calling on senators, representatives, and other prominent federal officials whose decisions affect GM's business interests. Both the advertising and (especially) lobbying efforts likely played important (albeit supporting) roles in taming the C/K issue for GM; however, these two dimensions are beyond the scope of this project and can be better pursued separately.
7. I am grateful to David Richardson, then CEO of Wirthlin Worldwide, and Kathryn Collins, retired director of communications research for GM, for information, review, and feedback about the Voice of the Public (VOP) surveys covered in this subsection. But I am ultimately responsible for the analysis presented here. The VOP was a project for which both people were the principal leaders in their respective organizations during the C/K pickup issue.
8. To enact a criticism of Harry Pearce's remarks as forensic discourse would be an insightful and enlightening exercise, but inappropriate for this chapter, because such an analysis is beyond the scope of this volume.
9. Ample coverage of and reactions to GM's press conference is available in newspapers and magazines published on and after February 9, 1993. Many of these articles address the effect of Pearce's remarks on GM's external constituencies. Others dwell on the nature and future of journalistic ethics.
10. This conclusion opens the door to an analysis of Pearce's remarks as corporate apologia (see Benoit & Brinson, 1994; Hearit, 1996; Ulmer, 1999; Ware & Linkugel, 1973). Such an approach would be very appropriate for this discourse example, as it amounts to a defense of GM. However, rhetorical criticism of Pearce's remarks as corporate apologia would, methodologically speaking, detract from my focus on dramatistic organizing and require additional theoretical explanation and critical analysis through methods like those prescribed by Hearit or Ware and Linkugel.
11. Through this critical analysis of a corporate speaker, I do not intend to suggest that Pearce and those with whom he worked consciously enacted the environment dramatistically. (In his review of the issue during an interview, Lechtzin, 1997, stated that he devised a separate three-phase view of the issue retrospec-

tively, which has helped in the planning and execution of communication for other issues.) However, I do foresee that this analysis suggests that the analytical method can be extended into the strategic planning of organizational discourse.

12. No mention of the C/K pickup issue is ever made in GM's annual reports, but vehicle safety is accented, as in the 1994 annual report that features a section entitled "Programs in the Public Interest." That section includes a short segment, "Motor Vehicle Safety," that describes how GM is working with automakers worldwide on vehicle safety standards that can be upheld by all nations rather than each nation having its own regulations.

13. This treatment of the writing process of the swat team is admittedly very brief and cursory; however, to go deeper into that subject would be too far afield for this project. An ethnographic investigation of the writing process of the team and, indeed, reader reception of the texts could prove to be a fruitful, separate research project that would befit the realm of research on nonacademic writing (see Johnson-Eilola & Selber, 2004; Odell & Goswami, 1985, Spilka, 1993).

14. Legal obligations for "informal disclosure" by publicly held companies, like GM, adds another dimension to the organizing behavior of public relations officials. This concept basically refers to the variety of ways, outside of those required by the U.S. Securities and Exchange Commission and other nations' similar regulatory bodies, that public companies communicate with their investors and the investing community in general. A very useful and detailed resource on this dimension is Walton (1996).

15. Fundamentally, CRM is a management approach used collaboratively across an enterprise to learn more about customers' needs and behaviors, develop stronger relationships with them (especially to retain the "right" customers), and get more new ones. CRM systems include processes, facilitated by specialized computer software, that help bring together a lot of information about customers, sales, marketing effectiveness, responsiveness, and market trends that affect the many operations of a company, from sales and planning to manufacturing and research and development. When used analytically, a CRM system "applies a variety of data analysis and modeling techniques to discover patterns and trends in customer data. It predicts potential variations so organizations can react to changes before it is too late. Decision makers and front-line employees use these deep insights to understand what their customers want and predict what they will do next" (Phalen, 2001, p. 108). Its power for public relations is essentially untapped but should be, especially for strategic planning discussed in Chapter 7.

16. In a bigger-picture way, van Ruler (2005) provided another explanation: "Why do practitioners seem so reluctant to adopt scholarly work? Why do senior practitioners and CEOs keep on hiring practitioners without any public relations oriented education and/or scholarly approach? It is not because practitioners and their clients are "obstinate," [sic] but because they hold totally different views on what makes a practitioner a professional. Public relations scholars usually describe a view on professionalism that has been focused on requirements as a well-defined body of scholarly knowledge, completion of some standardized and prescribed course of study, examination and certification by a state and oversight by a state agency which has disciplinary powers over practitioner's behaviors" (p. 160).

17. My use of this term is not in reference to the American philosophical tradition of pragmatism, as championed by the likes of William James, Richard Rorty, and others. Although the fit of this philosophy in my argument at this early point in my chapter could be developed, I refrain from doing so in the interest of staying focused on my thesis. In my use of the terms, *pragmatic* and *pragmatism*, I am using them in a sense and reference virtually synonymous with that of "practical" and "practicality" and reflecting something being usable, useful, and used.
18. Six sigma is a business performance-management approach that uses statistical methods about variation in data and processes (denoted by the lowercase Greek letter sigma) to ensure high quality and reliability of products, services, and transactions. All system components must perform to specific targets, and so too must each critical aspect of every component. The idea is that a system will produce less than 3.4 errors or defects per million—produce the right thing the right way 99.9997% of the time (six standard deviations), which is nearly perfect (see Pande et al., 2002).
19. Admittedly, this work echoes much of the discourse conventions required for academic publishing, which is a kind of survival skill in this profession. My goal for projects on which I am working is to have them be usable, useful and used by practitioners and scholars alike (see Smudde, 2004a).
20. This strategic planning approach works, as WPPI Energy uses it (Anne Rodriguez, personal communication, July 12, 2009) and I used it in my industry work before coming to academia full time in 2002. It was central to my portfolio presented as part of the requirements for my becoming accredited in public relations (APR) through the PRSA. The approach also has played well in my teaching and consulting.
21. From large, multinational organizations to small, local businesses, performance measurements are necessary to keep a company on track. Gore's (1997) study, *Serving the American Public: Best Practices in Performance Measurement*, was undertaken by the U.S. government to document what high-performance public and private organizations do to be so successful and, especially, how they measure their performance. The study's participants featured people from a large number of organizations in the private and public sectors in the United States, Canada, and the United Kingdom. According to the study, successful performance measurement systems are characterized by the following aspects:

- *Leadership* is critical in designing and deploying effective performance measurement and management systems, where such executive involvement is active and personal, especially when it comes to communicating expectations and results.
- *A conceptual framework* is needed for any performance measurement system, and it features ways to think about and apply specified performance measures, like matrix systems, target setting, benchmarking, criteria for the Malcolm Baldrige National Quality Award or the International Standards Organization's certification.
- *Effective internal and external communication* are keys to successful performance measurement systems, where it depends on and demands open, honest and multidirectional communication among all stakeholders.

- *Accountability for results* must be clearly assigned and well understood. Everyone understands what it takes to be successful and where they are responsible for achieving organizational goals.
- Performance measurement systems must provide *the most relevant, timely, and strategically important information* for decision makers, not just compile data, so they can accurately assess progress and take action to achieve objectives and goals.
- *Compensation, rewards, and recognition* should be linked to performance measurements, tying financial and nonfinancial incentives directly to performance.
- Performance measurement systems should be *positive, not punitive*, which means the systems are "learning" systems that help everyone to identify what works and what doesn't so that the best approaches are maintained and the ineffective ones are repaired or replaced.
- *Results and progress* toward program commitments should be openly shared with employees, customers and other stakeholders so they know, at a high level and without compromising sensitive information, where the company is headed, how it will get there, and how it will measure progress.

Organizational members from the top down must be committed to applying these concepts so that everyone in the company knows where the company is headed and how they are going to get there. Also notice how important public relations is, especially from an internal standpoint. Public relations also plays a role with external audiences when reporting corporate performance.

REFERENCES

Adler, B. J. (1993). *"They are us": Identification strategies in the rhetoric of two Lutheran church organizations.* Unpublished doctoral dissertation, Wayne State University, Detroit.

Ainspan, N., & Dell, D. (2000). *Employee communication during mergers* (Rep. No. R-1270-00-RR). New York: The Conference Board.

Albert, S., & Whetten, D. A. (1985). Organizational identity. *Research in Organizational Behavior, 7,* 263-295.

Aldrich, H., & Herker, D. (1977). Boundary spanning roles and organization structure. *Academy of Management Review, 2,* 217-230.

Allen, M. W., & Caillouet, R. H. (1994). Legitimation endeavors: Impression management strategies used by an organization in crisis. *Communication Monographs, 61,* 44-62.

American Institute of Certified Public Accountants Inc., & Maisel, L. S. (2001). *Performance measurement practices survey results.* Jersey City, NJ: Author.

American Productivity and Quality Center. (2002). *Performance measurement benefits.* Houston, TX: Author. http://www.apqc.org/pm/pmbenefits.cfm (accessed July 30, 2009).

Anthony, R. N. (1988). *The management control function.* Boston, MA: Harvard Business School.

Arthur W. Page Society (2007). *The authentic enterprise: Relationships, values and the evolution of corporate communications.* New York: Author. http://www.awpagesociety.com/images/uploads/2007AuthenticEnterprise.pdf (accessed Nov. 19, 2008).

Auto safety groups want GM C-K pickup truck deal scuttled. (1996, July 2). *NewsEDGE.* Waltham, MA: Desktop Data.

Bailey, B. (2000). *Spin tactics: A guide to guerrilla media relations.* Saginaw, MI: Glovebox Guidebooks of America.

Baker, A. (2000, February 2). Web-tracking: As accurate as you want it to be. *webPR.* Cambridge, MA: MediaMap. http://www.mediamap.com/webpr.

Bantz, C. R. (1989). Organizing and the social psychology of organizing. *Communication Studies, 40*, 231-240.

Bantz, C. R. (1990). Organizing and enactment: Karl Weick and the production of news. In S. R. Corman, S. P. Banks, C. R. Bantz, & M. E. Mayer (Eds.), *Foundations of organizational communication: A reader* (pp. 133-141). New York: Longman.

Bantz, C. R., & Smith, D. H. (1977). A critique and experimental test of Weick's model of organizing. *Communication Monographs, 44*, 171-184.

Bazerman, M. (1998). *Judgment in managerial decision making* (4th ed.). New York: Wiley.

Beard, M. (2001). *Running a public relations department* (2nd ed.). London: Kogan Page.

Berg, D. M., & Robb, S. (1992). Crisis management and the paradigm case. In E. L. Toth & R. L. Heath (Eds.), *Rhetorical and critical approaches to public relations* (pp. 93-110). Hillsdale, NJ: Erlbaum.

Benoit, W. L., & Brinson, S. L. (1994). AT&T: "Apologies are not enough." *Communication Quarterly, 42*, 75-88.

Birch, J. (1994). New factors in crisis planning and response. *Public Relations Quarterly, 39*, 31-34.

Bivins, T. H. (1999). *Handbook for public relations writings: The essentials of style and format*. Lincolnwood, IL: National Textbook Company.

Blaney, J. R., Benoit, W. L, & Brazeal, L. M. (2002). Blowout! Firestone's image restoration campaign. *Public Relations Review, 28*, 379-392.

Boorstin, D. J. (1958). *The Americans: The colonial experience*. New York: Vintage Books.

Bostdorff, D. M., & Vibbert, S. L. (1994). Values advocacy: Enhancing organizational images, deflecting public criticism, and grounding future arguments. *Public Relations Review, 20*, 141-158.

Botan, C. H. (1994). Lee Iacocca as internal issues manager in speeches to employees and dealers. In M. W. Seeger (Ed.), *I gotta tell you* (pp. 29-41). Detroit: Wayne State University Press.

Botan, C. (2006). Grand strategy, strategy, and tactics in public relations. In C. Botan & V. Hazleton (Eds.), *Public relations theory II* (pp. 223-247). Mahwah, NJ: Erlbaum.

Botan, C. H., & Hazleton, V., Jr. (Eds.). (1989). *Public relations theory*. Hillsdale, NJ: Erlbaum.

Botan, C. H., & Hazleton, V., Jr. (Eds.). (2006). *Public relations theory II*. Mahwah, NJ: Erlbaum.

Bovet, S. F. (1995, October). Forecast 2001: A golden age for public relations looms. *Public Relations Journal, 12-14*, 38.

Boyd, J. (2004). Organizational rhetoric doomed to fail: R. J. Reynolds and the principle of the oxymoron. *Western Journal of Communication, 68*(1), 45-71.

Brancato, C. K. (2004). *Improving communications between companies and investors* (Rep. No. SR-04-01). New York: The Conference Board.

Brinson, S. L., & Benoit, W. L. (1996). Dow Corning's image repair strategies in the breast implant crisis. *Communication Quarterly, 44*, 29-41.

Brock, B. L. (1985). Epistemology and ontology in Kenneth Burke's dramatism. *Communication Quarterly, 33*, 94-104.

Brock, B. L. (1990). Rhetorical criticism: A Burkean approach revisited. In B. L. Brock, R. L. Scott, & J. W. Chesebro (Eds.), *Methods of rhetorical criticism: A twentieth-century perspective* (3rd ed. rev., pp. 183-195). Detroit: Wayne State University Press.

Brock, B. L. (1995). Evolution of Kenneth Burke's criticism and philosophy of language. In B. L. Brock (Ed.), *Kenneth Burke and contemporary European thought: Rhetoric in transition* (pp. 1-33). Tuscaloosa: University of Alabama Press.

Brock, B. L. (1999). *Kenneth Burke and the 21st century*. Albany: State University of New York Press.

Brock, B. L., Burke, K., Burgess, P. G., & Simmons, H. W. (1985). Dramatism as ontology or epistemology: A symposium. *Communication Quarterly, 33*, 17-33.

Brock, B. L., Scott, R. L., & Chesebro, J. W. (Eds.). (1990). *Methods of rhetorical criticism: A twentieth-century perspective* (3rd ed. rev.) Detroit: Wayne State University Press.

Brothers, T., & Gallo, H. (Eds.). (1992). *Corporate strategies for effective communications* (Rep. No. 991). New York: The Conference Board.

Brown, M. E. (1969). Identification and some conditions of organizational involvement. *Administrative Science Quarterly, 14*, 346-355.

Brown, M. H., & McMillan, J. J. (1991). Culture as text: The development of an organizational narrative. *Southern Communication Journal, 57*, 49-60.

Budd, J. F., Jr. (2003). Public relations is the architect of its future: Counsel or courtier? Pros offer opinions. *Public Relations Review, 29*, 375-383.

Burke, K. (1966a). *Language as symbolic action: Essays on life, literature, and method*. Berkeley: University of California Press.

Burke, K. (1966b). Terministic screens. In K. Burke, *Language as symbolic action: Essays on life, literature and method* (pp. 44-62). Berkeley: University of California Press.

Burke, K. (1968a). *Counter-statement*. Berkeley: University of California Press.

Burke, K. (1968b). Dramatism. In D. L. Sills (Ed.), *International encyclopedia of the social sciences* (Vol. 7, pp. 445-452). New York: Macmillan.

Burke, K. (1969a). *A grammar of motives*. Berkeley: University of California Press.

Burke, K. (1969b). *A rhetoric of motives*. Berkeley: University of California Press.

Burke, K. (1970). *The rhetoric of religion: Studies in logology*. Berkeley: University of California Press.

Burke, K. (1973). *The philosophy of literary form*. Berkeley: University of California Press.

Burke, K. (1978). (Nonsymbolic) motion/(symbolic) action. *Critical Inquiry, 4*, 809-838.

Burke, K. (1984a). *Attitudes toward history* (3rd ed.). Berkeley: University of California Press.

Burke, K. (1984b). *Permanence and change: An anatomy of purpose* (3rd ed.). Berkeley: University of California Press..

Burke, K. (1985). Dramatism and logology. *Communication Quarterly, 33*, 89-93.

Burke, K. (1989). Poem. In H. W. Simons & T. Melia (Eds.), *The legacy of Kenneth Burke* (p. 263). Madison: University of Wisconsin Press.

Burns, R. G. (1997). *Denying harm: The social construction of image in the auto industry.* Unpublished doctoral dissertation, Florida State University, Tallahassee.

Cameron, G., & Sallot, L. (1996). Developing standards of professional performance in public relations. *Public Relations Review, 22*(1), 43-62.

Campbell, K. K., & Jamieson, K.H. (1986). Introduction (Special issue on genre criticism.) *Southern Speech Communication Journal, 51,* 293-299.

Cathcart, R. S. (1993). Instruments of his own making: Burke and media. In J.W. Chesebro (Ed.), *Extensions of the Burkean system* (pp. 287-308). Birmingham: University of Alabama Press.

Caywood, C. L. (Ed.). (1997). *The handbook of strategic public relations and integrated communications.* New York: McGraw-Hill.

Center for Automotive Safety. (1997, October 14). *Statement on 25th anniversary of GM firebomb pickups.* Washington, DC: Author.

Cheney, G. (1983a). On the various and changing meanings of organizational membership: A field study of organizational identification. *Communication Monographs, 50,* 342-362.

Cheney, G. (1983b). The rhetoric of identification and the study of organizational communication. *Quarterly Journal of Speech, 69,* 143-158.

Cheney, G. (1984, March). *Toward an ethic of identification.* Paper presented at The Burke Conference, Philadelphia, PA.

Cheney, G. (1988). On the facts of the text as the basis of human communication research. In J. A. Anderson (Ed.), *Communication yearbook* (Vol. 11, pp. 455-481). Newbury Park, CA: Sage.

Cheney, G. (1991). *Rhetoric in an organizational society: Managing multiple identities.* Columbia: University of South Carolina Press.

Cheney, G. (1992). The corporate person (re)presents itself. In E. L. Toth & R. L. Heath (Eds.), *Rhetorical and critical approaches to public relations* (pp. 165-183). Hillsdale, NJ: Erlbaum.

Cheney, G., & Dionisopoulos, G. N. (1989). Public relations? No, relations with publics: A rhetorical-organizational approach to contemporary corporate communication. In C. H. Botan & V. Hazleton, Jr. (Eds.), *Public relations theory* (pp. 135-157). Hillsdale, NJ: Erlbaum.

Cheney, G., & Frenette, G. (1993). Persuasion and organization: Values, logics, and accounts in contemporary corporate public discourse. In C. Conrad (Ed.), *The ethical nexus* (pp. 49-74). Norwood, NJ: Ablex.

Cheney, G., & McMillan J. J. (1990). Organizational rhetoric and the practice of criticism. *Journal of Applied Communication Research, 18,* 93-114.

Cheney, G., & Tompkins, P. K. (1987). Coming to terms with organizational identification and commitment. *Central States Speech Journal, 38,* 1-15.

Cheney, G., & Vibbert, S. L. (1987). Corporate discourse: Public relations and issue management. In F. M. Jablin, L. L. Putnam, K. H. Roberts, & L. W. Porter (Eds.), *Handbook of organizational communications: An interdisciplinary perspective* (pp. 165-194). Newbury Park, CA: Sage.

Chesebro, J. W. (1992). Extensions of the Burkean system. *Quarterly Journal of Speech, 78,* 356-368.

Christensen, L. T., & Cheney, G. (1994). Articulating identity in an organizational age. In J. A. Anderson (Ed.), *Communication yearbook* (Vol. 17, pp. 222-235). Newbury Park, CA: Sage.
Clintonites ram GM. (1993, April 14). *The Wall Street Journal* (Reprint).
Condit, C. M. (1992). Post-Burke: Transcending the sub-stance of dramatism. *Quarterly Journal of Speech, 78*, 349-355.
Corrado, F. M. (1993). *Getting the word out: How managers can create value with communications*. Homewood, IL: Business One Irwin.
Courtright, J. L., & Slaughter, G. Z. (2007). Remembering disaster: Since the media do, so must public relations. *Public Relations Review, 33*, 313-318.
Courtright, J. L., & Smudde, P. M. (Eds.). (2007). *Power and public relations*. Cresskill, NJ: Hampton Press.
Coveney, M., Ganster, D., Hartlen, B., & King, D. (2003). *The strategy gap: Leveraging technology to execute winning strategies*. Hoboken, NJ: Wiley.
Crable, R. E., & Vibbert, S. L. (1985). Managing issues and influencing public policy. *Public Relations Review, 11*, 3-16.
Crable, R. E., & Vibbert, S. L. (1995). Mobil's epideictic advocacy: "Observations" of Prometheus bound. In W. N. Elwood (Ed.), *Public relations inquiry as rhetorical criticism: Case studies of corporate discourse and social influence* (pp. 27-46). Westport, CT: Praeger.
Cragan, J. F., & Shields, D. C. (Eds.). (1981). *Applied communication research: A dramatistic approach*. Prospect Heights, IL: Waveland.
Cragan, J. F., & Shields, D. C. (1995). *Symbolic theories in applied communication research: Bormann, Burke and Fisher*. Cresskill, NJ: Hampton Press.
Croft, A.C. (2006). *Managing a public relations firm for growth and profit* (2nd ed.). Binghamton, NY: Best Business Books.
Cross, G. A. (1993). The interrelation of genre, text, and process in the collaborative writing of two corporate documents. In R. Spilka (Ed.), *Writing in the workplace: New research perspectives* (pp. 141-152). Carbondale: Southern Illinois University Press.
Cutlip, S. M. (1994). *The unseen power: Public relations, a history*. Hillsdale, NJ: Erlbaum.
Cutlip, S. M. (1995). *Public relations history: From the 17th to the 20th century, the antecedents*. Hillsdale, NJ: Erlbaum.
Cutlip, S. M. (1997). The unseen power: A brief history of public relations. In C. L. Caywood (Ed.), *The handbook of strategic public relations and integrated communications* (pp. 15-33). New York: McGraw-Hill.
Cutlip, S. M., Center, A. H., & Broom, G. M. (1994). *Effective public relations* (7th ed.). Upper Saddle River, NJ: Prentice-Hall.
D'Aprix, R. (1982). *Communicating for productivity*. New York: Harper & Row.
D'Aprix, R. (1996a). *Communicating for change*. San Francisco: Jossey-Bass.
D'Aprix, R. (1996b, January/February). The challenge of integration in the information age. *Communication World*, pp. 19-21.
D'Aprix, R. (1997, April/May). Partner or perish: A new vision for staff professionals. *Strategic Communication Management*, pp. 12-15.
D'Aprix, R. (2001, August-September). Reinventing the strategic communicator. *Strategic Communication Management*, pp. 32-35.

Darin, A.T. (1995, November 6). Ford loses $62.4 million Bronco II case. *Automotive News*, p. 2.

Davenport, T. H., & Beck, J. C. (2002). *The attention economy: Understanding the new currency of business*. Boston: Harvard University Press.

Deathridge, C. P., & Hazelton, V. (1998). Effects of organizational worldviews on the practice of public relations: A test of the theory of public relations excellence. *Journal of Public Relations Research*, 10(1), 57-71.

Deming, W. E. (1986). *Out of the crisis*. Cambridge: Massachusetts Institute of Technology Center for Advanced Engineering Study.

DeWaal, A. A. (2002). *Quest for balance: The human element in performance management systems*. New York: Wiley.

Dilenschneider, R.L. (Ed.). (1996). *Dartnell's public relations handbook* (4th ed.). Chicago: Dartnell Corp.

Dozier, D. M., Grunig, L. A., & Grunig, J. E. (1995). *Manager's guide to excellence in public relations and communications management*. Mahwah, NJ: Erlbaum.

Drucker, P. F. (1994). The theory of the business. *Harvard Business Review*, 72(5), 95-104.

Duncan, H. D. (1968). *Symbols in society*. New York: Oxford University Press.

Duncan, H. D. (1989). *Communication and social order*. New Brunswick, NJ: Transaction.

Eaton, R. J., Trotman, A., & Smith, J. F., Jr. (1994, November 10). Letter to the President of the United States.

Eggins, S., & Martin, J. R. (1997). Genres and registers of discourse. In T. A. Van Dijk (Ed.), *Discourse as structure and process* (pp. 230-256). London: Sage.

Elwood, W. N. (Ed.). (1995a). *Public relations inquiry as rhetorical criticism*. Westport, CT: Praeger.

Elwood, W. N. (1995b). Public relations is a rhetorical experience: The integral principle in case study analysis. In W. N. Elwood (Ed.), *Public relations inquiry as rhetorical criticism: Case studies of corporate discourse and social influence* (pp. 3-12). Westport, CT: Praeger.

Epstein, M. J., & Birchard, B. (2000). *Counting what counts: Turning corporate accountability to competitive advantage*. Cambridge, MA: Perseus.

Everett, J. L. (1994). Communication and sociocultural evolution in organizations and organizational populations. *Communication Theory*, 4, 93-110.

Ewen, S. (1996). Visiting with Edward Bernays. In S. Ewen, *PR! A social history of spin* (p. 18). New York: Basic Books.

Farrell, T. B., & Goodnight, G. T. (1981). Accidental rhetoric: The root metaphors of Three Mile Island. *Communication Monographs*, 48, 271-300.

Feds want GM pickup probe. (1992, December 3). *Detroit News*, p. 1.

Ferguson, S. D. (1999). *Communication planning: An integrated approach*. Thousand Oaks, CA: Sage.

Fialkow, J. (2000, March). See attached file...and other e-pitching no-nos. *Alert! Monthly Media & PR Bulletin*. Cambridge, MA: MediaMap.

Fink, S. (1986). *Crisis management*. New York: McGraw-Hill.

Filipczak, B. (1995, July). Obfuscation resounding: Corporate communication in America. *Training*, pp. 29-36.

Fisher, W.R. (1980). Genre: Concepts and applications in rhetorical criticism. *Western Journal of Speech Communication*, 44, 288-299.

Fitzpatrick, K. R., & Whillock, R. K. (1993). Assessing the impact of globalization on U.S. public relations. *Public Relations Review, 19*(4), 315-325.
Flower, L. S., & Hayes, J. R. (1982). Cognitive processes in writing. *College Composition and Communication, 32*, 365-387.
Foss, S. K. (1984). Retooling an image: Chrysler Corporation's rhetoric of redemption. *Western Journal of Speech Communication, 48*, 75-91.
Foss, S. K., Foss, K. A., & Trapp, R. (1991). Kenneth Burke. In *Contemporary perspectives on rhetoric* (2nd ed., pp. 169-207). Prospect Heights, IL: Waveland.
Foucault, M. (1972). *The archaeology of knowledge and the discourse on language* (A.M.S. Smith, Trans.). New York: Pantheon Books. (Original work published 1969)
Frazer, J. (1922, 1998). *The golden bough*. New York: Viking Press.
Garone, S. J. (Ed.). (1995). *Integrating business strategies with communications* (Rep. No. 1131-95-CH). New York: The Conference Board.
Garten, J. E. (2001). *The mind of the CEO*. New York: Basic, Perseus.
Gayeski, D.M. (1996). *Profiles in innovation: Managing corporate communication in changing times*. New York: OmniCom Associates.
Geishecker, L., & Zrimsek, B. (2002, July 18). *Use CPM to integrate the enterprise view* (ID No. LE-17-4266). Stamford, CT: Gartner.
General Motors Corporation. (1992). *1992 Annual report*. Detroit: Author.
General Motors Corporation. (1993a). *GM focus: Special report*. Detroit, MI: Author.
General Motors Corporation. (1993b, February 9). *GM this week*. Detroit, MI: Author.
General Motors Corporation. (1993c, June 16). *GM this week*. Detroit, MI: Author.
General Motors Corporation. (1993d, February 8). *In the matter of General Motors media briefing: Harry Pearce—2/8/93*. Unpublished transcript, Hamilton-Legato Deposition Centers, Troy, MI.
General Motors Corporation. (1994, November). *Voice of the public—Daily tracking*. Detroit, MI: Author.
General Motors Corporation. (1995, January 25). *Abbreviated chronology of key events that occurred regarding GM's 1973-1987 full-size C/K pickups*. Detroit: Author.
General Motors Corporation. (1996, December 26). *General Motors statement on status of the settlement agreement of class action litigation involving C/K pickups*. Detroit: Author.
German, K. M. (1995). Critical theory in public relations inquiry: Future directions for analysis in a public relations context. In W. N. Elwood (Ed.), *Public relations inquiry as rhetorical criticism: Case studies of corporate discourse and social influence* (pp. 279-294). Westport, CT: Praeger.
Gibson, D. C. (1995). Public relations considerations of consumer product recall. *Public Relations Review, 21*, 225-240.
GM says safety of some trucks was overstated. (1992, December 3). *Wall Street Journal*, p. C20.
GM pickup settlement offers $1,000. (1996, July 5). *USA Today*, p. 1B
Goldman, J. (1984). *Public relations in the marketing mix*. Lincolnwood, IL: NTC Business Books.
Gonzalez-Herrero, A., & Pratt, C. B. (1995). How to manage a crisis before—or whenever—it hits. *Public Relations Quarterly, 40*, 25-29.

Gonzalez-Herrero, A., & Pratt, C. B. (1996). An integrated symmetrical model for crisis-communications management. *Journal of Public Relations Research, 8*, 79-105.

Gore, A. (1997). *Serving the American public: Best practices in performance measurement.* Washington, DC: Office of the Vice President of the United States. http://govinfo.library.unt.edu/npr/library/papers/benchmrk/nprbook.html#strategies (accessed June 22, 2002).

Grabe, W., & Kaplan, R. B. (1996). *Theory and practice of writing: An applied linguistics perspective.* New York: Longman.

Gregg, R. B. (1978). Kenneth Burke's prolegomena to the study of the rhetoric of form. *Communication Quarterly, 26*, 3-13.

Grunig, J. E. (Ed.). (1992). *Excellence in public relations and communications management.* Hillsdale, NJ: Erlbaum.

Grunig, J. E. (1993a). Image and substance: From symbolic to behavioral relationships. *Public Relations Review, 19*, 121-139.

Grunig, J. E. (1993b). Implications for public relations for other domains of communication. *Journal of Communication, 43*, 164-173.

Grunig, J. E. (2005). *Alexander Hamilton Medal for lifetime achievement in public relations remarks of acceptance by James E. Grunig.* Retrieved June 17, 2008, from http://www.instituteforpr.org/files/uploads/2005_GrunigRemarks.pdf.

Grunig, J. E., Grunig, L. A., Sriramesh, K., Yi-Hui, H., & Lyra, A. (1995). Models of public relations in an institutional setting. *Journal of Public Relations Research, 7*, 163-186.

Grunig, J. E., & Hunt, T. (1984). *Managing public relations.* New York: Holt, Rinehart & Winston.

Grunig, L. A. (1992). Toward the philosophy of public relations. In E. L. Toth & R. L. Heath (Eds.), *Rhetorical and critical approaches to public relations* (pp. 65-92). Hillsdale, NJ: Erlbaum.

Grunig, L. A., Grunig, J. E., & Dozier, D. M. (2002). *Excellent public relations & effective organizations: A study of communication management in three countries.* Mahwah, NJ: Erlbaum.

Gusfield, J. R. (1989). *Kenneth Burke: On symbols and society.* Chicago: University of Chicago Press.

Guth, D. W. (1995). Organizational crisis experience and public relations roles. *Public Relations Review, 21*, 123-136.

Hall, D. T., & Schneider, B. (1972). Correlates of organizational identification as a function of career pattern and organizational type. *Administrative Science Quarterly, 17*, 340-350.

Hamilton, P. K. (1989). Application of a generalized persuasion model to public relations research. In C. H. Botan & V. Hazleton Jr. (Eds.), *Public relations theory* (pp. 323-334). Hillsdale, NJ: Erlbaum.

Hammond, K., & Larsen, S. (1998, March 3). Starr accused of obstructing justice in GM case. *Mother Jones, MoJo Wire.* www.mojones.com/news_wire.

Hannaford, P. (1986). *Talking back to the media.* New York: Facts on File.

Harlow, R. L. (1976). Building a public relations definition. *Public Relations Review, 2*, 29-42.

Hauss, D. (1995a, October). Career pointers for practitioners of the future. *Public Relations Journal,* pp. 20-21.

Hauss, D. (1995b, October). Technology forecast: Speed of information will impact all practice areas. *Public Relations Journal*, pp. 16-19.

Haseltine, P. W. (1993, March 24). *Remarks by Philip W. Haseltine, president, American Coalition for Traffic Safety Inc.* Transcript of a speech at the National Press Foundation Workshop on ethics for investigative journalists, Washington, DC.

Haseltine, P. W. (1994, May 5). *Litigation journalism and the motor vehicle*. Paper presented for a symposium on litigation journalism at Lehigh University, Schnecksville, PA.

Hearit, K. M. (1994). Apologies and public relations crises at Chrysler, Toshiba and Volvo. *Public Relations Review, 20,* 113-126.

Hearit, K. M. (1995). From "we didn't do it" to "it's not our fault": The use of apologia in public relations crises. In W. N. Elwood (Ed.), *Public relations inquiry as rhetorical criticism: Case studies of corporate discourse and social influence* (pp. 117-131). Westport, CT: Praeger.

Hearit, K. M. (1996). The use of counter-attack in apologetic public relations crises: The case of *General Motors vs. NBC. Public Relations Review, 22,* 233-248.

Heath, R. L. (1980). Corporate advocacy: An application of speech communication perspectives and skills—and more. *Communication Education, 29,* 370-377.

Heath, R. L. (1992a). Critical perspectives on public relations. In E. L. Toth & R. L. Heath (Eds.), *Rhetorical and critical approaches to public relations* (pp. 37-61). Hillsdale, NJ: Erlbaum.

Heath, R. L. (1992b). The wrangle in the marketplace: A rhetorical perspective of public relations. In E. L. Toth & R. L. Heath (Eds.), *Rhetorical and critical approaches to public relations* (pp. 17-36). Hillsdale, NJ: Erlbaum.

Heath, R. L. (1993). A rhetorical approach to zones of meaning and organizational prerogatives. *Public Relations Review, 19,* 141-155.

Heath, R. L. (1994). *Management of corporate communication: From interpersonal contacts to external affairs*. Hillsdale, NJ: Erlbaum.

Heath, R. L. (1997). *Strategic issues management: Organizations and public policy challenges*. Thousand Oaks, CA: Sage.

Heath, R. L. (2001). A rhetorical enactment rationale for public relations: The good organization communicating well. In. R. L. Heath (Ed.), *Handbook of public relations* (pp. 31-50). Thousand Oaks, CA: Sage.

Heath, R. L. (2006). A rhetorical theory approach to issues management. In C. Botan & V. Hazleton (Eds.), *Public relations theory II* (pp. 63-100). Mahwah, NJ: Erlbaum.

Heath, R. L., & Bryant, J. (1992). *Human communication theory: Concepts & contexts*. Hillsdale, NJ: Erlbaum.

Heath, R. L., Leth, S. A., & Nathan, K. (1994). Communicating service quality improvement: Another role for public relations. *Public Relations Review, 20,* 27-39.

Heath, R. L., & Nelson, R. A. (1986). *Issues management: Corporate public policymaking in an information society*. Beverly Hills, CA: Sage.

Hendrix, J. A., & Hayes, D. C. (2007). *Public relations cases* (7th ed.). Belmont, CA: Wadsworth.

Herrington, A., & Moran, C. (2005). The idea of genre in theory and practice: An overview of the work in genre in the fields of composition and rhetoric and new genres studies. In A. Herrington & C. Moran (Eds.), *Genre across the curriculum* (pp. 1-19). Logan: Utah State University Press.

Hipple, J. R. (2007, August). Public relations: The critical link to successful business strategy. *Public Relations Tactics*, p. 17.

Hodder, I. (1994). The interpretation of documents and material culture. In N. K. Denzin & Y. S. Lincoln (Eds.), *Handbook of qualitative research* (pp. 393-402). Thousand Oaks, CA: Sage.

Hollihan, T. A., & Riley, P. (1989). *Argument and corporate advocacy: The influences of organizational culture on public discourse*. Paper presented at the Sixth SCA/AFA Conference on Argumentation, Anaheim, CA.

Holstein, W. J. (2008). *Manage the media (don't let the media manage you)*. Boston: Harvard Business Press.

Holtz, S. (2000, February/March). Integrating technology with the traditional: Shall the 'twain e'er meet? *Communication World*, pp. 17-21.

Holtz, S. (2002). *Public relations on the net* (2nd ed.). New York: Amacom.

Holtz, S. (2006a). *Blogging for business: Everything you need to know and why you should care*. New York: Kaplan Business.

Holtz, S. (2006b). Communicating in the world of Web 2.0. *Communication World, 23*(3), 24-26.

Holtz, S., & Hobson, N. (2007). *How to do everything with podcasting*. New York: McGraw-Hill.

Hoover, J. D. (1994). The Japanese trade imbalance: Lee Iacocca and corporate advocacy. In M. W. Seeger (Ed.), *I gotta tell you* (pp. 167-177). Detroit: Wayne State University Press.

Hoover, J. D. (Ed.). (1997). *Corporate advocacy: Rhetoric in the information age*. Westport, CT: Quorum Books.

Horton, J. (2006). What's it worth? Publicity metrics reconsidered (revised). http://www.online-pr.com/Holding/Publicity_Metrics_Reconsidered_REVISED.pdf (accessed June 28, 2008).

Howard, C. M. (1995). "Building cathedrals"—reflections on three decades in corporate PR and a peek at the future. *Public Relations Quarterly, 40*, 5-12.

Howard, C. M., & Mathews, W. K. (2000). *On deadline: Managing media relations* (3rd ed.). Prospect Heights, IL: Waveland Press.

Ihlen, Ø. (2002a). Defending the Mercedes A-class: Combining and changing crisis-response strategies. *Journal of Public Relations Research, 14*, 185-206.

Ihlen, Ø. (2002b). Rhetoric and resources: Notes for a new approach to public relations and issues management. *Journal of Public Affairs, 2*(4), 259-269.

Ihlen, Ø. (2004). Norwegian hydroelectric power: Testing a heuristic for analyzing symbolic strategies and resources. *Public Relations Review, 30*, 217-223.

Ingrassia, P., & White, J. B. (1995). *Comeback: The fall and rise of the American automobile industry*. New York: Touchstone.

Jaksa, J. A., & Pritchard, M. S. (1994). *Communication ethics: Methods of analysis* (2nd ed.). Belmont, CA: Wadsworth.

Janis, I. (1972). *Victims of groupthink: A psychological study of foreign decisions and fiascoes*. Boston: Houghton Mifflin.

Japp, P. M. (1999). "Can this marriage be saved?": Reclaiming Burke for feminist scholarship. In B. L. Brock (Ed.), *Kenneth Burke and the 21st century* (pp. 113-130). Albany: State University of New York Press.

Jensen, B. (1995, August). Are we necessary? The case for dismantling corporate communication. *Communication World*, pp. 14-18, 30.
Johannesen, R. L. (1990). *Ethics in human communication* (3rd ed.). Prospect Heights, IL: Waveland.
Johnson-Eilola, J., & Selber, S. A. (2004). *Central works in technical communication*. New York: Oxford.
Kaplan, R. S., & Norton, D. P. (1996). *The balanced scorecard: Translating strategy into action*. Boston: Harvard Business School Press.
Katz, D., & Kahn, R. L. (1966). *The social psychology of organizations*. New York: Wiley.
Kay, J. (1994). Lee Iacocca as debater and storyteller: Speeches concerning the problems and future of the automobile industry. In M. W. Seeger (Ed.), *I gotta tell you* (pp. 119-131). Detroit: Wayne State University Press.
Kelleher, T. (2007). *Public relations online: Lasting concepts for changing media*. Thousand Oaks, CA: Sage.
Keller, M. (1993). *Collision: GM, Toyota, Volkswagen and the race to own the 21st century*. New York: Currency.
Kent, M. L. (2008). Critical analysis of blogging in public relations. *Public Relations Review, 34,* 32-40.
Kiley, D. (1988, October 24). How Suzuki swerved to avoid a marketing disaster. *Adweek's Marketing Week*, pp. 27-28.
Killingsworth, M. J., & Gilbertson, M. K. (1992). *Signs, genres, and communities in technical communication*. Amityville, NY: Baywood.
Kohl, S. (2000). *Getting attention: Leading-edge lessons for publicity and marketing*. Boston: Butterworth-Heinemann.
Kreps, G. L. (1980). A field experimental test and reevaluation of Weick's model of organizing. In D. Nimmo (Ed.), *Communication yearbook* (Vol. 4, pp. 389-398). New Brunswick, NJ: Transaction.
Kreps, G. L. (1989). Reflexivity and internal public relations: The role of information in directing organizational development. In C. H. Botan & V. Hazleton Jr. (Eds.), *Public relations theory* (pp. 265-279). Hillsdale, NJ: Erlbaum.
Kreps, G. L. (2007). A Weickian approach to public relations and crisis management. In T. L. Hansen-Horn & B. D. Neff (Eds.), *Public relations: From theory to practice* (pp. 20-30). Boston: Pearson Allyn & Bacon.
Kruckeberg, D. (1995). The challenge for public relations in the era of globalization. *Public Relations Quarterly, 40,* 36-38.
Kuhn, T. S. (1970). *The structure of scientific revolutions* (2nd ed.). Chicago: University of Chicago Press.
Lacey, J. P., & Llewellyn, J. T. (1995). The engineering of outrage: Mediated constructions of risk in the Alar controversy. In W. N. Elwood (Ed.), *Public relations inquiry as rhetorical criticism: Case studies of corporate discourse and social influence* (pp. 47-68). Westport, CT: Praeger.
Landes, L. (1997). People. Systems. Truth. Trust. *The Public Relations Strategist, 3,* 47-49.
Larkey, L., & Morrill, C. (1995). Organizational commitment as symbolic process. *Western Journal of Communication, 59,* 193-213.
Larkin, T. J., & Larkin, S. (1994). *Communicating change*. New York: McGraw-Hill.

Larkin, T. J., & Larkin, S. (1995, April). Everything we do is wrong. *Across the Board*, pp. 32-36.
Larkin, T. J., & Larkin, S. (1996a, May). Are your people getting the message? *Across the Board*, pp. 16-20.
Larkin, T. J., & Larkin, S. (1996b, May-June). Reaching and changing frontline employees. *Harvard Business Review*, pp. 95-104.
Larsen, S. (1998, June 3). Jury sees Starr docs, finds GM liable for death. *Mother Jones, MoJo Wire*. www.mojones.com/news_wire.
Larsen, S., & Hammond, K. (1998, Feb. 27). Starr helped GM cover up possible perjury. *Mother Jones, MoJo Wire*. www.mojones.com/news_wire.
Lauterborn, R. F. (1996). The product nobody wanted to buy: A corporate marketing public relations case history. *Journal of Corporate Public Relations*, 6-8.
Lauzen, M. M. (1994). Public relations practitioner role enactment in issue management. *Journalism Quarterly, 71*, 356-369.
Lauzen, M. M. (1995a). Public relations managers' involvement in strategic issue diagnosis. *Public Relations Review, 21*, 287-304.
Lauzen, M. M. (1995b). Toward a model of environmental scanning. *Journal of Public Relations Research, 7*, 187-203.
Lauzen, M. M., & Dozier, D. M. (1994). Issues management mediation of linkages between environmental complexity and management of the public relations function. *Journal of Public Relations Research, 6*, 163-184.
Lechtzin, E. (1992, December 14). [Interoffice memorandum, General Motors Corporation]. Detroit: Author.
Lechtzin, E. S. (1993). One year after the infamous *Dateline NBC* test-crash show, GM executive tells how automaker "swatted" back. *TJFR Business News Reporter, 7*, 1, 4-5, 8.
Lechtzin, E. S. (1997, August 25). Personal interview transcript.
Ledingham, J. A., & Bruning, S. D. (Eds.). (2000). *Public relations as relationship management: A relational approach to the study and practice of public relations*. Mahwah, NJ: Erlbaum.
Leichty, G., & Springston, J. (1993). Reconsidering public relations models. *Public Relations Review, 19*, 327-339.
Lesly, P. (Ed.). (1998). *Lesly's handbook of public relations and communications* (5th ed.). Lincolnwood, IL: National Textbook Company.
L'Etang, J. (1994). Public relations and corporate social responsibility: Some issues arising. *Journal of Business Ethics, 13*, 111-123.
L'Etang, J., & Pieczka, M. (2006). *Public relations: Critical debates and contemporary practice*. Mahwah: NJ: Erlbaum.
Levin, D. P. (1989). *Irreconcilable differences: Ross Perot versus General Motors*. Boston: Little, Brown.
Lindenmann, W. K. (2006). *Public relations research for planning and evaluation*. Gainesville, FL: Institute for Public Relations Research. http://www.instituteforpr.org/research_single/relations_research_planning/ (accessed June 15, 2007).
Ling, D. A. (1970). A pentadic analysis of Senator Edward Kennedy's address to the people of Massachusetts, July 25, 1969. *Central States Speech Journal, 21*, 81-86.
Long, L. W., & Hazelton, V., Jr. (1987). Public relations: A theoretical and practical response. *Public Relations Review, 8*, 3-13.

Lukaszewski, J. E. (1995). Managing litigation visibility: How to avoid lousy trial publicity. *Public Relations Quarterly, 40*, 18-24.

Lukaszewski, J. E. (1996). Public relations to handle litigation. *Vital Speeches of the Day, 63*, 144-148.

Lukaszewski, J. E. (2001a, April-May). Demystifying strategy: How to develop the mind of a strategist: Part 1 of 3. *Communication World*, pp. 13-15.

Lukaszewski, J. E. (2001b, June-July). Having strategic impact: How to develop the mind of a strategist: Part 2 of 3. *Communication World*, pp. 26-28.

Lukaszewski, J. E. (2001c, August-September). See you at the table: How to develop the mind of a strategist: Part 3 of 3. *Communication World*, pp. 9-11.

Lukaszewski, J. E. (2008). *Why should the boss listen to you? The seven disciplines of the trusted strategic advisor.* San Francisco: Jossey-Bass.

Matthews, G. (1995). Epideictic rhetoric and baseball: Nurturing community through controversy. *Southern Communication Journal, 60*, 275-291.

McElroy, J. (1994, August) GM public relations. *Automotive Industries*, p. 5.

McNelly, C. (1996). The implications of employee portability: A new role for employee communicators. *Journal of Corporate Public Relations*, 30-35.

MediaMap. (2000a). *How to get coverage on the web.* Cambridge, MA: Author.

MediaMap. (2000b). *How to get press coverage using editorial calendars.* Cambridge, MA: Author.

Middleberg, D. (2001). *Winning PR in the wired world: Powerful communications strategies for the noisy digital space.* New York: McGraw-Hill.

Miller, C. R. (1984). Genre as social action. *Quarterly Journal of Speech, 70*, 151-167.

Miller, G. R. (1989). Persuasion and public relations: Two "Ps" in a pod. In C. H. Botan & V. Hazleton Jr. (Eds.), *Public relations theory* (pp. 45-66). Hillsdale, NJ: Erlbaum.

Mintzberg, H. (1994). *The rise and fall of strategic planning.* New York: The Free Press.

Mitroff, I. I., Harrington, L. K., & Gai, E. (1996, September). Thinking about the unthinkable. *Across the Board*, pp. 44-48.

Moffitt, M. A. (1999). *Campaign strategies and message design: A practitioner's guide from start to finish.* Westport, CT: Praeger.

Moran, T. (1993, April). GM burns itself. *The American Lawyer*, pp. 68-83.

Morgan, G. (1986). *Images of organization.* Newbury Park, CA: Sage.

Moss, D., Vercic, D., & Warnaby, G. (2000). *Perspectives on public relations research.* New York: Routledge.

Murray, D. (2007). *Industry great questions social media.* Regan.com. http://www.raganinc.com/ME2/Sites/dirmod.asp?sid=&nm=&type=MultiPublishing&mod=PublishingTitles&mid=5AA50C55146B4C8C98F903986BC02C56&tier=4&id=9E3790ABAF1A4A94896392E41738F15C&SiteID=DC81DAE7AA324947A48EAA072CA239A7 (accessed November 12, 2007).

Nader, R. (1965). *Unsafe at any speed: The designed-in dangers of the American automobile.* New York: Pocket Books.

NBC admits truck test used incendiary device. (1993, February 9). *Washington Post*, p. A1.

Nemec, R. (1999, February/March). Leaders, take us to your communicator. *Communication World*, pp. 29-32.

Nemec, R. (2000, October/November). Transfer your communication skills to cyber space. *Communication World*, pp. 25-28.

Newsom, D., & Carrell, B. (1997). *Public relations writing: Form and style*. Belmont, CA: Wadsworth.

Newsom, D., & Haynes, J. (2008, February). Writing the PR plan: Defining success for your organization. *Public Relations Tactics*, pp. 16-17.

NHTSA: You call this science (1993, May 2). *The Detroit News* [reprint].

Oates, D. B. (2006, October). Measuring the value of public relations: Tying efforts to business goals. *Public Relations Tactics*, p. 12.

Odell, L., & Goswami, D. (Eds.). (1985). *Writing in nonacademic settings*. New York: Guilford.

Oliver, S. (2007). *Public relations strategy* (2nd ed.). London: Kogan Page.

Olson, W. K. (1993a, March). Are GM's full-size pickups rolling firebombs? *Consumers' Research*, pp. 24-25.

Olson, W. K. (1993b, June 21). It didn't start with *Dateline NBC*. *National Review*, pp. 41-45.

O'Neill, W. J. (1993, March 16). Internal memorandum about C/K pickup truck special report [General Motors Corporation, North American Operations]. Warren, MI: Author.

Orlikowski, W. J., & Yates, J. (1994). Genre repertoire: The structuring of communicative practices in organizations. *Administrative Science Quarterly, 39*, 541-574.

Pacanowsky, M. E., & O'Donnell-Trujillo, N. (1982). Communication and organizational cultures. *Western Journal of Speech Communication, 46*, 115-130.

Pacanowsky, M. E., & O'Donnell-Trujillo, N. (1983). Organizational communication as cultural performance. *Communication Monographs, 50*, 126-147.

Paine, K. D., Draper, P., & Jeffrey, A. (2008). *Using public relations research to drive business results*. Coral Gables, FL: Institute for Public Relations. http://www.instituteforpr.org/files/uploads/UsingResearch_DriveBusiness.pdf (accessed June 24, 2008).

Pande, P. S., Neuman, R. P., & Cavanagh, R. R. (2002). *The six sigma way team fieldbook: An implementation guide for process improvement teams*. New York: McGraw-Hill.

Pavlik, J. V. (1987). *Public relations: What research tells us*. Newbury Park, NJ: Sage.

Pfeffer, J. (1981). Management as symbolic action: The creation and maintenance of organizational paradigms. In L. L. Cummings & B. M. Straw (Eds.), *Research in organizational behavior* (Vol. 3, pp. 1-52). Greenwich, CT: JAI Press.

Phalen, S. (2001, June 15). *Increasing customer value: Harness the power of predictive CRM*. Montgomery Research Inc. http://www.crmproject.com/documents.asp?grID=170&d_ID=327 (accessed June 12, 2002).

Potter, L. (1998, September). Strategic communication: Dead or in demand as never before? *Communication World*, pp. 14-17.

Potter, L. R. (2006). Strategic planning: Timeless wisdom still shapes successful communication programs. In T. L. Gillis (Ed.), *The IABC handbook of organizational communication: A guide to internal communication, public relations, marketing, and leadership* (pp. 80-92). San Francisco: Jossey-Bass.

Pratt, C. B. (1997). *Food Lion Inc. v. ABC News Inc.*: Invasive deception for the public interest? *Public Relations Quarterly, 42*, 18-20.

Public Citizen Litigation Group (1995). *1994 Annual Report*. Washington, DC: Author.
Public Relations Society of America Foundation. (PRSA). (2000). *The national credibility index: Making personal investment decisions*. New York: Author.
Putnam, L. L. (1982). Paradigms for organizational communication research: An overview and synthesis. *Western Journal of Speech Communication, 46*, 192-206.
Putnam, L. L. (1989). Negotiation and organizing: Two levels of analysis within the Weickian model. *Communication Studies, 40*, 249-257.
Putnam, L. L., & Sorenson, R. L. (1982). Equivocal messages in organizations. *Human Communication Research, 8*, 114-132.
Quirke, B. (2008). *Making the connections: Using internal communication to turn strategy into action* (2nd ed.). Hampshire, UK: Gower.
Robert, M. (1998). *Strategy pure & simple II: How winning companies dominate their competitors*. Hightstown, NJ: McGraw-Hill.
Robert, M. (2006). *The new strategic thinking: Pure and simple*. New York: McGraw-Hill.
Rotondi, T., Jr. (1975). Organizational identification: Issues and implications. *Organizational Behavior and Human Performance, 13*, 95-109.
Rueckert, W.H. (1982). *Kenneth Burke and the drama of human relations* (2nd ed.). Berkeley: University of California Press.
Ryan, M. (2003). Public relations and the web: Organizational problems, gender, and institution type. *Public Relations Review, 29*, 335-349.
Saffir, L. (1993). *Power public relations: How to get PR to work for you*. Lincolnwood, IL: NTC Business Books.
Sallot, L., & Cameron, G. (1997). Professional standards in public relations: A survey of educators. *Public Relations Review, 23*(3), 197-217.
Sallot, L., Cameron, G., & Weaver-Lariscy, R. (1998a). PR educators and practitioners identify professional standards. *Journalism & Mass Communication Educator, 53*(2), 19-30.
Sallot, L., Cameron, G., & Weaver-Lariscy, R. (1998b). Pluralistic ignorance and professional standards: Underestimating professionalism of our peers in public relations. *Public Relations Review, 24*(1), 1-18.
Schiemann, W. A., & Lingle, J. H. (1999). *Bullseye! Hitting your strategic targets through high-impact measurement*. New York: The Free Press.
Schuetz, J. E. (1997). Argumentation and corporate advocacy: A synthesis. In. J. D. Hoover (Ed.), *Corporate advocacy: Rhetoric in the information age* (pp. 237-252). Westport, CT: Quorum Books.
Seeger, M. W. (1986). The Challenger tragedy and search for legitimacy. *Central States Speech Journal, 37*, 136-146.
Seeger, M. W. (Ed.). (1994a). *"I gotta tell you."* Detroit: Wayne State University Press.
Seeger, M. W. (1994b). Lee Iacocca as business statesman. In M. W. Seeger (Ed.), *"I gotta tell you"* (pp. 15-25). Detroit: Wayne State University Press.
Seeger, M. W. (1997a). *Ethics and organizational communication*. Cresskill, NJ: Hampton Press.
Seeger, M. W. (1997b). Straight talk: Lee Iacocca as corporate rhetor. In. J. D. Hoover (Ed.), *Corporate advocacy: Rhetoric in the information age* (pp. 73-87). Westport, CT: Quorum Books.

Seeger, M. W. (2006). Best practices in crisis communication: An expert panel process. *Journal of Applied Communication Research, 34*(3), 232-244.

Seeger, M. W., & Bolz, B. J. (1991). *Pre-crisis, crisis, and post-crisis communication in the Bhopal-Union Carbide industrial accident.* Unpublished manuscript.

Seeger, M W., Sellnow, T. L., & Ulmer, R. R. (1998). Communication, organization, and crisis. In M.E. Roloff (Ed.), *Communication yearbook* (Vol. 21, pp. 231-275). Thousand Oaks, CA: Sage.

Seitel, F. P. (1998). *The practice of public relations* (7th ed.). Upper Saddle River, NJ: Prentice Hall.

Sellnow, T. L. (1993). Scientific argument in organizational crisis communication: The case of Exxon. *Argumentation and Advocacy, 30,* 28-42.

Sellnow, T. L., & Ulmer, R. R. (1995). Ambiguous argument as advocacy in organizational crisis communication. *Argumentation and Advocacy, 31,* 138-150.

Serini, S. A. (1994). Power networks and surveillance: Viewing service as an interactive component of public relations professionalism. *Public Relations Review, 20,* 43-54.

Simon, R., & Zappala, J. (1996). *Public relations workbook: Writing and techniques.* Lincolnwood, IL: National Textbook Company.

Sinickas, A. D. (1997). *How to measure your communication programs* (2nd ed.). San Francisco: Sinickas Communications.

Sloan, A. P., Jr., & Sparkes, B. (1940). *Adventures of a white-collar man.* New York: Doubleday, Doran.

Smircich, L., & Stubbart, C. (1985). Strategic management in an enacted world. *Academy of Management Review, 10,* 724-736.

Smith, A. L. (1991). *Innovative employee communication: New approaches to improving trust, teamwork and performance.* Englewood Cliffs, NJ: Prentice Hall.

Smith, R. D. (1993). Psychological type and public relations: Theory, research, and applications. *Journal of Public Relations Research, 5,* 177-199.

Smudde, P. M. (1991). A practical model of the document-development process. *Technical Communication, 38,* 316-323.

Smudde, P. M. (1993). Downsizing technical communication staff: The risks to corporate success. *Technical Communication, 40,* 35-41.

Smudde, P. M. (2001). Issue or crisis: A rose by any other name.... *Public Relations Quarterly, 46*(4), 34-36.

Smudde, P. M. (2004a). Concerning the epistemology and ontology of public relations literature. *Review of Communication, 4*(3-4), 163-175.

Smudde, P. M. (2004b). Implications on the practice and study of Kenneth Burke's idea of a "public relations counsel with a heart." *Communication Quarterly, 52,* 420-432.

Smudde, P. M. (2005). Blogging, ethics and public relations: A proactive and dialogic approach. *Public Relations Quarterly, 50*(3), 34-38.

Smudde, P. M. (2007). Public relations' power as based on knowledge, discourse, and ethics. In J. L. Courtright & P. M. Smudde (Eds.), *Power and public relations* (pp. 207-238). Cresskill, NJ: Hampton Press.

Smudde, P. M. (2008). The "logological organizing" of corporate discourse: A Burkean case-study analysis. In R. Wess & J. Selzer (Eds.), *Kenneth Burke and his circles.* West Lafayette, IN: Parlor Press.

Smudde, P. M., & Courtright, J. L. (2008). Time to get a job: Helping image repair theory begin a career in industry. *Public Relations Journal, 2*(1). http://www.prsa.org/prjournal/Vol2No1/SmuddeCourtright.pdf (accessed February 1, 2008).

Smudde, P. M., & Courtright, J. L. (in press). A holistic approach to stakeholder management. In B. Sowa & W. T. Coombs (Eds.), *Public relations management and case studies*. Thousand Oaks, CA: Sage.

Spilka, R. (Ed.). (1993). *Writing in the workplace: New research perspectives*. Carbondale: Southern Illinois University Press.

Springston, J. K., & Leichty, G. (1994). Boundary spanning activities in public relations. *Journalism Quarterly, 71,* 697-708.

Sproule, J. M. (1989). Organizational rhetoric and the public sphere. *Communication Studies, 40,* 258-265.

Stertz, B. A. (1991, February 5). Chrysler plans big campaign to deflect fallout from negative magazine review. *Wall Street Journal*, p. B6.

Stacks, D. W. (2002). *A primer of public relations research*. New York: Guilford.

Steyn, B. (2003). From strategy to corporate communication strategy: A conceptualisation. *Journal of Communication Management, 8*(2), 168-184.

Steyn, B. (2006). Contributions of public relations to organizational strategy formulation. In E. L. Toth (Ed.), *The future of excellence in public relations & communication management* (pp. 137-172). Mahwah, NJ: Erlbaum.

Strnad, P. (1987, April 3). Audi tags $80M to steer clear of image problems. *Advertising Age*, p. 98.

Strobel, L. P. (1980). *Reckless homicide? Ford's Pinto trial*. South Bend, IN: And Books.

Swales, J. M. (1990). *Genre analysis: English in academic & research settings*. Cambridge: Cambridge University Press.

Swedish Public Relations Association. (1996). *Return on communications*. Stockholm: Author.

Terry, V. (2001). Lobbyists and their stories: Classic PR practitioner role models as functions of Burkean human motivations. *Journal of Public Relations Research, 13*(3), 235-263.

The C/K battle: A litmus test for recalls? (1994, November 28). *Automotive News*, pp. 1, 33.

Tompkins, P. K. (1984). Functions of human communication in organizations. In C. Arnold & J. W. Bowers (Eds.), *Handbook of rhetorical and communication theory* (pp. 659-713). New York: Allyn & Bacon.

Tompkins, P. K. (1987). Translating organizational theory: Symbolism over substance. In F. M. Jablin, L. L. Putnam, K. H. Roberts, & L. W. Porter (Eds.), *Handbook of organizational communications: An interdisciplinary perspective* (pp. 70-96). Newbury Park, CA: Sage.

Tompkins, P. K., & Cheney, G. (1985). Communication and unobtrusive control in contemporary organizations. In R. D. McPhee & P. K. Tompkins (Eds.), *Organizational communication: Traditional themes and new directions* (pp. 179-210). Beverly Hills, CA: Sage.

Tompkins, P. K., & Cheney, G. (1993). On the limits and substance of Kenneth Burke and his critics. *Quarterly Journal of Speech, 79,* 225-231.

Tompkins, P. K., Fisher, J. Y., Infante, D. A., & Tompkins, E. L. (1975). Kenneth Burke and the inherent characteristics of formal organizations: A field study. *Speech Monographs, 42*, 135-142.

Toth, E. L. (1992). The case for pluralistic studies of public relations: Rhetorical, critical, and systems perspectives. In E. L. Toth & R. L. Heath (Eds.), *Rhetorical and critical approaches to public relations* (pp. 3-16). Hillsdale, NJ: Erlbaum.

Toth, E. L. (2007). *The future of excellence in public relations and communication management: Challenges for the next generation.* Mahwah, NJ: Erlbaum.

Toth, E. L., & Heath, R. L. (Eds.). (1992). *Rhetorical and critical approaches to public relations.* Hillsdale, NJ: Erlbaum.

Toth, E. L., Serini, S. A., Wright, D. K., & Emig, A. G. (1998). Trends in public relations roles: 1990-1995. *Public Relations Review, 24*(2), 148-163.

Troy, K. (1988). *Employee communications: New top-management priority* (Rep. No. 919). New York: The Conference Board.

Troy, K. (1993). *Managing corporate communications in a competitive climate* (Rep. No. 1023). New York: The Conference Board.

Ulmer, R. R. (1999). Responsible speech in crisis communication: The case of *General Motors v. Dateline NBC.* In M. W. Seeger (Ed.), *Free speech yearbook* (Vol. 37, pp. 155-168). Washington, DC: National Communication Association.

van Dijk, T. A. (1997). Discourse as interaction in society. In T. A. van Dijk (Ed.), *Discourse as social interaction* (pp. 1-37). London, UK: Sage.

van Ruler, B. (2005). Commentary: Professionals are from Venus, scholars are from Mars. *Public Relations Review, 31*, 159-173.

VanLeuven, J. K. (1989). Theoretical models for public relations campaigns. In C. H. Botan & V. Hazleton, Jr. (Eds.), *Public relations theory* (pp. 193-202). Hillsdale, NJ: Erlbaum.

Vasquez, G. M. (1993). A *homo narrans* paradigm for public relations: Combining Borman's symbolic convergence theory and Grunig's situational theory of publics. *Journal of Public Relations Research, 5*(3), 201-216.

Walton, W. S. (1996). *Corporate communications handbook: A guide to press releases and other informal disclosure for public companies.* Deerfield, IL: Clark, Boardman, Callaghan.

Ware, B. L., & Linkugel, W. A. (1973). They spoke in defense of themselves: On the generic criticism of apologia. *Quarterly Journal of Speech, 59*, 273-283.

Warren, R. S., & Kaden, L. B. (1993, March 21). *Report of inquiry into crash demonstrations broadcast on* Dateline NBC *November 17, 1992.* Unpublished manuscript.

Watson, T., & Noble, P. (2005). *Evaluating public relations: A best practice guide to public relations planning, research and evaluation.* London: Kogan Page.

Weick, K. E. (1969). *The social psychology of organizing.* Reading, MA: Addison-Wesley.

Weick, K. E. (1979a). Educational organizations as loosely coupled systems. *Administrative Science Quarterly, 21*, 1-19.

Weick, K. E. (1979b). *The social psychology of organizing* (2nd ed.). New York: McGraw-Hill.

Weick, K. E. (1988). Enacted sensemaking in crisis situations. *Journal of Management Studies, 25*, 305-317.

Weick, K. E. (1995). *Sensemaking in organizations*. Thousand Oaks, CA: Sage.
Weick, K. E. (1996, May-June). Prepare your organization to fight fires. *Harvard Business Review*, pp. 143, 148.
Weiser, B. (1993, February 23). Does TV news go too far? A look behind the scenes at NBC's truck crash test. *Washington Post*, p. A1.
White, A. (1969). *Assassination of the Corvair*. New Haven, CT: Readers Press.
Whitwell, K., & Argenbright, L. (1998, August/September). Ten tips for becoming a great communication consultant (or a communication consultant). *Communication World*, pp. 44-45.
Wilcox, D. L., Ault, P. H., & Agee, W. K. (1996). *Public relations: Strategies and tactics* (4th ed.). New York: HarperCollins.
Wilcox, D. L., Nolte, L. W., & Jackson, P. (1996). *Public relations writing and media techniques* (3rd ed.). Reading, MA: Addison-Wesley.
Wilder, C. (1989). Introduction to the Transaction edition. In H. D. Duncan, *Communication and social order* (pp. vii-xxvii). New Brunswick, NJ: Transaction Books.
Williams, D. E., & Tredaway, G. (1992). Exxon and the Valdez accident: A failure in crisis communication. *Communication Studies, 43*, 56-64.
Williams, J. (1996, March). On becoming a strategic partner with management. *Communication World*, p. 31.
Witmer, D. F. (2000). *Spinning the web: A handbook for public relations on the Internet*. New York: Addison Wesley Longman
Xifra, J., & Huertas, A. (2008). Blogging PR: An exploratory analysis of public relations weblogs. *Public Relations Review, 34*, 269-275.
Young, M., & Post, J. E. (1993). Managing to communicate, communicating to manage: How leading companies communicate with employees. *Organizational Dynamics, 22*, 31-43.
Zagaroli, L. (1997, October 14). Consumer groups call side-mounted GM truck fuel tanks "lethal." *The Detroit News*. www.detroitnews.com.
Zucker, L. G. (1987) Institutional theories of organization. *Annual Review of Sociology, 13*, 443-464.

ABOUT THE AUTHOR

Pete Smudde ("smood-dee") is assistant professor of public relations at Illinois State University. In 2002 he moved to academia full time after 16 years in industry, gaining experience in planning, writing, and editing a full range of public relations, marketing, executive, and technical discourse for companies of various sizes and in many industries. He has operated his own consulting practice and served numerous clients over the years. Pete's held an executive-level position in corporate communications and worked in corporate, agency, and entrepreneurial enterprises, ranging from General Motors to family-owned businesses.

Smudde is accredited in public relations (APR) through the Public Relations Society of America. He holds a PhD in communication (minor in linguistics), focusing on rhetorical theory and communication theory from Wayne State University (2000); a master's of science degree in writing from Illinois State University (1989); and bachelor of arts degree in English and philosophy from Illinois State University (1986). He had served as adjunct faculty at Edgewood College, University of Michigan Business School, and Wayne State University.

Smudde has published many articles, presented numerous papers, and been a guest speaker on public relations and other topics. He and Dr. Jeffrey L. Courtright (Illinois State University) published *Power and Public Relations* by Hampton Press. The two are publishing *Inspiring Cooperation and Organizations: Genres, Message Design, and Strategy in Public Relations* also with Hampton Press in 2011. Smudde has a another book, *Humanistic Critique of Education: Teaching and Learning as Symbolic Action*, published in 2010 by Parlor Press.

The author has won many awards for his industry work, including awards from the Public Relations Society of America, the International Association for Business Communication, and the Society for Technical Communication. He also received a Wisconsin Teaching Fellowship in 2005 for a project developing a unique approach to teaching and learning in public relations courses.

AUTHOR INDEX

Adler, B.J., 22, 23, *205*
Agee, W.K., 9, 46, *223*
Ainspan, N., 9, *205*
Albert, S., 22, *205*
Aldrich, H., 14, 16, 137, *205*
Allen, M.W., 16, *205*
American Institute of Certified Accountants, 174, *205*
American Productivity and Quality Center, 175, *205*
Anthony, R.N., 147, *205*
Argenbright, L., 18, *223*
Arthur W. Page Society, 146, *205*
Ault, P.H., 9, 46, *223*

Bailey, B., 17, 86, 132, *205*
Baker, A., 19, *205*
Bantz, C.R., 26, 37, 38, *206*
Bazerman, M., 147, *206*
Beard, M., 9, *206*
Beck, J.C., 144, *210*
Benoit, W.L., 7, 10, 11, 89(n10), *206*
Berg, D.M., 16, *206*
Birch, J., 9, *206*
Birchard, B., 172, 174, *210*
Bivins, T.H., 46, 131, *206*
Blaney, J.R., 7, *206*
Bolz, B.J., 10, *220*
Boorstin, D.J., 150, *206*

Bostdorff, D.M., 16, *206*
Botan, C.H., 3, 11, 13, 144, *206*
Bovet, S.F., 16, *206*
Boyd, J., 23, 152, *206*
Brancato, C.K., 9, *206*
Brazeal, L.M., 7, *206*
Brinson, S.L., 10, 11, 89(n10), *206*
Brock, B.L., 21, 22, 23, 32(n3), 33, 35, 42, 55, 157, 162, *206*, *207*
Broom, G.M., 5, 9, 46, 126, 142, *209*
Brothers, T., 9, *207*
Brown, M.E., 22, *207*
Brown, M.H., 3, *207*
Bruning, S.D., 18, *216*
Bryant, J., 139, *213*
Budd, J.F., 16, 18, 32(n3), 144, 145, *207*
Burgess, P.G., 32(n3), 162, *207*
Burke, K., 4, 7, 19, 20, 21, 22, 24, 25, 32, 32(n3), 33, 34, 39, 40, 41, 43, 45, 46, 54, 57, 58, 71, 82, 133, 138, 143, 156, 157, 159, 161, 162, 164, *207*
Burns, R.G., 5, *208*

Caillouet, R.H., 16, *205*
Cameron, G., 17, *208*, *219*
Campbell, K.K., 45, *208*
Carrell, B., 46, *218*
Cathcart, R.S., 53, *208*
Cavanagh, R.R., 153, 153(n18), *218*

Caywood, C.L., 46, 172, *208*
Center for Automotive Safety, 60, 70, *208*
Center, A.H., 5, 9, 46, 126, 142, *209*
Cheney, G., 3, 5, 12, 14, 15, 16, 19, 23, 24, 32, 39, 42, 54, 89, 134, 137, 139, 142, 152, 161, *208*, *209*, *221*
Chesebro, J.W., 32, 32(n3), 35, 55, *207*, *208*
Christensen, L.T., 24, *209*
Condit, C.M., 32, *209*
Corrado, F.M., 17, *209*
Courtright, J.L.,13, 152, 153, 155, *209*, *221*
Coveney, M., 175, *209*
Cragan, J.F., 25, 152, *209*
Croft, A.C., 9, *209*
Cross, G.A., 47, 121, *209*
Cutlip, S.M., 5, 9, 46, 126, 142, 143, *209*

D'Aprix, R., 16, 17, 18, 145, 155, *209*
Darin, A.T., 7, *210*
Davenport, T.H., 144, *210*
Deathridge, C.P., 17, *210*
Dell, D., 9, *205*
Deming, W.E., 151, *210*
DeWaal, A.A., 174, *210*
Dilenschneider, R.L., 46, *210*
Dionisopoulos, G.N., 16, 134, 139, 152, 161, *208*
Dozier, D.M., 14, 15, 16, 18, 146, *210*, *212*, *216*
Draper, P., 173, *218*
Drucker, P.F., 148, 149, *210*
Duncan, H.D., 32, 129, 157, *210*

Eaton, R.J., 69, *210*
Eggins, S., 132, 160, *210*
Elwood, W.N., 3, 13, 16, 54, 152, *210*
Emig, A.G., 17, *222*
Epstein, M.J., 172, 174, *210*
Everett, J.L., 28, 37, *210*
Ewen, S., 142, *210*

Farrell, T.B., 9, *210*
Ferguson, S.D., 17, 18, 133, 144, 161, *210*
Fialkow, J., 19, *210*

Filipczak, B., 17, *210*
Fink, S., 9, *210*
Fisher, J.Y., 22, 41, *222*
Fisher, W.R., 45, *210*
Fitzpatrick, K.R., 17, *211*
Flower, L.S., 136, *211*
Foss, K.A., 33, 34, *211*
Foss, S.K., 22, 33, 34, *211*
Foucault, M., 46, *211*
Frazer, J., 57, *211*
Frenette, G., 24, *208*

Gai, E., 9, *217*
Gallo, H., 9, *207*
Ganster, D., 175, *209*
Garone, S.J., 9, 18, *211*
Garten, J.E., 145, *211*
Gayeski, D.M., 18, *211*
Geishecker, L., 173, *211*
General Motors Corporation, 6, 60, 62, 63, 64, 65, 66, 67, 68, 69, 70, 74, 87, 88, 89, 96, 194, *211*
German, K.M., 16, *211*
Gibson, D.C., 16, *211*
Gilbertson, M.K., 53, *215*
Goldman, J., 17, *211*
Gonzalez-Herrero, A., 9, 16, *211*, *212*
Goodnight, G.T., 9, *210*
Gore, A., 174(n21), *212*
Goswami, D., 121(n13), *218*
Grabe, W., 45, *212*
Gregg, R.B., 32, 33, 34, 53, *212*
Grunig, J.E.,3, 4, 9(n2), 15, 16, 17, 18, 143, 146, 152, *210*, *212*
Grunig, L.A., 14, 15, 16, 17, 18, 146, *210*, *212*
Gusfield, J.R., 32, *212*
Guth, D.W., 16, *212*

Hall, D.T., 23, *212*
Hamilton, P.K., 14, *212*
Hammond, K., 71, *212*, *216*
Hannaford, P., 17, *212*
Harlow, R.L., 16, *212*
Harrington, L.K., 9, *217*
Hartlen, B., 175, *209*
Haseltine, P.W., 111, *213*
Hauss, D., 17, *212*, *213*

Hayes, D.C., 153, 167, *213*
Hayes, J.R., 136, *211*
Haynes, J., 146, *218*
Hazelton, V., 13, 16, 17, 137, *206, 210, 216*
Hearit, K.M., 3, 5, 12, 16, 46, 67, 89(n10), 152, *213*
Heath, R.L., 3, 5, 9, 13, 14, 15, 16, 81, 131, 137, 139, 152, 160, *213*
Hendrix, J.A., 153, 167, *213*
Herker, D., 14, 16, 137, *205*
Herrington, A., 46, *213-214*
Hipple, J.R., 145, 146, 155, *214*
Hobson, N., 19, *214*
Hodder, I., 8, *214*
Hollihan, T.A., 16, *214*
Holstein, W.J., 155, *214*
Holtz, S., 18, 19, *214*
Hoover, J.D., 3, 11, 16, *214*
Horton, J., 173, *214*
Howard, C.M., 16, 17, *214*
Huertas, A., 19, *223*
Hunt, T., 143, *212*

Ihlen, O., 7, 152, *214*
Infante, D.A., 22, 41, *222*
Ingrassia, P., 6, *214*

Jackson, P., 46, *223*
Jamieson, K.H., 45, *208*
Janis, I., 83, *214*
Japp, P.M., 32, *214*
Jaska, J.A., 5, *214*
Jeffrey, A., 173, *218*
Jensen, B., 16, 18, *215*
Johannesen, R.L., 139, *215*
Johnson-Eilola, J., 121(n13), *215*

Kaden, L.B., 64, 96, *222*
Kahn, R.L., 3, *215*
Kaplan, R.B., 45, *212*
Kaplan, R.S., 175, *215*
Katz, D., 3, *215*
Kay, J., 11, *215*
Kelleher, T., 19, *215*
Keller, M., 6, *215*
Kent, M.L., 19, *215*
Kiley, D., 7, *215*
Killingsworth, M.J., 53, *215*

King, D., 175, *209*
Kohl, S., 17, *215*
Kreps, G.L., 16, 26, 27, *215*
Kruckeberg, D., 17, *215*
Kuhn, T.S., 20, 46, *215*

Lacey, J,P., 16, *215*
Landes, L., 18, *215*
Larkey, L., 28, 42, *215*
Larkin, S.,16, *215*
Larkin, T.., 16, *215*
Larsen, S., 71, *212, 216*
Lauterborn, R.F., 9, *216*
Lauzen, M.M., 16, *216*
Lechtzin, E.S., 63, 66, 68, 73, 79, 80, 82, 83, 84, 87, 88, 89(n11), 90, 91, 94, 95, 96, 110, 111, 117, 122, 198, *216*
Ledingham, J.A., 18, *216*
Leichty, G., 14, 16, *216, 221*
Lesly, P., 46, *216*
L'Etang, J., 13, 16, *216*
Leth, S.A., 9, *213*
Levin, D.P., 6, *216*
Lindemann, W.K., 135, *216*
Ling, D.A., 133, 163, *216*
Lingle, J.H., 174, *219*
Linkugel, W.A., 3, 16, 46, 89(n10), *222*
Llewellyn, J.T., 6, *215*
Long, L.W., 16, 137, *216*
Lukaszewski, J.E., 9, 18, 145, 155, *217*
Lyra, A., 17, *212*

Maisel, L.S., 174, *205*
Martin, J.R., 132, 160, *210*
Mathews, G., 3, 11, 12, *217*
Mathews, W.K., 17, *214*
McElroy, J., 100, *217*
McMillan, J.J., 3, 24, *207, 208*
McNelly, C., 9, *217*
Media Map, 17, *217*
Middleberg, D., 19, *217*
Miller, C.R., 53, *217*
Miller, G.R., 13, 152, *217*
Mintzberg, H., 146, *217*
Mitroff, I.I., 9, *217*
Moffitt, M.A., 144 *217*
Moran, C., 46, *213-214*
Moran, T., 46, 63, *213, 217*

Morgan, G., 3, *217*
Morrill, C., 28, 42, *215*
Moss, D., 13, *217*
Murray, D., 145, *217*

Nader, R., 7, *217*
Nathan, K., 9, *213*
Nelson, R.A., 15, 137, *213*
Nemec, R., 18, *217*, *218*
Neuman, R.P., 153, 153(n18), *218*
Newsom, D., 46, 146, *218*
Noble, P., 131, 135, *222*
Nolte, L.W., 46, *223*
Norton, D.P. 175, *215*

Oates, D.B., 145, 173, *218*
Odell, L., 121(n13), *218*
O'Donnell-Trujilllo, N., 3, *218*
Oliver, S., 18, 144, *218*
Olson, W.K., 70, 111, *218*
O'Neill, W.J., 68, *218*
Orlikowski, W.J., 53, *218*

Pacanowsky, M.E., 3, *218*
Paine, K.D., 173, *218*
Pande, P.S., 153, 153(n18), *218*
Pavlli, J.V., 8, *218*
Pfeffer, J., 14, *218*
Phalen, S., 130(n15), *218*
Pieszka, M., 13, *216*
Post, J.E., 17, *223*
Potter, L., 18, 14, *218*
Pratt, C.B., 9, 2, 13,16, 67, 126, *211*, *212*, *218*
Pritchard, M.S., 5, *214*
Public Citizen Litigation Group, 7, 60, *219*
Public Relations Society of America Foundation, 124, *219*
Putnam, L.L., 26, 27, *219*

Quirke, B., 16, 17, 147, *219*

Riley, P., 16, *214*
Robb, S., 16, *206*
Robert, M., 148, *219*
Rotondi, T., 23, *219*
Rueckert, W.H., 40, 57, *219*
Ryan, M., 19, *219*

Saffir, L., 9, *219*
Sallot, L., 17, *208*, *219*
Schiemann, W.A., 174, *219*
Schneider, B., 23, *212*
Schuetz, J.E., 24, 124, 134, *219*
Scott, R.L., 55, *207*
Seeger, M.M., 3, 5, 9, 10, 11, 16, 27, 79, 139, *219*, *220*
Seitel, F.P., 5, *220*
Selber, S.A., 201(n13), *215*
Sellnow, T., 3, 9, 10, 16, 79, *220*
Serini, S.A., 17, *220*, *222*
Shields, D.C., 25, 152, *209*
Silber, S.A., 121(n13), *215*
Simmons, H.W., 32(n3), 162, *207*
Simon, R., 46, *220*
Sinickas, A.D., 131, 135, *220*
Slaughter, G.Z., 152, *209*
Sloan, A.P., 111, *220*
Smircich, L., 27, *220*
Smith, A.L., 17, *220*
Smith, D.H., 26, *206*
Smith, J.F., 69, *210*
Smith, R.D., 16, *220*
Smudde, P.M., 4, 13, 19, 40, 42, 121, 127, 137, 153, 153(n19), 155, 156, *209*, *220*, *221*
Sorenson, R.L., 27, *219*
Sparkes, B., 111, *220*
Spilka, R., 121(n13), *221*
Springston, J., 14, 16, *216*, *221*
Sproule, J.M., 26, 41, *221*
Sriramesh, K., 17, *212*
Stacks, D.W., 131, 135, *221*
Stertz, B.A., 7, *221*
Steyn, B., 144, *221*
Strnad, P., 7, *221*
Strobel, L.., 7, *221*
Stubbart, C., 27, *220*
Swales, J.M., 45, *221*
Swedish Public Relations Association, 173, *221*

Terry, V., 16, 17, 152, *221*
Tompkins, L.K., 22, 41, *222*
Tompkins, P.K., 22, 24, 32, 41, 42, 48, 137, 201, *208*, *221*, *222*
Toth, E.L., 3, 13, 14, 15, 17, 152, *222*

Author Index

Trapp, R., 33, 34, *211*
Tredaway, G., 3, 9, *223*
Trotman, A., 69, *210*
Troy, K., 9, 89(n10), *222*

Ulmer, R.R., 3, 5, 10, 12, 16, 79, 89(n10), *220*, *222*

van Dijk, T.A., 129, 157, *222*
van Ruler, B., 17, 149(n16), *222*
VanLeuven, J.K., 16, *222*
Vasquez, G.M., 16, 152, *222*
Vercic, D., 13, *217*
Vibbert, S.L., 3, 5, 14, 15, 16, 19, 137, 139, 142, *206*, *208*

Walton, W.S., 46, 125(n14), *222*
Ware, B.L., 3, 16, 46, 89(n10), *222*
Warnaby, G., 13, *217*
Warren, R.S., 64, 96, *222*
Watson, T., 131, 135, *222*
Weaver-Lariscy, R., 17, *219*
Weick, K.E., 3, 14, 10, 25, 26, 27, 36, 39, 40, 41, 42, 129, 137, 151, 157, 162, *222*, *223*

Weiser, B., 61(f), *223*
Whetten, D.A., 22, *205*
Whillock, R.K., 17, *211*
White, A., 7, *223*
White, J.B., 6, *214*
Whitwell, K., 18, *223*
Wilcox, D.L., 9, 46, *223*
Wilder, C., 35, *223*
Williams, D.E., 3, 9, *223*
Williams, J., 18, *223*
Witmer, D.F., 19, 233
Wright, D.K., 17, *222*

Xifra, J., 19, *223*

Yates, J., 53, *218*
Yi-Hui, H., 17, *212*
Young, M., 17, *223*

Zagaroli, L., 69, 70, *223*
Zappala, J., 46, *220*
Zrimsek, B., 173, *211*
Zucker, L.G., 3, *223*

SUBJECT INDEX

abstract, abstraction, 35, 40, 41
acceptance (frame of), 20, 33-35, 41, 43, 59, 94, 106, 143
accounting, 128, 140, 173
accuracy, 12, 13, 107
adaptation, 28, 37
administrative rhetoric, 39
advertising, 22, 23, 172, 174, 200
advertorials, 47, 51
advocacy, 11, 16, 24, 25, 113, 124
agencies (federal/public or independent/private), 17, 19, 84, 87, 117, 142
ambassadors, 68, 101, 102, 134
ambiguity, 20, 41, 44, 199
analyzing performance data, 148
apologia, 12, 16, 46, 200
applied research, 8, 9
argument, 8, 9, 12, 16, 20, 62, 65, 69, 72, 88, 94, 106, 145, 154, 199, 202
assembly rules, 36 (see also "rules")
attitude, 13, 19-21, 25, 32-33, 59, 74-79, 86, 97, 104, 126, 135, 137, 144, 150-151, 153, 161, 163, 166, 167
attorneys, 60, 69-71, 82, 85, 88, 93, 95-96, 107-109, 112-113, 120, 157
audiences, 6-7, 11-12, 45-47, 49, 51-53, 77, 87-88, 91, 110, 117, 130-136, 140, 156, 159-161, 163, 165-168, 171, 203
audience (key), 165

audio news releases, 47, 48
authority, 20, 69, 93, 101, 107, 130, 160
awareness, 63, 65, 70, 74-79, 93, 121, 124, 167

backgrounders, 47, 49, 105-107, 108, 114, 118, 125, 159, 162, 172
bargaining, 26
basic research, 9, 13, 16
behaviors, 13, 14, 16, 21, 23, 33, 37, 74-75, 103, 135, 161, 166-167
behavior (organizing), 6, 25, 26-27, 41, 81, 125, 140, 145, 151, 162, 201
behavior (communication), 10, 36, 55, 131, 1, 37
best practices, 154, 202
Big 3, 115-116
biographical statements (bios), 47, 49
blogs, 19, 47, 52
bottom-up planning, 147
boundary spanning, 14, 137, 149
budgets, budgeting, 63, 141, 147-150, 170-171, 173
bureaucratizing, 20
business, 3, 9, 14-15, 18-19, 22, 32, 59, 81, 85-86, 88, 112, 115, 131-132, 139, 142-150, 153-155, 157, 167-169, 172-176, 200, 202

227

campaigns, 8-9, 15, 22-23, 70, 100-101, 113, 137, 150, 167, 173
case studies, 3, 5-6, 9-10, 13, 23, 32, 47, 50, 57, 73-74, 122-123, 126-130, 132-134, 156, 174, 176
causal linkages, 25, 36-37, 127, 135
causal loops, 36
cause maps, 36, 44, 135
Center for Automotive Study (CAS), 60, 63, 66-67, 69-70, 93, 100, 104, 107, 113, 120, 128
change, 6, 15-16, 21, 24, 26, 36-37, 39, 46, 74, 77, 106, 108, 131, 135, 137, 140, 149, 153, 158-159, 161, 168-169, 175, 201
channels, 46, 51, 66, 93, 103, 144, 168, 171
Chrysler Corporation, 7, 11, 22, 60, 69, 108, 115, 117
cluster analysis, 21, 34, 162
coach of attitudes, 20
comic corrective, 143
commodity, economic, 144
communication plan, 131-133, 166, 171-172
community, 12, 15, 18, 45-47, 52-53, 128, 134, 152, 174, 179
complaints, 17, 96, 115
conflict, 26-27, 35, 133, 161
consensual validation, 36, 42, 83, 138
consensus, 17, 36-37
consolidating performance data, 148
constituents, 115
consubstantiality, 20, 29, 33, 43, 121, 138, 161, 178
consumers, 7, 25, 49, 58-60, 65, 71-72, 76, 109, 167
context, 3-6, 20, 23, 25, 29, 33, 37, 39, 42, 44, 46, 49, 53-57, 71, 75-76, 80, 83, 85, 89, 92, 100, 104-110, 121, 125-126, 128-133, 135, 138-139, 144, 155-157, 159-162, 164-168, 170
control, 36, 80, 84, 94, 102, 133, 139, 147, 149, 164, 168, 173-174
conversations, 6, 47, 52, 92-94, 103, 112, 169, 172
corporate communications, 7, 9, 13, 16, 46, 103, 112-113, 119, 131, 140, 151

corporate culture, 3
corporate image pieces, 47, 51
corporate image pieces (advertisements), 10, 51
corporate image pieces (brochures), 51
corporate image pieces (websites), 52
corporate planning, 18
corporate reports, 47, 51
corporate reports (annual report), 40, 51, 75, 101, 201
corporate reports (public interest report), 51
corporate rhetor, 11-12
corporate rhetoric, 5, 12, 15
corporate social responsibility, 16
corporate themes, 26
coupons, 73, 90, 98, 120
credibility, 7, 9, 66, 73, 107, 124-125, 134, 158, 169
crisis management, 9, 16, 79, 164
critical method, 4-5, 31-32, 38, 80, 136-137, 154, 199
critical success factors (CSF), 135, 149, 169, 171
criticism, 3, 6, 10-11, 13, 23, 32, 35, 41, 54, 55, 62, 94, 117, 153-154, 156, 200
customer relationship management (CRM), 130, 174, 201
cyberspace, 18
cycles, 24, 26-27, 36, 43, 137, 140

damage (image), 10, 89, 169
damage (legal), 12-13, 67, 88
damage (physical), 58
dancing of an attitude, 21, 33, 161
Dateline NBC, 12, 63, 66-68, 72-73, 76-77, 79, 83, 87-100, 102-103, 106, 114-116, 118-119, 122, 199
dealers, automotive, 7, 41, 58, 67-68, 87, 89, 101, 114-115, 119-121
decentering, 12, 89
decision-making, 14, 147, 154
defamation, 66, 88, 96, 99-100, 102, 117
defects, 7, 11, 180
defects (C/K pickup fuel system), 4, 6, 58-60, 62-66, 68, 70-72, 83, 85, 87, 88, 94-95, 98, 104-106, 108, 116, 118, 124

Subject Index

dialogic communication, 11, 14, 16, 19, 109, 139 (*see also* "face-to-face communication")
discourse genre, 6, 29, 31, 44-47, 51, 56, 73, 80, 90, 121, 129, 133, 136, 138, 159, 162, 168
discourse conventions, 40, 44-45, 47, 52-53, 202
discourse development, 4, 40, 140
discursive action, 40, 44, 52, 94, 130-133, 135, 154, 164
disorder, 34, 58-60, 71 (*see also* "order")
Dodge, 64, 85-86, 107, 114
dominant coalition, 146
donations, 150
double interacts, 26, 36, 38
Dow Corning, 10-11
drama, 5, 7, 14, 21, 33-34, 53, 57, 71, 73, 80-81, 85-86, 90-92, 94-95, 99, 101, 105-107, 110, 114, 116, 121, 125-126, 129-133, 136, 138, 156-157, 159-164, 166
dramatism, 4-6, 14, 21, 24, 25, 32-35, 38-39, 43-44, 53-55, 87, 89, 91, 97, 108, 121, 123, 125-126, 133, 136-137, 140, 156-157, 161-164, 199, 200
dramatistic organizing, 30, 31-56, 122, 126-128, 132, 140, 142, 147, 155-156, 164, 171, 172, 176, 178
duty, 41, 59, 93 (*see also* "ethics")

ecological change, 26, 37, 137, 140
e-commerce, 18
editors, 51, 100
education, 150, 174, 201
empirical data, 73, 85, 87, 107, 112, 118, 125
employees, 7, 9, 12-14, 16, 27, 46, 51, 65, 67-68, 89, 100-103, 114-116, 119, 121, 132, 140, 147-148, 169, 171, 173, 175, 199, 201, 203
empowerment, 20
enacted environment, 4-5, 7, 10, 27-29, 36-37, 40-45, 53-54, 66-67, 80, 85, 87, 89-90, 92, 94-95, 97-107, 109, 112, 114, 116, 121, 125, 129-130, 136-138, 140-141, 149, 151, 155, 159, 162, 200

enactment, 4, 10, 14, 26, 28-29, 37-42, 44, 54, 82-85, 89, 116, 119, 129, 136-137, 140, 144, 151, 157
engineering, engineers, 62, 65, 70, 82, 84, 88, 100, 113, 155, 157
entitlement, 24
environment, 4, 5, 10-11, 15-16, 19, 23, 26-27, 29, 36-38, 41-43, 51, 55, 66, 73, 78-82, 85, 87, 89, 93-95, 106-107, 117, 121, 124-126, 128-131, 134-135, 137, 139, 142, 148, 154, 157, 159, 162-165, 169, 200 (*see also* "enacted environment" and "equivocal environment")
epideictic, 16
epistemology, 21, 55, 199
equipment for living, 33
equivocal environment, 5, 26, 80-81, 94-95, 117, 124-126, 129, 157
equivocality, 25-27, 35-38, 41, 44, 83, 136, 139
ethical equivocality, 27, 139
ethics, 5, 17, 24, 27, 131 (*see also* "duty")
ethics (journalistic), 12, 67, 73, 87-88, 90, 116, 200
ethics (public relations), 13, 16, 131-134, 139, 141, 144, 151, 154-155, 159-161, 163-164, 166, 171
ethnography, 140, 201
evaluation, 8, 25, 30, 56, 113, 127, 131, 134-135, 149, 153, 160, 164, 169-171, 173
evolution, 25, 28-29, 37, 42, 44, 54-55, 57, 71-72, 91, 112, 128, 137, 142, 156-157
excellence theory of public relations, 14-15, 17
executives, 16, 69, 86, 108, 115, 146, 172
expenses, 13, 63, 150, 170, 173
experiences, 1, 7-8, 18, 33, 49, 50, 104, 119, 132, 136, 141, 143-144, 147-148, 152, 168-169, 175, 199
experience: smooth flow, 36-40, 129, 138, 157
exposé, 12, 64, 76-77, 92, 94-96 (*see also* "*Dateline NBC*")

face-to-face communication, 52, 168 (*see also* "dialogic communication")
fact sheets, 47, 49, 51, 65, 106, 114-115, 168
Failure Analysis Associates (FaAA), 64, 85
fantasy theme analysis, 14, 17
Federal Motor Vehicle Safety Standards (FMVSS), 59, 60-61, 64, 84, 93, 108
financial performance measures, 74, 76, 150-151, 172-175
fires, post-collision, 60, 62-64, 68, 70, 85-86, 98, 100, 102, 114, 119
fliers, 47, 49
Ford Motor Company, 7, 60, 64, 69, 85-86, 95, 107-108, 114-115, 117
forecasting, 147-148, 175
form, 3, 10, 21, 32, 33-35, 40, 44-45, 53, 89, 95, 97, 99, 106, 118, 125, 134, 137, 146, 157, 161-162
frames of reference, framing, 24, 26, 33, 39-42, 83, 87, 93, 94, 99, 106, 116, 129, 133, 143, 151, 157, 164
free speech, 12
frequently asked questions (FAQ), 47, 49, 98, 104, 108-109
friends, 21, 73, 89, 102, 104, 125, 134
fuel system (C/K pickups), 4, 6, 29, 60-62, 65-66, 69-70, 72, 76, 81, 84-85, 87, 93, 95, 97-98, 104-105, 107, 112-113, 124 (*see also* "fuel tanks")
fuel tanks, 58, 60, 63-65, 69, 71, 87-88, 96, 98, 100 (*see also* "fuel system")

General Motors (GM), 1, 4, 6, 7-8, 12-13, 29-31, 41, 53-136, 141, 155, 176
genre repertoire, 53
globalization, 16
GM family, 73, 101-103, 112, 115-116, 119, 125, 134
goaded by hierarchy, 21, 34, 43, 57 (*see also* order and "hierarchy" and "order")
goals, 10-12, 17, 131-132, 135-137, 139, 147, 149, 159-161, 167, 169, 171, 173-174, 202, 203

hexad, 25, 163
hierarchy, 21-22, 28, 34-35, 38, 41-44, 57, 168 (*see also* "goaded by hierarchy" and "order")
human (definition), 21
humanism, 20, 138

identification, 5, 12, 13-14, 21-25, 28, 29, 32-33, 35, 39, 41-44, 54-55, 73, 89, 110, 111, 125-126, 129-131, 133-134, 136-138, 140, 145, 156-157, 159-164, 166
identity, 12, 21-24, 42, 139
image, 7, 10-12, 22, 47, 51, 67, 75-76, 78, 86, 89, 137, 143, 151, 153, 158, 169, 200
information processing, 14, 27
interlocked behaviors, 25, 28, 35-36, 137
Internet, 18-19, 48, 140, 168
intertextuality, 134, 154, 161
interviews, 12, 29, 47, 48, 50, 52, 64, 67, 70, 88, 140, 170, 200
intranet, 18, 102
introspective research, 9, 16-17
investors, 7, 40, 175, 201
investor communications, 9, 47
issue management, 3, 16

journalism, journalists, 5, 17, 47-48, 50-51, 66-67, 86-87, 89-90, 92, 94, 96, 99, 108, 111, 113-114, 116, 131, 143-144, 168, 200

key messages, 29, 51-52, 67, 73, 81, 84-86, 98-101, 103, 105, 111, 114-116, 121, 124, 130-135, 155, 159-161, 163, 166, 169
knowledge, 6, 8, 10, 14, 17, 21, 26, 37, 54, 132, 138, 141, 147, 151-152, 160, 167, 201

labor, 24, 42, 170
labor unions, 19, 142
labor movement, 143
language, 11, 21, 24, 26, 32-35, 38, 41-45, 51-55, 82, 91, 102, 118, 125, 132, 134, 141, 146, 155, 159-163, 171, 175
lawsuits, 62, 66, 77, 93-94, 98-100, 102, 117

leadership, 83, 155, 180
leading indicators, 135, 149, 169-171, 173-174
legitimacy, legitimation, 10, 16, 137
litigation, 9, 62-63, 70, 79, 83, 85, 94, 96, 99, 104-105, 112, 124, 200
lobbyists, 17, 200
loci of communication, 38-40
logological context, 55, 160, 162, 165-166, 168
logology, 5, 55, 57, 199
loose coupling, 41-42, 44, 137

magazines, 47, 52, 200
management (organizational), 4, 14, 17, 40, 67, 82, 89, 94, 104, 108, 137, 138, 141-142, 144-148, 151, 154-155, 157, 173, 175-176
management control process, 147, 149, 173
managers, 16-17, 24, 27, 41-42, 102, 141, 145, 147, 168
mass media, 11, 19, 50, 51, 53, 87
matte releases, 47, 49
media advisories, 47, 48
media coverage, 12, 63, 72, 76-77, 83, 111, 124, 170-171
meetings, 16, 47, 50-51, 83, 151, 168, 173
message design, 16 (see also "key messages")
metaphor, 9, 34, 40, 141
mission, 149-150, 171
mortification, 22, 35, 57-59, 65, 71, 129, 157
Moseley v. GM, 63, 67, 69, 70, 73, 77, 79, 83, 90, 92, 96, 97, 100, 119, 200
motivation, 17, 21, 23, 25, 34, 38, 44, 86-87, 162
mystery, 22, 34, 41

naming, 21, 33, 42, 129, 162
narrative paradigm, 14
National Broadcasting Company (NBC), 12, 62-64, 66-68, 72-73, 76-77, 79, 83, 87-100, 102-103, 106, 114-119, 122, 177

National Highway Traffic Safety Administration (NHTSA), 7, 60, 62-66, 68-70, 72-74, 76-78, 83-86, 90, 93, 100-101, 105, 108-113, 116, 118, 122-124, 128
negotiation, 26, 109, 102, 125, 134
neighbors, 73, 89
new economy, 18
newsletters, 47, 51, 68, 87, 101-103, 115, 119, 134, 161
nonfinancial performance measures, 172-175, 203

objectives (communication planning), 9, 68, 111, 120-121, 132, 134-135, 137, 139, 149, 153, 155, 157, 159, 161, 164-167, 169-171, 173, 174-176, 203
ontology, 21, 199
operating activity, 147
order, 4-5, 10, 19, 21-22, 24-25, 29, 32, 34-35, 37-39, 41-44, 46, 53-56, 57-60, 62-63, 65, 68-69, 71-72, 76, 83, 87, 107, 128-130, 133, 137-138, 142, 156-159, 163, 165, 178 (see also "disorder," "goaded by hierarchy" and "hierarchy")
organizational commitment, 28
organizational communication, 3, 6, 8, 14, 17, 19, 22, 24-28, 32, 41, 45, 53, 159
organizational culture, 14, 16, 28
organizational functions, 14, 46, 127, 148, 150, 155, 173
organizing (process), 4-6, 25-30, 31, 35-44, 53-57, 71, 81-85, 89, 93, 97, 99, 111, 121-129, 131-132, 135-140, 145, 149, 151, 156-157, 162, 164, 199-200, 201
outcomes, 100, 112, 120
outgrowths, 5
outputs, 137, 173-174

paradigm shifts, 20, 46
paradox, 40, 42, 43
passivity (frame of), 33, 42
pentad, 21-22, 25, 34-35, 43-44, 56, 90, 102, 126, 133, 137, 156, 161-164, 166
Pepsi, 79, 80

perfection, 21, 34, 156
performance management, 27, 172, 175, 202
performance measurement, 173-174, 176, 202, 203
persuasion, 11, 13, 21, 24, 32, 39, 137, 143, 159
petition, 60, 64, 93-94, 118, 128
photo news releases, 47, 48
pitch calls, 47, 51, 110-111, 114
pitch letters, 47, 51, 111, 114
plaintiffs, 84, 113
plans, 4, 79, 80, 146, 148-149, 167, 171, 172
podcasts, 47, 52
policies, 7, 25, 51, 154
posters, 47, 49
postmodernism, 28
power, 13, 19, 34, 108, 110, 117, 134, 154, 201
practitioners, 4, 8, 14, 16-20, 23, 45-47, 53-54, 56, 126-129, 131-141, 143-145, 149-150, 152-157, 160-164, 172, 201, 202
pragmatism, 150-151, 202
prediction, 17, 154
prepared statements, 47, 48, 92-94, 99, 103-105, 107-108
press conferences, 35, 47, 50, 66-67, 77-78, 82, 86-87, 89, 97-100, 102, 107, 110, 114-115, 117, 159, 162, 199, 200
press kits, 47, 50, 51, 98, 101, 106-107, 113-114, 116, 119
press releases, 40, 47, 48, 49, 51, 98-99, 107, 114, 125, 159, 162, 168, 172, 174
PrimeTime Live, 12, 98
procedures, 10, 94, 154, 175
professionalism, 12, 18, 201
propositions, 25
Public Citizen, 7, 60, 62-63, 66, 69-70, 93, 107, 113, 120, 128
public policy, 15, 159, 165
public service announcements (PSA), 47, 51
publicists, 20

qualitative study, 4, 17, 54-55, 74, 130, 145-146, 151, 153, 160, 170, 174-176

quantitative study, 65, 73-74, 130, 145-146, 151, 153, 160, 170, 174-176
ratio (pentadic), 34, 87-89, 94, 112, 116-117
recalls (product), 59-61, 68-69, 73, 76-78, 82-84, 86, 90, 93-96, 100-101, 105, 107-108, 110, 112, 115-117, 120, 128, 151
recipes (organizing), 25, 36, 129-131, 146,157
rejection (frame of), 20, 33-35, 41, 43, 87, 93, 94, 106, 143
reputation, 7, 67,74, 83-84, 87-89, 117, 121, 151, 158, 169, 172
resources (allocation of), 12, 146, 173, 179
retention, 26, 37-43, 83, 89, 93, 129-130, 137, 151, 157, 160, 173, 201
retirees, 7, 68, 89, 101, 114-115, 119, 140
rhetorical criticism, 10, 13, 23, 35, 54-55, 153, 200
rhetorical equivocality, 129, 137, 157, 162
rules (organizing), 25, 36-37, 39-40, 45, 108, 120, 145

safety (product), 5, 11, 29, 58, 60, 62-73, 75-76, 79, 81-88, 90, 93-96, 98, 100, 102, 104-109, 112-114, 116, 118-120, 124, 199, 201
sales, 46, 75, 79, 150, 167, 172, 174, 179
satellite media tours (SMT), 47, 50
satisfaction, 23, 117, 144, 174
scapegoats, scapegoating, 35, 57, 73, 90
secular prayers, 20, 133, 164
selection, 26, 37, 40, 89, 137
self-image, 23
sensemaking, 5, 10, 25, 27-29, 31, 36-44, 83, 87-89, 101-102, 121, 123, 129, 132, 137, 140, 157, 162
situation analysis, 149, 164, 169
speeches, 11, 40, 47, 50, 55, 145, 159
spin, 96, 143
stakeholder analysis, 130, 160
stakeholders, 3, 5, 14, 16, 24, 51, 52, 68, 87, 89, 97, 130, 155, 160, 175, 200, 202, 203

statistics, 27, 62, 64-67, 86, 102, 104, 107, 111-114, 124, 145, 202
stockholders, 7, 40, 65-66, 87, 101, 119, 121
strategic planning process, 4, 14, 132, 138-142, 145, 147-149, 153, 156, 159, 173, 201, 202
strategic plans, 121, 146-149, 155, 159, 161, 164, 172-176 (*see also* "plans")
strategic thinking, 141, 147
strategies, 7, 12, 15, 19-20, 27, 29, 33, 45, 67-68, 73, 80-82, 85-87, 89-90, 97, 141, 144, 146-147, 149, 155, 167-168, 176
substance, 21, 24, 33, 43, 159
supervisors, 16, 168
swat team, 73, 82-85, 87-90, 92-95, 97, 99, 101-103, 105-107, 109-111, 114, 116, 118, 120-123, 125-126, 136, 140, 201
symbolic action, 5-8, 14, 21-22, 24-26, 28-29, 31-35, 38-39, 41-45, 53-55, 57, 71, 81, 89, 92-93, 110-111, 121, 123, 126-126,128-129, 136-138, 140, 156-157, 159-160, 162-166, 199, 200
symbolic convergence theory, 16
symbolic superstructures, 20
symbolic tinkering, 33
symbolism, 8, 11, 22, 33
symmetrical communication, 14 (*see also* "dialogic communication")

tactics, 9, 46, 99, 141-151, 167-168, 171, 174
talk, talking, 7, 25-26, 36-39, 42, 67, 80, 103, 108, 110
task control process, 147, 149, 168, 173
technician (role), 17

technology, 16, 18-19, 52, 84, 102, 155, 168, 172, 174, 177
terministic center, 34
terministic screen, 34, 143
textual analysis, 24, 28-29, 31-32, 44, 54, 56, 81, 91, 106, 118
thought leaders, 134
timing, 132, 141
tip sheets, 47, 49
top-down planning, 147-148
trust, 10, 139, 143-145, 155
Tylenol, 79, 80, 143
U.S. Department of Transportation (DOT), 68, 106-108, 113-114, 118-120
uncertainty, 10, 69, 115, 117, 129, 137, 157
Union Carbide, 10

value chain, 173
value (contribution), 8, 142, 144, 148, 153, 172-173
victimage, 22, 35, 57-58, 65, 71, 129, 157
video news programs, 47, 51, 99-100
video news releases, 47, 48
vision, 141,148-150, 173-174
Voice of the Public (VOP) surveys, 74-75, 78-79, 174, 200

white papers, 47, 50
wikis, 47, 52
Wirthlin Worldwide, 74, 200
worldviews, 17, 133, 163
writing process, 11, 201
written correspondence, 47, 52, 106, 115-116,119-121

Zelenuk v. GM, 62-63, 93-94

CPSIA information can be obtained at www.ICGtesting.com
Printed in the USA
LVOW100617020512

279977LV00001B/4/P

```
HD          Smudde, Peter M.
59
.S537       Public relations as
2011           dramatistic
               organizing.

                            35019000031541
```

DATE			

BAKER & TAYLOR